Intersectionality and Creative Business Education

Bhabani Shankar Nayak
Editor

Intersectionality and Creative Business Education

Inclusive and Diverse Cultures in Pedagogy

Editor
Bhabani Shankar Nayak
Business School for the Creative Industries
University for the Creative Arts
Epsom, UK

ISBN 978-3-031-29951-3   ISBN 978-3-031-29952-0   (eBook)
https://doi.org/10.1007/978-3-031-29952-0

This Palgrave Macmillan imprint is published by the registered company Springer Nature Switzerland AG.
The registered company address is: Gewerbestrasse 11, 6330 Cham, Switzerland

This volume is dedicated to the creative power, abilities and skills of the working people.

Acknowledgements

I am thankful to the University for the Creative Arts for providing research funding to organise a day-long workshop from which this text emerged. I am thankful to all my colleagues in the Business School for the Creative Industries for their participations and contributions in the making of this volume. I particularly thank Victoria Kelley, Philip Powell, Mark O'Connor, Katie Griffiths, Julian Sims, Jennifer Perumal and Elizabeth Baxter for all their support. Thanks to Liz Barlow and Divya for all their support.

About the Volume

This volume intends to engage with the 'role of inclusive and diverse culture(s) in Creative Business Education'. It specifically deals with different forms of inequalities based on class, gender, race, region, religion and belief, sexual orientations, and disabilities in teaching and learning. The book advances different theoretical trends within 'intersectionality' and limits of its praxis. It is important to articulate and outline the critical lineages of intersectionality within creative business education and its progressive potentials for an egalitarian pedagogical transformation.

Contents

Notes on Contributors

Katherine Appleford joined UCA in 2022, as Senior Lecturer in Consumer Behaviour. Her research bridges sociology, cultural studies, human geography and fashion theory. She is particularly interested in the ways in which fashion is used to construct and communicate social identity, and how consumption practices are shaped by gender, race and class. Her doctoral research analyses the ways social class is mobilised through contemporary fashion practices, consumption and tastes, demonstrating how class shapes women's understandings and performance of gender, space and mothering. More recently her work has considered young women's shifting attitudes around body image and beauty ideals, and the role of celebrity and social media in cultivating new body image standards. This research considers important intersections between the body, gender and race and critically analyses the concept of body positivity and its use across fashion marketing campaigns.

Ghulam Ali Arain is Associate Professor of Leadership and Organisational Agility at the United Arab Emirates University, UAE. He holds a PhD from Aix-Marseille University, France. He is an editor-in-chief of the *Journal of Economic and Administrative Sciences*. His research has been published in the *Journal of Business Ethics, Journal of Knowledge Management, Applied Psychology, International Journal of Human Resource*

Management, Group and Organization Management, European Journal of Work and Organisational Psychology and many other leading journals.

Caglar Bideci is Lecturer in Business and Marketing at Business School for the Creative Industries at University for the Creative Arts (UCA). Bideci has a PhD in business management from Swansea University. Before joining UCA, he worked at Swansea University and Rabat Business School. Bideci taught at undergraduate and postgraduate levels and supervised several student projects, including MSc and MPhil theses. Much of his current works focus on consumer experience and experience design. He is working on sustainability in business and digital marketing and how sustainability can be integrated into the consumer experience within the designing experience. His passion is to enhance his research portfolio and develop an interactive and engaging learning environment in business and marketing where students can progress to their highest potential. He has teaching experience in design and marketing. He is working on experience, sustainability, gender issues and alternative hedonism.

Julie Blanchard-Emmerson is a white, feminist researcher and lecturer at UCA, teaching fashion histories and theories. Her study about pre-teen girls, fashion, age and temporality has resulted in a book chapter and academic articles in world-renowned journals and important periodicals in her field, such as *Sociology* and the *Journal of Fashion Practice*. She was also invited to present at an AHRC-funded workshop at the Victoria & Albert Museum, alongside other experts in the field. Her research in relation to students of colour and pedagogy aims to improve equity in fashion management education and has received funding from UN PRME (Principles of Responsible Management Education).

Mark Brill works as Senior Lecturer in Creative Advertising at the Business School for the Creative Industries, University for the Creative Arts, UK. He lectures on BA (Hons) Advertising degree at UCA Farnham. His specialism is in digital and emerging advertising channels. His research focus is on creative innovation and specifically on how the Internet of Things can be used to create meaningful experiences. Brill has a background in advertising agency and brand creative and strategy with nearly 25 years of experience in the field. Working with early adoption, he has developed innovative campaigns in emerging sectors, from early websites through to mobile and most recently in connected devices. He is a fellow of the HEA and is a regular keynote speaker and media commentator on topics around emerging media.

Simon Dancey has worked in the cultural sector for more than 25 years, initially as a professional musician, promoter and community activist and subsequently at the highest levels of leadership and governance, as a CEO and research academic (https://www.simondancey.com/). His research explores culture, conflict, inequality, power and the social construction of reality through imaginaries: our imaginaries and ideas and how they shape the external world and can be utilised for social transformation. He takes a multidisciplinary approach to research, exploring how often different disciplines, ideas, epistemologies and groups can shed new light and new solutions to global problems.

Sara Leal de Matos-Powell is a politics and international relations graduate from University College London. Her research revolves around social policy and European politics. Her interests in politics are practical as well as theoretical, and she was one of the youngest candidates in Portugal's legislative elections in 2022.

Frank Fitzpatrick works as Senior Lecturer in Management and Organisational Behaviour at the Business School for the Creative Industries, University for the Creative Arts, UK. Fitzpatrick has recently joined the UCA Business School after an accomplished overseas career in international management in education and cultural relations. He has recently published *Understanding Intercultural Interaction: An Analysis of Key Concepts* and has published peer-reviewed articles in *Critical Perspectives in International Business Journal*. His main research interests are cross-cultural adjustment, interculturality, third culture identity, international HRM and international relocation and mobility. He is the subject lead for the MA/MSc in Human Resource Management in Creative Industries. He has extensive experience of working in leadership and academic roles in international business and education across several continents and diverse cultural contexts. He holds a PhD in cross-cultural business communication and a master's degree in business administration (MBA) and has published internationally on intercultural issues in the globalised workplace.

Imran Hameed is a professor in the Faculty of Business Administration at Lahore School of Economics, Lahore, Pakistan. He holds a PhD degree in management sciences from Aix Marseille University, France. His research interests include organisational identification, organisational change, psychological well-being and knowledge-hiding. His research has been published in the *Journal of Management, Journal of Knowledge Management, Applied Psychology, Group and Organization Management, European Journal of Work and Organisational Psychology, Review of Public Personnel Management* and many other leading journals.

Kathleen Hinwood is a senior lecturer at the University for the Creative Arts, Business School for the Creative Industries. She is working across a number of different courses, primarily marketing and advertising for both UG and PG courses. Hinwood is also the course lead for Level 4 & 5 Advertising. Previously, she worked in both creative advertising and strategic marketing roles in both corporate and agency environments for over 20 years. She is able to share her expertise and unique experiences with the students, enabling them to keep up to date with contemporary marketing and advertising practices. In July 2021, she completed her PhD registration and is due to complete her doctorate in 2025. She has a postgraduate certificate in creative education (UCA 2020) and a bachelor of arts degree and a graduate diploma in fine art (University of Melbourne). She is a fellow of the Higher Education Authority and a qualified external examiner.

Laura Holme is a lecturer at the University for the Creative Arts, Business School for the Creative Industries. She is the subject lead for the MA/MSc Global Marketing and Communications course and provides supports for UG advertising courses. She is also a visiting lecturer at University of Arts London (UAL), Ravensbourne, and Point Blank Music

School. She has 35 years of experience in the advertising industry, working for several global agency networks, and she now has her own consultancy focused on agencies and clients. Her professional practice enables her to keep abreast of the contemporary landscape and bring this knowledge and real-time experience into her teaching practice. She holds a postgraduate certificate in creative education (UCA 2021), a postgraduate diploma in advertising from Watford College and a bachelor of arts degree from Leicester University. She is a fellow of the Higher Education Authority and a qualified external examiner.

Bhabani Shankar Nayak is a political economist and works as Professor of Business Management and Programme Director of Strategic Business and Management at the University for the Creative Arts, UK. His research interests consist of closely interrelated and mutually guiding programmes surrounding political economy of development, religion, business and capitalism. He is the author of *Political Economy of Gender and Development in Africa* (2023), *Creative Business Education* (2022), *Political Economy of Development and Business* (2022), *Modern Corporations and Strategies at Work* (2022), *Disenchanted India and Beyond* (2020), *China: The Bankable State* (2021), *Hindu Fundamentalism and the Spirit of Global Capitalism in India* (2018) and *Nationalising Crisis: The Political Economy of Public Policy in India* (2007).

Philip Powell is Professor of Creative Business and Director of the Business School for the Creative Industries at the University for the Creative Arts, UK. Philip Powell stood down after ten years as executive dean, pro vice-master and Professor of Management at Birkbeck, University of London. Powell was Deputy Dean of the School of Management at the University of Bath and previously worked at Warwick Business School, Goldsmiths, Adelaide, Southampton and Nova de Lisboa Universities. Powell's research into management, information systems, operations and higher education management has led to more than 360 published outputs. He is a fellow of the British Computer Society, Academy of Social Sciences, Centre for Online and Distance Education, and Higher Education Academy. He is a senior scholar of the Association of Information Systems. He was editor-in-chief of the *Information Systems*

Journal. He has held an honorary chair at the University of Groningen in the Netherlands for the past 16 years and is a visiting professor at the University of Stirling.

Shajara Ul-Durar works as Senior Lecturer in Management and Organisational Behaviour at University of Sunderland, UK. The researcher is an emerging early career researcher with expertise in organisational behaviour, business ethics and environmental management. She is the projects' lead of the Association of Physicians and Surgeons of the UK. She is a Fellow of Higher Education Academy (HEA) as a fellow, Chartered Management Institute as CMgr MCMI, Chartered Association of Business Schools as Certified Management and Business Educator, Academic Associated CIPD, Professional Member Young Professionals' Society and a member of the British Academy of Management. She is an enthusiastic interdisciplinary researcher who wants to create an impact through research. She is experienced in cross-cultural researches. She has won several research grants/projects and has published in high-profile international academic journals.

Anita Walsh is Professor of Work-Based Learning at Birkbeck, University of London, and a UK National Teaching Fellow. She sees herself as a practitioner researcher, in that her research interests focus on epistemologies of practice and the pedagogies required to support the recognition of the full range of knowledges, both conceptual and applied, in the academic curriculum. Walsh is an internationally recognised expert on pedagogies associated with the academic recognition of experiential learning and has national recognition for her expertise in innovative curriculum design.

List of Figures

Introduction

Intersectionality: Which Way Now?

On 25 May, Derek Chauvin, a White American police officer, killed George Floyd, a 46-year-old Black man in Minneapolis, Minnesota. It was in broad daylight that Floyd pressed his knee on Floyd's neck, like a colonial trophy hunter. There were eighteen complaints against him, and he has now been charged with second-degree murder. Three of his other colleagues who stood by and did nothing to stop the cold-blooded murder are also facing charges. Chauvin is the first White police officer to be charged for the murder of a Black civilian in Minnesota. But Floyd isn't the first man to be murdered by a White cop in the US. On 17 July 2014, Eric Garner was killed by a White police officer in New York. "I Can't Breathe" were the last words of both Floyd and Garner before their death. These are among many institutional murders in the US that have now sparked worldwide protests. It revealed the inherent and institutional structures of racism in the country. "I Can't Breathe" did not die with Floyd and Garner. These words became anthems of anti-racism and social justice movements worldwide.

The Black Lives Matter movement, which emerged in 2013, continues to campaign against racism within and outside the US. It derives its inspiration from historic political struggles for equality, liberty and justice, and continues to represent the legacies of anti-colonial struggles, civil rights movement other progressive and radical socio-political movements. The protests across the US, Europe and other regions across the world reflect the frustration and despair of people of colour in the face of pervasive racism in different parts of the world. Despite earlier movements for racial equality, Black, Asian and minority ethnic communities in the US, Europe and Asia continue to face various forms of institutionalised discrimination and structural violence in their everyday lives. White supremacy, as an ideal, owes its origins within the historical events of transatlantic slavery and European colonialism that still inform and underpin racial and other forms of discrimination within and outside the western world. Therefore, movements like #BlackLivesMatter carry global significance.

The Black Lives Matter movement has also opened up wounds of all other forms of discrimination in different societies across the world. Discrimination against Muslims, Kashmiris, Dalits (untouchables) and tribals in India; non-Bengalis and religious minorities in Bangladesh; Ahmadis, Baluch, Hindus, Sikhs and Christians in Pakistan; Tamils in Sri Lanka; Rohingya in Myanmar; and Tibetans and Uighur Muslims in China—besides other forms of discrimination based on gender, sexualities, dress and food habits—remains rampant. They form the unadulterated reality of our unequal capitalist world. The forward march towards an egalitarian and non-discriminatory world depends on people's resolve to fight against all forms of discrimination based on prejudice.

In recent times, there has been a global upsurge in right-wing politics and reactionary movements, which give patronage to the politics of hate and othering. They breed discrimination, violence and inequalities in different parts of the world. The liberal and right-wing commentators offer Eurocentric Lockean social contract as an alternative to re-establish peace and social order based on ideals of hierarchy and domination. The progressive, democratic and emancipatory political forces and their movements are divided on different ideological sectarian lines. The social, cultural, religious, racial, gender and economic divisions in the society echo within the weak and divided emancipatory political struggles.

Many radical, socialist and progressive movements consider identity politics as the cultural logic of failed capitalism. They argue that identity politics destroys the unity of the working classes and marginalised communities' fight against the capitalism system. In reality, these two ideological trends of progressive and radical movements need to understand that race, ethnicity, gender and class intersect with each other within a capitalist system. Intersectionality helps us understand the existence of multiple and overlapping forms of exploitation, violence and oppression. This realisation is important to develop clear emancipatory political strategies. The intersectionality of race, gender, class, caste, sexuality and other marginalised communities is an important indicator to understand different layers of exploitations and oppressions within the hierarchy of capitalist systems. The different forms of identities-based discrimination, oppression and exploitation exist not in separation, but in unity with different structures and processes of capitalism.

The politics of intersectionality ignores the role of pre-existing unequal social relations in shaping conditions of production and reproduction within capitalism. The failure of class politics and defeat of revolutionary movements during the 1990s led to the rise of intersectionality as an approach to understand exploitation and discrimination based on personal characteristics of individuals, like race, gender, sexuality, caste, region, territoriality and ethnicity. The postmodern and post-structural theories provide the ideological foundation to intersectionality identity politics. The idea of intersectionality attempts to find alternatives within existing capitalist system that reproduces the gender, class, caste and race-based inequalities and exploitations that result in precarity and proletarianisation. The existing archetype of intersectionality debates and discourses has failed to locate the fluidity of power relations and sites of struggles against identity-based violence, exploitations, dominance and discriminations within and outside the communities.

The intersectionality approach to movement is ahistorical, as it does not look at the inherent and historical roots of different forms of exploitation with capitalism. So, deradicalisation is an inadvertent outcome of intersectionality as a political approach to emancipatory struggles. The critiques of intersectionality do not reject and disregard the realities of multiple forms of power structure that exploit, discriminate and kill on the basis of individual identities. The ideas of identities are not just about atomised, abstract and individual self-reflections. They also involve the individual identity's organic relationship and interactions with environment and fellow beings. The individual builds relationships with others to fulfil their own desires and needs that give meaning to their life. This generates the foundation of collective identity based on voluntary but natural relationships. These relationships are territorialised and de-territorialised by multiple identities created and destroyed as per the requirements of the neoliberal capitalism under globalisation. For example, the identity issues of displaced person, refugees and internal and external migrants are direct or indirect products of capitalism. So, there are material conditions that shape identity politics. Hence, the mindless criticisms of identity politics are also dangerous. It is important to separate two different ideological trends of identity politics.

The growth of European reactionary nationalist politics led by the British Nationalist Party and English Defence League in the UK, UKIP in England, the National Front in France, New Dawn in Greece and Jobbik in Hungary are classic examples of reactionary identity politics that promotes a cultural logic of failed capitalism. The politics of Upper Caste Hindus led by the Bharatiya Janata Party (BJP) in India and White supremacists in Europe and the US are reactionary identity politics, which needs to be discarded. The Scottish Nationalist Party (SNP) follows both regressive and progressive aspects of identity politics, which add to the complexities of identity politics. Four centuries of globalisation led to the normalisation of precarity, and the emancipatory labour and trade union movements have become wage bargaining movements, promoting representative careerism in the name of affirmative actions. Such an approach helps hide the institutional discriminatory practices of capitalist structures led by the patriarchy of White supremacists in Europe and Americas and the Brahmanical Hindu caste order in the Indian subcontinent.

The Dalit and tribal movements in India, LGBTQIA+ movements, anti-racism movements, women's movements and indigenous movements to save their land, livelihood and forests are emancipatory identity politics. Therefore, it is important to embrace progressive aspects of identity politics, develop intersectionality and transcend differences as a political strategy to strengthen emancipatory struggles for liberty, equality, justice and fraternity. The progressive ideological engagements with intersectionality politics can reduce the isolationist approach of identity politics. It is impossible to fight racial, gender and caste discrimination without fighting capitalism. The academic left and their privileged politics must get on with it without creating further mirage of theoretical complexities.

The struggle against racism, patriarchy, caste, sexism and all other forms of discriminations and exploitations are struggles against capitalism. Let the everyday realities of people with their subjective and objective conditions guide an organised and united struggle for alternatives to all dehumanising structures of capitalism. Finally, as the significance of the #BlackLivesMatter movement goes global with its open and inclusive approach, it is important to call for a borderless revolutionary internationalism based on experiences of local sites of struggles against all forms of inequalities, injustices and exploitations. The local, national, regional and global alliance of revolutionary collectives can only help in democratising the world and ensure peace and prosperity for one and all.

Intersectionality, Creative Industries and Creative Business Education

The curriculum of business education is rebranding itself, and expanding into creative business education by incorporating areas of advertisement, journalism, digital media, fashion, branding, singing, photography, music, film making, script writing and communication and so on. It follows new language but old spirit of business. The language of profit brings old business education curriculum and new creative business education curriculum together in essence. The production of value and its transformation into price helps in the commodification of labour in creative industries to ensure processes of the accumulation of profit. In this process of accumulation, creative business within creative industries produces alienation by separating actors from their films, musicians from their music and singers from their songs. Such a separation is crucial for capitalism to flourish and expand itself further by creating an intimate form of alienation where singers follow their passion but controlled by the record companies. The process is same for other workers in different creative industries. The workers think that they are following their passion, but the producers and owners of creative industries transform worker's passion into profit. Therefore, it is in the interests of the creative business education to engage with such an alienating process to expand a more critical and radical curriculum combining the essence and emancipatory potentials of creative industries' workers.

The people of colour, women, working-class people, sexual and other minorities are marginalised within creative industries and ignored within the curriculum of the emerging creative business education. The diverse work force within creative industries finds themselves in a condition which is managed, controlled and conceptualised by the 'white' leadership. The majority of studios, private TV channels, production houses, recording companies, directors, producers, distribution channels, press, advertisement and fashion industries and training centres of creative industries are owned by few 'white men'. The lopsided ownership pattern within creative industries creates conditions of non-inclusive work culture within the sector, where diverse work force is domesticated by few White owners and managers.

The McKinsey's recent research on 'the Black experience in corporate America' shows the marginalisation of creative Black population within creative industries in the US. The study further argues that there is minimal representation of minorities and Black within top management and board. There are structural barriers for BME communities within creative industries. The Black talents and emerging artists are undervalued and marginalised within the creative corporate sector in the US. The Dalits, tribals, women and working-class people are not only undervalued but also marginalised within Indian creative industries. The experience is no different within creative industries in other parts of the world. The multiple facets of marginalised identity of a creative worker are within discriminatory structure, institutions and processes of creative industries.

Therefore, 'intersectionality' is crucial to understand, explain and overcome different forms of exploitation and discrimination within creative industries. In this context, it is important to shape creative business education curriculum that reflects the realities of everyday lives of labour within creative industries. The essence and emancipatory agendas of creative business education and its success depend on its abilities to democratise, decolonise and dismantle the structures and processes of discrimination and exploitation. The praxis of 'intersectionality' as an approach can help to develop and enrich critical norms, values, practices and processes within the curriculum of creative business education. Because intersectional experience of discrimination, exploitation and subordination within creative industries can only be addressed by taking intersectionality into account.

In spite of being a critical tool of analysis, intersectionality has failed to understand and explain the historical roots of different forms of discrimination and exploitation within capitalism. Therefore, it is important for creative business education to understand the limits of 'intersectionality' and its emancipatory projects. The intersectionality approach to movement is ahistorical, as it does not look at the inherent and historical roots of different forms of exploitation with capitalism. So, deradicalisation is an inadvertent outcome of intersectionality as a political approach to emancipatory struggles.

This volume introduces intersectionality into the teaching and research praxis on creative business education and creative industries. The analytical framework of intersectionality helps to understand the predicaments of BME workers within creative industries and their non-representation within the curriculum of creative business education. This volume engages with the "*role of inclusive and diverse culture(s) in Creative Business Education*". It specifically deals with different forms of inequalities based on class, gender, race, region, religion and belief, sexual orientations and disabilities in teaching and learning. The book advances different theoretical trends within '*intersectionality*' and limits of its praxis. It is important to articulate and outline the critical lineages of intersectionality within creative business education and its progressive potentials for pedagogical transformation.

It is within this context that the volume attempts to engage with intersectionality to understand different forms and layers of exploitation that are being either ignored or undermined within creative industries and creative business education. Chapter 1 by Katherine Appleford has outlined the challenges of class in creative business education. The chapter argues to unpack class in classrooms for the students to understand the ways in which it operates and how it impacts on their lives. Caglar Bideci in Chap. 2 has summarised different forms of discrimination and disadvantage intersecting and overlapping experiences of students in creative education. Bideci is proposing a new system approach to provide optimum intersectionality in higher (creative) education settings in order to create an inclusive environment for all while enhancing the learning experience. In Chap. 3, Anita Walsh, Philip Powell and Sara Leal de Matos-Powell have explored the concept of intersectionality while investigating social class as a disadvantage in higher education. The chapter assesses the role of work-based learning as a potential mitigator and introduces the concept of tempered radicalism.

Julie Blanchard-Emmerson in Chap. 4 has argued that fashion is an industry complicit with racism and racial inequality. She questioned the existing literature where teaching about fashion's social responsibility to racialised minorities is seemingly absent. The chapter supplements the lack by drawing together sustainability and responsibility pedagogy with literature about safety in the classroom and decoloniality of the curriculum. Julie Blanchard-Emmerson suggests that embedding anti-racist and sustainability ethics throughout academic institutions is necessary to create an inclusive teaching environment, particularly for students of colour. In the future, research with students of colour about their educational needs should actively listen to their voices and centre those voices, rather than the author's own. In Chap. 5, Frank Fitzpatrick explores interculturality to promote inclusive and diverse perspectives in international higher education. He argued that "recognition and appreciation of different perspectives on the learning process can feed back into both pedagogical and administrative practice to the benefit of educational policy and strategy, including staff development and growth. Fostering *interculturality* can enrich the perspective of both the learner and the provider of instruction and governance, as well as delivering an inspiring educational experience that facilitates intercultural development for all students and practitioners."

In Chap. 6, Kathleen Hinwood and Laura Holme have argued to develop intercultural understanding and awareness in teaching and learning to develop a more inclusive professional practice in the age of internationalisation of higher education. The chapter advocates for the Community of Practice as a core approach to inclusive teaching practices.

It further argues that "a widening set of intercultural principles, and inclusive teaching practices must be firmly rooted throughout the entire institution to meet the individual needs of students based on their experiences and attainment levels which in turn will benefit HEIs in terms of student satisfaction, reputation and recruitment".

Imran Hameed, Shajara Ul-Durar and Ghulam Ali Arain in Chap. 7 help us to understand the tradition and practices of knowledge-hiding in academia from an intersectionalist's perspective. It identifies and explains different antecedents and outcomes of knowledge-hiding in academia to understand why academics are involved in such behaviour and how it impacts individual and organisational results. The chapter also discusses the role of individuals' demographics in causing knowledge-hiding behaviour by looking at the effect of gender and local versus foreign (i.e., employee nationality), concluding with intersectionality as a critical area of future research in knowledge-hiding literature.

Mark Brill has studied digital health applications for people living with dementia in Chap. 8. It argues that the digital application designers and developers need to address a disparate range of questions and challenges of people living with dementia. The themes discussed in this chapter reflect on issues in health and ageing, including the efficacy of the proposed solutions, practical requirements in the development of appropriate digital technologies and questions of intersectionality in ageism, diversity and digital inclusion. Chapter 9 by ST Dancey argues that the artificial separation and dominance of the creative industries, as separate from publicly funded art, is problematic. This is best observed in policy and structure, with the separation of institutions such as the UK Arts Councils and Creative Industries institutions. In reality there is a constant move of individuals working and creating between industry and publicly subsidised arts, but the policy is enacted often in silos, with the social construct of the creative industries always dominating.

The final chapter (Chap. 10) by Bhabani Shankar Nayak has outlined the limits of intersectionality as a theoretical framework within the context of creative industries and creative business education. The radical politics and its grand narratives based on emancipatory theories of Marxism and Feminisms have failed to adopt an inclusive and diverse approach to understand, analyse and explain different complexities and layers of capitalist exploitation within the structural and post-structural forms of capitalist systems. 'Intersectionality' has emerged as a theoretical framework to fill the gap within theoretical narratives of radical politics. 'Intersectionality' has helped to understand different layers of social, political, economic, cultural and religious exploitation within capitalism. It engages with different levels of hierarchy within the individual experience moving beyond narrow silo of identity in search of alternative politics and theory. However, this chapter outlines the limits of intersectionality as it has failed to identify the structure and fluidity of power relations within capitalism. It has failed to document different sites of struggles against majoritarian and dominant identity-based violence, exploitation, supremacy and discrimination within and outside communities. The 'intersectionality' as an approach is ahistorical, as it does not look at the roots of the different forms of exploitation with capitalism. Therefore, deradicalisation is an inadvertent outcome of intersectionality as a political and theoretical approach to emancipatory struggles.

1

The 'C' Word: The Challenges of Class in Creative Business Education

Katherine Appleford

Introduction

In my teaching roles, I have often looked to engage my students in discussions around social class. I have devised tasks that ask students to consider how social class impacts consumer tastes and attitudes, how class is mobilised in artistic spaces and creative careers, and how structural class inequality creates challenges in everyday life, work, and education. These tasks allow students to consider whether class exists, how it exists, and to reflect on their own class experiences, thinking through the ways that class intersects with their other forms of social identity, such as gender, race, sexuality, disability, and body image. These exercises can generate quite different responses, but I have generally found that while students can articulate the ways they have been stereotyped, disadvantaged, or

K. Appleford (✉)
Business School for the Creative Industries, University for the Creative Arts, Epsom, UK
e-mail: Katie.Appleford@uca.ac.uk

© The Author(s), under exclusive license to Springer Nature Switzerland AG 2023
B. S. Nayak (ed.), *Intersectionality and Creative Business Education*,
https://doi.org/10.1007/978-3-031-29952-0_1

excluded due to differing forms of social identity, when it comes to class their responses are often less forthcoming.

The 'c' word, as academics acknowledge (e.g. Reay, 2005; Savage, 2000; Stuber, 2006), can pose specific challenges in the classroom. Firstly, there is the challenge of defining class. Finding a way to make sense of class in terms of occupation or economic, cultural, and social capital can be difficult, and some students may lack a sense of class awareness, leading them to question if class even exists. Then, there is the challenge of talking about class. Students often face difficulties navigating the nuances of class and may also experience some anxiety with using the 'c' word. There is also the reluctance amongst some students to identify with class, as this may mean being positioned by class themselves. This leads some to talk about class as a political issue that exists 'out there' rather than in relation to their class identity. For others, particularly working-class students, there is a desire to dis-identify and distance themselves from class, while for others obstacles are posed by the morality of class.

I have also faced some of these negotiations around the 'c' word in my research. In my conversations with women about their fashion practices and the ways they evaluate other women's dress, my respondents did talk about class and their comments demonstrated how class intersects with notions of (appropriate) femininity and (appropriate) dress (Appleford, 2022). The conversations illustrated the significance of class and how class is mobilised. Yet, talking about class openly, using the 'c' word, was difficult for them and me. I had to think carefully about how I approached the subject of class. I needed to gauge when it was appropriate to use the 'c' word, and for my participants, there was a tendency to discuss class in ways that were more indirect and ambivalent (Payne & Grew, 2005).

In this chapter then, I look to address the 'c' word in creative business education in two ways. I first want to make the case for talking about issues pertaining to social class and class inequality, within the framework of intersectionality, with respect to creative careers. Though the 1980s and early 1990s saw a move away from class analysis, since the 2000s academics have embraced a more Bourdieuan understanding of class, which not only considers disparities in economic position but demonstrates the important role habitus, taste, and cultural and social capital play in class inequalities. Indeed, within the creative industries, academics have shown the critical role cultural and social capital play when embarking on creative careers and moving up the career ladder. Thus, this work suggests that within creative business education, it is vital to provide opportunities for students to develop social networks and understandings of the creative work environment, which they may not otherwise have but to do it in ways that take into account the different ways they are disadvantaged and the competing pressures they face.

Secondly, I want to address some of the challenges of using the 'c' word in the classroom. These challenges include the fuzzy nature of class definitions, the unconscious character of class, the stigma and shame which surround class identities, and the tendency to view class as a political issue that exists 'out there' rather than a form of individual social identity. I argue that it is important within creative business education to find ways to address class despite these challenges. As academics writing about both creative industries and education have argued, class and conversations concerning inequality are often 'unspeakable' (Allen et al., 2013), but in order to confront the obstacles, creative business educators, institutions, and partners need to be more conscious and candid about class inequalities and the ways that they are mobilised through the sector.

The chapter starts by looking at shifts in class analysis and its role in debates concerning intersectionality. Here, I outline the move towards a Bourdieuan model of class, which bring together economic dimensions of class with cultural practices and tastes. Then I look to consider the role of class in debates concerning intersectionality. As authors such as Anthias (2013) note, while early black feminist theorists debating intersectionality looked to bring class into the intersectional conversation, there has been a tendency for academics to consider class separately from issues of race, gender, and other forms of identity. This is due, in part, to the wide appropriation of Bourdieu's model of class. Yet within the creative industries, there is a growing body of work that looks to use Bourdieu's concepts to consider the intersection between race and class to understand attitudes towards art and the visiting of artistic spaces. Moreover, as I discuss in the third section of this chapter, the significance of class and class inequality in the creative industries has been well documented in recent research which demonstrates the ways in which success in creative industries is shaped by class backgrounds and access to social networks.

As such, this work suggests that it is important to consider the role of class in creative business and education and to create opportunities for creative business students to develop their cultural and social capital. However, as I discuss in the final section, addressing the 'c' word can be challenging for a multitude of reasons, and thus tackling the concept of class and class inequality requires a sensitive approach. That does not mean however that class should be overlooked, rather it demands an openness to class debates and recognition of the inequality that exists.

Understanding Class and Intersectionality

In the late 1980s and early 1990s within British Sociology there was a drift away from class debates. As McLeod et al. (2009) suggest, class had 'fallen out of academic and political fashion', with authors such as Beck (1992), Gorz (1980), Pakulski and Walters (1996) suggesting that we had moved beyond the class concept and that it was now a 'zombie category' (Beck & Beck-Gernsheim, 2002: 203–4). This drift had been triggered by several factors. The decline in the manufacturing industry and growth of service sector work; the feminisation of the labour market; the rise in affluence and access to education; and the difficulties traditional Marxist models posed for understanding the class location of managers and supervisors all played a role. Consequently, attention moved to understanding social inequality through other lenses, such as risk, gender, and race.

For a significant number of British academics (e.g. Crompton, 2008; Devine & Savage, 2005; Reay, 1997; Skeggs, 1997), however, class remained an important and valuable concept for understanding social lives. As O'Neill and Wayne (2018) suggest, whilst the nature of work, the composition of workers, and the technology they use can all change, this change alone does not result in the abolition of class relations. Rather, changes in the nature of work demand that the models of class are revised so that they do not rely only on occupation. Moreover, regardless of any significant shifts in work and education, understanding class only in terms of work, or one's relationship to the means of production, is problematic as it fails to recognise how class is a lived experience. As contemporary research shows, class is mobilised through choices of lifestyle and cultural tastes and practices (e.g. Skeggs, 1997; Friedman, 2014; Parsons, 2016; Appleford, 2022); it exists in individuals' psyches as it is experienced in emotional ways (Reay, 2005).

Therefore, class cannot be understood as a simple category based on income or occupation. As Savage (2015) and others note, class is messy and complex, and it is a form of identity that develops and shifts across life histories. So, cultivating a contemporary model of class is immensely challenging. Certainly, Marxist models which focus primarily on individuals' relationship with the 'means of production' fail to capture the nuanced and fuzzy ways that class operates. Hence, British sociology has looked for alternatives with many turning to Bourdieu as his model arguably better reflects the various dynamics of class and how it is mobilised through tastes and cultural practice. Indeed, for Bourdieu (1989, 1996 [1984]), it is through everyday ways of being, cultural practices, and tastes that class distinctions are made, as taste operates as a marker of class.

Outlined in his work *Distinction: A Social Judgement of Taste* (1996 [1984]), Bourdieu's concept of class acknowledges its material relations, but also recognises class as a cultural phenomenon, arguing that class is embedded in social relations and day-to-day activities (Block & Corona, 2014). Class, he suggests, is dependent on an individual's level of capital which exists in three different forms. First is economic capital, which refers to income, wealth, and property. Second is cultural capital, which can be embodied in the individual's actions and attitudes, objectified in the form of cultural goods, such as books and musical instruments, or institutionalised in the form of educational qualifications. And third is social capital, drawn from social networks that bring some form of 'credential', either economic or cultural (Bourdieu, 1989). Together, Bourdieu (1996 [1984]) argues that these forms of capital cultivate a person's 'conditions of existence', which can be understood as circumstances that define their 'distance from necessity', giving rise to particular lifestyles and cultural tastes. In addition, these circumstances are also said to shape an individual's 'habitus', which Bourdieu (1990) describes as a structure that 'generates' internalised practices and perceptions. These perceptions or understandings give rise to distinctive or classifiable behaviours, attitudes, and practices, which are used to locate individuals in the social hierarchy. Individuals develop an appreciation for differing tastes which then enables them to classify others; just their own practices work to classify themselves. Moreover, within a wider social context these cultural tastes also sit within a hierarchy in which those which demonstrate a greater 'taste of freedom' have greater 'legitimated superiority' (1996 [1984]: 56). In recent years this understanding of class has gained immense popularity, and although it is not without limitations, it is generally considered the most relevant model for contemporary western societies with Devine and Savage (2005) regarding its wide adoption as a 'cultural turn' in class analysis.

Intersectionality and Class

At the same time that important shifts have taken place in the understandings of class, within feminist work there has been increasing recognition of the importance of intersectionality. Coined by Crenshaw (1989), intersectionality is a concept which captures a problem long recognised by black feminists, namely that by understanding subordination or disadvantage only 'along a single categorical axis' (Crenshaw, 1989: 140) academics fail to acknowledge the experiences of those who face multiple forms of oppression, specifically black women. Using the analogy of the traffic intersection, Crenshaw argues that when considering discrimination against black women, it can be difficult to disentangle that which results from race, and that which results from gender. The harm or injury caused is the result of discrimination operating on multiple axes, which takes place at the intersection. Traditionally, however, academics have tended to focus on just one category of social identity at a time (e.g. gender, race, or class) when looking at social inequality and often from the position of those who are advantaged in other ways (e.g. by race). As a result, their work fails to recognise how discrimination is the consequence of the intersection (e.g. gender and race), and at the same time, this has the effect of universalising the experience of social groups, which further results in marginalising the experiences of those whose discrimination flows from different sources and in different directions.

> With Black women as the starting point, it becomes more apparent how dominant conceptions of discrimination condition us to think about subordination as disadvantage occurring along a single categorical axis. I want to suggest further that this single-axis framework erases Black women in the conceptualization, identification and remediation of race and sex discrimination by limiting inquiry to the experiences of otherwise-privileged members of the group. In other words, in race discrimination cases, discrimination tends to be viewed in terms of sex- or class-privileged Blacks; in sex discrimination cases, the focus is on race- and class-privileged women. (Crenshaw, 1989: 140)

Instead, then, an intersectional approach calls on academics to 'acknowledge the interaction between gender, race, and other categories of difference in individual lives, social practices, institutional arrangements, and cultural ideologies and the outcomes of these interactions in terms of power' (Davis, 2008: 68).

Crenshaw's (1989) early work understandings and applications of intersectionality have rapidly expanded, with some suggesting that it has been one of 'the most important contributions to feminist scholarship' (Davis, 2008: 57) in recent years. However, as Davis (2008) acknowledges, it is also a concept that creates much confusion about what it actually means and how it should be applied. In a bid to unpack this, authors such as McCall (2005) and Hancock (2007) have sought to provide further clarification by outlining their respective 'intra-categorical, anti-categorical, and inter-categorical' and 'unitary, multiple or intersectional' methodological approaches, while Anthias (2013) proposes using a 'translocational lens' to address some of the problems of balance between types of social identity. One of the challenges intersectionality raises is the question of which social identities should be included and to what extent (Valentine, 2007), and this is particularly relevant when considering the role of social class. As Walby et al. (2012: 228) note, early work which largely sought to address the previously neglected issue of race, often did so 'at the expense of class' and arguably there continues to be 'ambivalence as to the location of class in the analysis of the intersection of gender with other inequalities' (2012: 231). Although early debates from black feminist authors such as Collins and Davis were keen to explore the class dynamics alongside gender and race intersections, 'interest in class has faded' since, and academic debates concerning class and intersectionality often 'remain separate' (Anthias, 2013: 132).

While Walby et al. (2012) suggest that the separation of class debates and intersectionality may be due to the complicated nature of class, and the fact it is not a protected characteristic in discrimination acts, Anthias suggests that the strong emphasis on Bourdieu's concept of class analysis is also significant. Although, as already discussed, Bourdieu is seen to offer a valuable model for contemporary class analysis, this work does not speak as strongly to issues of race or gender, which are critical to intersectional debates. That does not mean to say that Bourdieu's concepts of capital, field, or habitus are not relevant. As Wallace (2017: 908) argues, across Bourdieu's work there is some recognition of the ways '"race" and racism as social factors … complicate class (dis)advantage', and equally, as research into the creative industries has demonstrated, his concept of capital can be extended, so that it includes other forms of capital such as 'black capital' or 'ethical capital' (Anthias, 2007; Rollock et al., 2014; Shah et al., 2010). Indeed, the extension of his concepts makes the relevance of Bourdieu to intersectional debates more obvious, but it does require intersectional academics to engage with his work more closely to draw out its value.

Class and Intersectionality in Creative Industries and Education

Interestingly within academic research pertaining to the arts and creative industries and in the sociology of education, there has been an increase in research that addresses class together with race, using Bourdieu's concepts. The work of Banks, for example, considers the attitudes and experiences of black American middle-class families towards the arts. This research demonstrates the ways that black middle-class parents cultivate cultural capital amongst their children by 'actively' nurturing 'their children's appreciation and understanding of fine art by arranging for them to attend exhibitions and activities at arts organizations, and by involving them in art collecting' (2012: 61). Banks (2010, 2012) suggests that these parents not only expose their children to legitimate culture in similar ways to white middle-class parents but also place emphasis on African American art. In this way, arts participation as a form of cultural capital is not only important for 'solidifying' class boundaries, but also a means for defining and mobilising racial and ethnic identities. Moreover, she suggests that owning black art operates as a means for racial unity and forms part of a greater project of racial uplift and can thus be understood as a form of 'black cultural capital'.

The idea of consuming black culture as a form of uplift and 'black cultural capital' is also noted in the work of Meghji (2020), who suggests that the consumption of some cultural forms can be used as a means of anti-racism. For Meghji (2019, 2020) all too often research into cultural capital takes a colour blind approach failing to acknowledge the ways in which dominant culture is often perceived by black people as 'white culture', which exists in cultural spaces (such as art galleries and museums) which black people can feel excluded from. Unlike Anderson (2015), however, who suggests that black people will typically view these white spaces as off-limits, Meghji claims that black middle-class people look to consume this dominant 'white' culture 'in order to establish equity with whites' (2020: 596), and at the same time will also look to consume black middle-class culture (e.g. literature, art, music by black artists), 'black cultural capital', to affirm their ethno-racial identity. In this way, Meghji suggests that black middle classes use cultural consumption as a means of anti-racism, by establishing a footing in traditionally white-only spaces whilst also highlighting positive depictions and diverse examples of black culture, thus contesting the 'white supremacist imageries of blackness and black people' (2020: 609) and uplifting black representation.

The ways in which black middle classes look to navigate the white space are also evidenced in work on education, with academics such as Rollock et al. (2011) and Wallace (2017) suggesting that black parents and students look to 'deploy' cultural capital in order to 'survive WhiteWorld' (2011: 1085). This involves black parents and students adopting and embodying (white) cultural capital and distancing themselves from racially defined cultural practices to secure some degree of status and legitimacy, routinely afforded to their white counterparts. Heavy emphasis is placed on speech, tone of voice, and (middle-class) accent, articulating thoughts and ideas 'properly' (2011), but other characteristics such as style, dress, and 'codes of walking' are also important (Wallace, 2017). Mobilising forms of black cultural capital is also key, however, and this involves asserting racial identity within the context of conventional cultural capital. By demonstrating knowledge of black history, black literature, and black thinkers for example, black middle-class individuals look to 'de-code and re-code dominant cultural capital' (Rollock et al., 2014) in a way that acknowledges their racial identity whilst also disrupting the stereotypical 'narratives of struggle, conflict, and underachievement' by exceeding expectations (Wallace, 2018: 475).

This growing body of work which considers the 'colour of class' (Rollock et al., 2014) has made a significant contribution towards intersectional understandings of class, and clearly illustrates how Bourdieu's theoretical ideas can be extended. As Wallace (2018) argues, however, there is still more work to be done. Certainly, within creative business education there is scope to consider how different identities look to 'play the game' (Bourdieu, 1996 [1984]) and how students and staff look to navigate the academic space in respect of both race and class. Moreover, across the academy there is a drive to reflect on how the curriculum legitimises some cultural forms over others to examine how the courses require certain types of cultural knowledge and to scrutinise course materials to diversify and decolonise the curriculum and provide greater space for traditionally marginalised voices. As Hegamin argues, however, in her discussion of creative writing, diversifying academic staff and extending a reading list is not enough. Rather, higher education institutions need 'to examine how students experience the classroom, how their expression is valued or dismissed' (Hegamin, 2017: 133), to challenge the dominant culture, and provide space for alternative expression. By doing this, creative business education may be able to bring about greater change not only within higher education but within the culture and creative industry sector, in both its workforce makeup and opportunities for career progression, but as with intersectional research, this shift requires academics and educators to take a more creative and critical approach.

Importance of Class in Creative Careers and Creative Business Education

The case for change within creative business education and in creative industries is strong and increasingly compelling. Though the role of class in creative careers had been largely overlooked up until the 2000s, more recent academic research and policy have shone a light on the lack of diversity in the cultural and creative sector workforce and the high levels of inequality across the sector in respect of class, race, gender, and disability (Bull & Scharff, 2017; Brook et al., 2020a, 2020b). According to Brook et al. (2018) class inequality and a lack of social mobility have been a 'longstanding problem' resulting in an industry dominated by middle and upper classes, whether it be in advertising or acting (McLeod et al., 2009; Grugulis & Stoyanova, 2012; Randle, 2015; Friedman et al., 2017). This social inequality has been brought about by a range of factors that speak to individuals' differing levels of economic, cultural, and social capital.

The 'placement system' and expectation that individuals will work for free in 'a precarious, penurious apprenticeship' to gain experience, for example, is a barrier to those with working-class backgrounds as they do not have the financial resources to enable them to work for free for any period (McLeod et al., 2009: 1031; Allen et al., 2013). Unlike their wealthy middle-class counterparts, working-class individuals are much less likely to be able to call upon friends or family to help them out with everyday bills whilst they gain experience in the field. However, the reliance on friends and acquaintances to gain these internships and placements in the first place puts them at a disadvantage from the outset. Moreover, the precarious nature of work in the creative sector, particularly in the early stages of a career, feeds into working-class parental anxieties around job security, making them less inclined to support their children's aspirations of embarking on a creative career (Bull & Scharff, 2017).

Although the cultural and creative sector may give the impression of being open, supportive, and anti-discriminatory, the data reflects an industry where 'entry is denied to those without affluence (in the form of unpaid internships), those without social connections (usually in the form of elite education), and those deviating from a norm of able-bodied youthfulness' (Taylor & O'Brien, 2017: 30). Indeed, it is not only in respect of placement and experience that the social and cultural capital of the middle class offer an advantage. As Grugulis and Stoyanova (2012: 1312) maintain, work opportunities are 'effectively hoarded by middle class professionalised' as they circulated through established social networks, between those with 'shared understandings … middle class educational experience and cultural capital'. The project-based model of working, which is common across many creative industries, further intensifies the significance of social networks and also contributes to the precarity of work and poor pay. Project teams are brought together for specific ventures and dissolved upon completion, meaning that employment is largely temporary, and because the budgets for such projects are often very tight, recruiting known and trusted colleagues is critical, meaning there is a preference for working with people within a tight social circle (Eikhof & Warhurst, 2013). Analysis of the 2014 Labour Force Survey also identified under-representation of those from working-class origins across the board, but particularly within publishing and music, and further suggested that a 'class origin pay gap' existed (O'Brien et al., 2016). This means that when those from working-class backgrounds do find work in areas such as museums, galleries, libraries, and IT, they typically receive lower rates of pay than those from middle-class origins. Moreover, these class inequalities and pay gaps intersect with gender, race, and disability, and are particularly acute in parts of the sector such as film, television, radio, and photography (Taylor & O'Brien, 2017).

According to Brook et al. (2018) and Taylor and O'Brien (2017), this lack of diversity further results in a lack of reflexivity within the industry. Those within the sector are largely immune to the class dynamics at play and therefore tend to view the creative sector as meritocratic, rewarding those who have innate talent and work hard. As a result, class inequalities in the industry go unrecognised, unchallenged, and thus persist. Bringing attention to these inequalities is therefore a crucial step in tackling (class) inequality. Moreover, as academic work has shown, class inequalities need to be better recognised not only within the cultural and creative industries but within the education sector too.

Within higher education broadly, and within arts and creative disciplines, there are also significant class inequalities at play, with Allen et al. (2013) claiming that some of these inequalities are actually reproduced by the very initiatives which seek to redress them. One such example is the use of work placements as a way of boosting students learning about the industry and developing social capital. However, rather than offering a means for developing social capital, Allen et al. (2013) maintain that placements, particularly those which are unpaid or low paid, can also operate as 'a "filtering site" in which students are evaluated through classifying practices that privilege middle class ways of being' (2013: 433). Being able to take up an unpaid or low paid placement and being able to demonstrate commitment to the role depends on economic resources and a supportive environment. While middle-class students' experience of placements may not be problem-free, for working-class students 'a lack of economic capital makes them more dependent on part-time employment, which hinders their capacity to undertake meaningful CV-building activities … (especially unpaid placements), thereby limiting opportunities for acquiring relevant social capital' (2013: 442). Furthermore, working-class students' reliance on part-time employment throughout their studies means that they are less flexible when it comes to the demand of placements too as they are less able to work long and unsociable hours as this often conflicts with their paid work. Added to this, they are less likely to have parents who encourage their subject choice and see it as a viable future career option, and who are consequently willing to find ways to accommodate and support the take-up and completion of such internships. Yet, rather than recognising the economic and social barriers that these students face, educators and employers are more likely to read these students as not being 'committed enough' and lacking motivation, characteristics which are conversely knowingly and successfully performed by their middle-class counterparts.

Allen et al. (2013) are not alone in these findings. Within specific areas of cultural and creative education such as music others (e.g. Bull & Scharff, 2017) have also found the experiences of working-class students lacking, limited by their lack of economic capital, differing cultural values, and lower levels of support and encouragement at home. Yet, despite the research which demonstrates that being able to pursue education in the creative sphere is linked to the home environment and economic capital, the perception of creativity as a product of innate talent persists. For working-class students this means that when they do pursue creative disciplines they can often feel uncomfortable, as they experience a sense of not quite fitting in or feeling that their performance is not quite right. As Skeggs (1997) writes, differences in habitus and cultural capital can create the feeling of a coat that does not fit, but since these class dynamics go unacknowledged, working-class students' experiences are read as a lack of talent or attributed to personal shortcomings and individual failure.

In setting out a series of recommendations for addressing some of these class issues in creative education, Allen et al. identify one of the key problems as the 'unspeakability' of class. Drawing attention to class inequality, they claim, is 'not recognised as legitimate resistance but as deficit weakness' (2013: 449) and this is compounded by students' lack of class vocabulary and safe spaces which enable them to share and explore their class experiences. Therefore, in order to tackle class inequality, institutions need to find ways that allow students to identify the way that class has shaped their knowledge and experience, to acknowledge and unpack how their success or failure is shaped by wider social structures and barriers, and is not just the result of individual failings. Moreover, providing this vocabulary and creating a safe space is not only necessary for understanding class inequality but its intersections too. However, as academic work on class and education has often noted and as I have found in my own teaching and research, addressing class in teaching brings its challenges and thus tackling the 'unspeakability' of class inequality does not necessarily mean using the 'c' word.

Using the 'C' Word in Creative Business Education

As I discuss in my work on fashion and class (Appleford, 2016, 2022), the 'c' word is messy and complex. It is both an academic concept and a term mobilised in people's ordinary and everyday life. As such, it is a category that is familiar to people, especially in British society, which is seen to have something of class obsession (Savage, 2015), but it is also a very loaded term because it raises 'issues of relative worth' (Sayer, 2002: 1.2) and involves expressions of cultural difference along with judgements of respectability and self-control (Sayer, 2002; Skeggs, 1997, 2004). As a result, talking about class can be difficult. In fact, 'class cannot always be articulated' and people are arguably more comfortable talking about class in indirect ways or as a political issue in society, rather than explicitly in terms of their own class identity (Devine & Savage, 2005; Payne & Grew, 2005). This does not mean that class does not exist, as the earlier sections of this chapter demonstrate that class plays a very significant role in creative education and is also an important part of people's lived experiences (Skeggs, 1997; Morley, 2021; Reay, 2005, 2021). Nevertheless, it does mean that using the 'c' word is tricky. Consequently, as Devine suggests, researchers (and educators) need to be attuned to the 'noise' which surrounds class conversations, that is, individuals' reactions to questions, intonation, and body language, and listen keenly to individuals' conversations in order draw out their experiences of class inequality, paying close attention to the coded words people used to talk about class in indirect ways (Payne & Grew, 2005).

Moreover, work focus on class and education suggests that for working-class students who have attended university with the hope of social mobility (Lehmann, 2009) matters of class identity can be more confusing because of the discrepancy which exists between their educational qualifications, cultural and social values, and economic capital or occupation. I found in my research, too, that for those who had been socially mobile, the question of class identity was particularly complex. Several of the women talked of being middle class now but were from a working-class background, in order to try and navigate differing economic and social aspects of class, and their feelings of ambiguity around their class location. In the case of working-class students, there can be a painful dislocation between an old working-class habitus and a newly evolving middle-class one (Baxter & Britton, 2001; Lehmann, 2009; Reay et al., 2009), resulting in a feeling of social unease, as these students negotiate the 'conflicts around prior identities and new identities in the university context' (Reay, 2021: 60).

Indeed, Reay et al. (2009) highlight the way that working-class students, and particularly those who are first-generation students, can face a considerable 'emotional cost' in their transition to university. Applications and entrance to higher education bring mixed emotions of fear and anxiety over their choice of degree, institution, and being in a 'strange and unfamiliar space', and at the same time as generating a feeling of excitement, pride, and anticipation as students consider what their study might mean for the future. This mix of conflicting emotions can continue once at university. Working-class students can lack academic confidence and experience feelings of inferiority. They may have a sense of 'not being good enough' (Reay, 2021: 57) and face tension between their university life and life at home, resulting in social isolation. Asking students directly about their class identity and to reflect on their class experience, then, can be quite uncomfortable as they may already feel anxious about not fitting in and this can lead to a defensive reaction, which may also be driven by an awareness of negative connotations associated with being working class. As Skeggs (1997:77) argues, class is a difficult issue to discuss for those 'who do not want to be reminded of their social positioning in relation to it'. Openly talking about class has the potential to expose individuals to social scrutiny and judgements about their own relative social worth (Sayer, 2002), and thus it has the potential to alienate students who are already struggling with fitting in.

Moreover, it may be as Lehmann's (2009) and Reay's (2005) work suggest that these students do not necessarily have a strong political class consciousness. Despite the inequalities they face, they may see class identity as 'inconsequential' or display a contradictory understanding of class difference, recognising and anticipating it on the one hand and denying it or dismissing it on the other. In Lehmann's (2009) research with Canadian students, he found that there was a tendency to reconstruct structural disadvantage as a moral advantage, with students stressing how their working-class experiences had helped cultivate their 'stronger work ethic, higher level of maturity, responsibility and independence' (2009: 639). Though these students 'vaguely related' these characteristics to their position, to a large extent these moral advantages were individualised, meaning that they believed that middle-class students could also potentially embody this same work ethic.

More generally, there appears to be a reticence in individuals to acknowledge the ways in which their class identity and their class history impact their lives and relationships. Here, Bourdieu's writings on habitus may provide a useful analysis, as he suggests that habitus can operate unconsciously (1990: 53). Though he acknowledges that our actions and perceptions can be driven by strategic decisions, Bourdieu suggests that responses of the habitus are in the first instance instinctive, and consequently have a feeling of 'correctness' and a constancy about them. The habitus is 'embodied history … internalised as a second nature and so forgotten as history', indeed it 'is the active presence of the whole past of which it is the product' (1990: 56). As such, an individual's way of being, mannerisms, tastes, and practices appear normal and natural, and are largely taken for granted because they are the learned response that has developed over the individual's lifetime. As Bourdieu explains, '[W]e don't directly feel the influence of … past selves because they are so deeply rooted within us' (1990: 56). Consequently, an individual may not be conscious of the degree to which their actions or experiences are 'classed' actions or shaped by their class history. Rather, it is only when asked about the role of class that they are encouraged to reflect on the extent to which class has shaped their experiences.

This unconscious nature of the habitus does not mean that individuals cannot identify differences between their tastes and practices and those of others. Indeed, Bourdieu strongly suggests that one of the consequences of the habitus is that it enables the identification of difference and further operates as a structure in which different practices are located in a social hierarchy (Bourdieu, 1996 [1984]). However, the recognition of difference or distinction does not necessarily mean that there is constant self-awareness or self-reflection on the ways in which class is operating in one's ordinary and everyday life.

Moreover, Bourdieu also suggests that habitus has a 'defence against change' (1990: 61), arguing that the habitus orientates away from information or situations which call it into question. Instead, the habitus encourages choices that reinforce it. This again means that individuals are less likely to engage with the ways class is shaping their experiences, attitudes, or practices, as they are not confronted by challenges to these perceptions or orientations.

> Through the systematic "choices" it makes among the places, events, and people that might be frequented, the *habitus* ends to protect itself from crises and critical challenges by providing itself with a milieu to which it is as pre-adapted as possible, that is, a relatively constant universe of situations tending to reinforce its dispositions by offering the market most favourable to it products. (Bourdieu, 1990: 61)

Yet, working-class students, in the context of higher education, are exposed to the unfamiliar and here they will face these 'crises and critical challenges'. Lacking a 'feel for the game', they may experience anxiety, self-doubt, and withdraw from social encounters, in the way Reay details, although they may still not fully recognise or be able to articulate the degree to which class is at play.

> The students were constantly engaged in an exhausting process of self-surveillance in order to monitor their behaviour and conform to unfamiliar, and sometimes inexplicable codes of behaviour. As they struggled with a sense of not fitting in socially, of failing to find a place to belong culturally within elite higher education, the least stressful option was often to remove themselves physically from the causes of their discomfort—the privileged majority. (Reay, 2021: 59)

Consequently, while it is important, as Allen et al. (2013) argue, to make class 'speakable', this does not necessarily mean using the 'c' word.

Instead, educators need to create space in which students can share and discuss their thoughts and anxieties, providing access to representation and offering routes to hear the student's voice. To encourage them away from an individualised understanding of success or failure, there needs to be greater acknowledgement amongst staff of the structural barriers in play, and both staff and students need to have a fuller understanding of issues concerning diversity and (in)equality within higher education. Allen et al. advocate a module within creative courses dedicated to this debate. Moreover, they also suggest that there is a need for greater levels of transparency around placement schemes and internships, in respect of pay, hours, and commitment alongside greater understanding from staff and businesses about the pressures working-class students face and how these impact their engagement, perhaps with a view to offering greater support and mentoring.

Conclusion

'Class remains a factor that profoundly shapes individuals' lives, their experiences and ultimately their identities' (Lehmann, 2009: 633). Using a Bourdieuan model of class, which considers the economic dimensions alongside cultural knowledge and experience and social networks, research from across the creative industries and creative education demonstrate that there is a significant level of class inequality at play, affecting university experiences, employment, and rates of pay. High levels of cultural and social capital are key to success in creative business, benefiting those in the middle class and disadvantaging those from working-class origins. Moreover, while class has often been considered separately from other forms of inequality, more recent work demonstrates the way in which Bourdieu's concepts can be used to interrogate the intersections between class, race, gender, and disability. When looking at the impact of class through an intersectional lens, it is clear that these disadvantages are compounded by inequalities in respect of other forms of identity.

Drawing on the literature within the Sociology of education, which considers the experiences of working-class students generally, and within creative education, it is evident that a lack of cultural and social capital adversely impacts working-class students. Yet, challenging the 'c' word in creative business education is not easy, for there is an 'unspeakability' which surrounds class and arguably an 'unconsciousness' about the way in which class disadvantages students. Simply highlighting the impact of class to staff or students, or looking to address 'c' word within teaching is not sufficient. Instead, creative business education needs to consider ways in which working-class students can develop capital in its various guises—cultural, social, black, ethical, and so, and it needs to do this in ways which acknowledge and accommodate the additional challenges these students face. Placements are useful, but unpaid internships present specific problems for working-class students, so being transparent about what a placement can offer and finding ways to mitigate the work pressures that some students experience is important. Moreover, institutions need to consider how they can develop their students' cultural and social capital in other ways, within the course curriculum, through field trips, project work for external clients, and guest speakers.

Just as providing space for students to share their experiences and anxieties is important, providing students with a voice so that they can move away from individualising failure and success towards better understanding the shared nature of their experiences and the structural inequalities at play is crucial as well. While individual students may not fully recognise the ways that their emotional response to higher education is being shaped by the class, it is evident in the work of Reay (2005) and others that there is a psychological dimension which needs to be addressed, and thus by sharing their thoughts with others, perhaps within modules that focus on equality and diversity within creative industries and education, there is a way to tackle the 'the shame, and fear of shame', which 'haunts working class relationships to education' (2005: 923).

References

Allen, K., Quinn, J., Hollingworth, S., & Rose, A. (2013). Becoming employable students and 'ideal' creative workers: Exclusion and inequality in higher education work placements. *British Journal of Sociology of Education, 34*(3), 431–452.

Anderson, E. (2015). The white space. *Sociology of Race and Ethnicity, 1*(1), 10–21.

Anthias, F. (2007). Gender, ethnicity and class: Reflecting on intersectionality and translocational belonging. *The Psychology of Women Review, 9*(1), 2–11.

Anthias, F. (2013). Hierarchies of social location, class and intersectionality: Towards a translocational frame. *International Sociology, 28*(1), 121 138. https://doi.org/10.1177/0268580912463155

Appleford, K. (2016). Being seen in your pyjamas: The relationship between fashion, class, gender and space. *Gender, Place & Culture, 23*(2), 162–180.

Appleford, K. (2022). *Classifying fashion, fashioning class: Making sense of Women's practices, perceptions and tastes.* Taylor & Francis Group.

Banks, P. A. (2010). Black cultural advancement: Racial identity and participation in the arts among the black middle class. *Ethnic and Racial Studies, 33*(2), 272–289.

Banks, P. A. (2012). Cultural socialization in black middle-class families. *Cultural Sociology, 6*(1), 61–73. https://doi.org/10.1177/1749975511427646

Baxter, A., & Britton, C. (2001). Risk, identity and change: Becoming a mature student. *International Studies in Sociology of Education, 11*(1), 87–104.

Beck, U. (1992). *Risk society.* Sage.

Beck, U., & Beck-Gernsheim, E. (2002). *Individualization: Institutionalized, individualism and its social and political consequences.* Sage.

Block, D., & Corona, V. (2014). Exploring class-based intersectionality. *Language, Culture and Curriculum, 27*(1), 27–42.

Bourdieu, P. (1989). Social space and symbolic power. *Sociological Theory, 7*(1), 14–25.

Bourdieu, P. (1990). *The logic of practice.* Polity.

Bourdieu, P.. [1984] (1996). *Distinction: A social critique of the judgement of taste.* Routledge & Kegan Paul.

Brook, O., O'Brien, D., & Taylor, M. (2018) *Social class, taste and inequalities in the creative industries. Panic! It's an arts emergency report.* Retrieved April 20, 2020, from https://createlondon.org/wp-content/uploads/2018/04/Panic-Social-Class-Taste-and-Inequalities-in-the-Creative-Industries1.pdf

Brook, O., O'Brien, D., & Taylor, M. (2020a). *Culture is bad for you.* Manchester University Press.

Brook, O., O'Brien, D., & Taylor, M. (2020b). "There's no way that you get paid to do the arts": Unpaid labour across the cultural and creative life course. *Sociological Research Online, 25*(4), 571–588. https://doi.org/10.1177/1360780419895291

Bull, A., & Scharff, C. (2017). 'McDonald's music' versus 'serious music': How production and consumption practices help to reproduce class inequality in the classical music profession. *Cultural Sociology, 11*(3), 283–301. https://doi.org/10.1177/1749975517711045

Crenshaw, K. (1989). *Demarginalizing the intersection of race and sex: A black feminist critique of antidiscrimination doctrine, feminist theory and antiracist politics* (Vol. 8, pp. 139–167). University of Chicago Legal Forum.

Crompton, R. (2008). *Class and stratification* (3rd ed.). Polity.

Davis, K. (2008). Intersectionality as buzzword: A sociology of science perspective on what makes a feminist theory successful. *Feminist Theory, 9*(1), 67–85.

Devine, F., & Savage, M. (2005). The cultural turn, Sociology and class analysis. In M. S. J. Savage & R. Crompton (Eds.), *Rethinking class: Culture, identities and lifestyles*. Palgrave Macmillan.

Eikhof, D. R., & Warhurst, C. (2013). The promised land? Why social inequalities are systemic in the creative industries. *Employee relations., 35*(5), 495–508. https://doi.org/10.1108/ER-08-2012-0061

Friedman, S. (2014). *Comedy and distinction: The cultural currency of a good sense of humour*. Routledge.

Friedman, S., O'Brien, D., & Laurison, D. (2017). 'Like skydiving without a parachute': How class origin shapes occupational trajectories in British acting. *Sociology, 51*(5), 992–1010.

Gorz, A. (1980). *Farwell to the working class*. Pluto Press.

Grugulis, I., & Stoyanova, D. (2012). Social capital and networks in film and TV: Jobs for the boys? *Organization Studies, 33*(10), 1311–1331.

Hancock, A. M. (2007). When multiplication doesn't equal quick addition: Examining intersectionality as a research paradigm. *Perspectives on Politics, 5*(1), 63–79.

Hegamin, T. C. (2017). "We don't need no creative writing": Black cultural capital, social (in) justice, and the devaluing of creativity in higher education. In S. Vaderslice & R. Manery (Eds.), *Can Creative writing really be taught*. Bloomsbury.

Lehmann, W. (2009). Becoming middle class: How working-class university students draw and transgress moral class boundaries. *Sociology, 43*(4), 631–647.

McCall, L. (2005). The complexity of intersectionality. *Signs: Journal of Women in Culture and Society, 30*(3), 1771–1800.

McLeod, C., O'Donohoe, S., & Townley, B. (2009). The elephant in the room? Class and creative careers in British advertising agencies. *Human Relations, 62*(7), 1011–1039.

Meghji, A. (2019). Encoding and decoding black and white cultural capitals: Black middle-class experiences. *Cultural Sociology, 13*(1), 3–19.

Meghji, A. (2020). Contesting racism: How do the black middle-class use cultural consumption for anti-racism? *Identities, 27*(5), 595–613.

Morley, L. (2021). Does class still matter? Conversations about power, privilege and persistent inequalities in higher education. *Discourse: Studies in the Cultural Politics of Education, 42*(1), 5–16.

O'Brien, D., Laurison, D., Miles, A., & Friedman, S. (2016). Are the creative industries meritocratic? An analysis of the 2014 British labour force survey. *Cultural Trends, 25*(2), 116–131.

O'Neill, D., & Wayne, M. (2018). *Considering class: Theory, culture and the media in the 21st century.* Brill.

Pakulski, J., & Walters, M. (1996). *The death of class.* Sage.

Parsons, J. M. (2016). *Gender, class and food: Families, bodies and health.* Palgrave Macmillan.

Payne, G., & Grew, C. (2005). Unpacking 'class ambivalence' some conceptual and methodological issues in accessing class cultures. *Sociology, 39*(5), 893–910.

Randle, K. (2015). Class and exclusion at work: The case of UK film and television. In *The Routledge companion to the cultural industries* (pp. 346–360). Routledge.

Reay, D. (1997). Feminist theory, habitus, and social class: Disrupting notions of classlessness. *Women's Studies International Forum, 20*(2), 225–233.

Reay, D. (2005). Beyond consciousness? The psychic landscape of social class. *Sociology, 39*(5), 911–928.

Reay, D. (2021). The working classes and higher education: Meritocratic fallacies of upward mobility in the United Kingdom. *European Journal of Education, 56*(1), 53–64.

Reay, D., Crozier, G., & Clayton, J. (2009). 'Strangers in paradise'? Working-class students in elite universities. *Sociology, 43*(6), 1103–1121.

Rollock, N., Gillborn, D., Vincent, C., & Ball, S. (2011). The public identities of the black middle classes: Managing race in public spaces. *Sociology, 45*(6), 1078–1093.

Rollock, N., Gillborn, D., Vincent, C., & Ball, S. J. (2014). *The colour of class: The educational strategies of the black middle classes.* Routledge.

Savage, M. (2000). *Class analysis and social transformation.* Open University.

Savage, M. (2015). *Social class in the 21st century.* Pelican.

Sayer, A. (2002). 'What are you worth?' Why class is an embarrassing subject. *Sociology Research, 7*(3). www.socresonline.org.uk/7/3/sayer.html

Shah, B., Dwyer, C., & Modood, T. (2010). Explaining educational achievement and career aspirations among young British Pakistanis: Mobilizing 'ethnic capital'? *Sociology, 44*(6), 1109–1127.

Skeggs, B. (1997). *Formations of class and gender: Becoming respectable*. Sage.

Skeggs, B. (2004). *Class, self, culture*. Routledge.

Stuber, J. M. (2006). Talk of class: The discursive repertoires of white working- and upper-middle-class college students. *Journal of Contemporary Ethnography, 35*(3), 285–318.

Taylor, M., & O'Brien, D. (2017). 'Culture is a meritocracy': Why creative workers' attitudes may reinforce social inequality. *Sociological Research Online, 22*(4), 27–47.

Valentine, G. (2007). Theorizing and researching intersectionality: A challenge for feminist geography. *The Professional Geographer, 59*(1), 10–21.

Walby, S., Armstrong, J., & Strid, S. (2012). Intersectionality: Multiple inequalities in social theory. *Sociology, 46*(2), 224–240.

Wallace, D. (2017). Reading 'race' in Bourdieu? Examining black cultural capital among black Caribbean youth in South London. *Sociology, 51*(5), 907–923.

Wallace, D. (2018). Cultural capital as whiteness? Examining logics of ethnoracial representation and resistance. *British Journal of Sociology of Education, 39*(4), 466–482.

2

The Union of Different Kinds: Classless Classes

Caglar Bideci

Introduction

When it comes to system creation where people are involved with individual differences within order (Miller, 1987), the intersectionality theory (Crenshaw, 1990) has opened a sincere discussion about inclusivity in the social environment and learning experience. The concept of intersectionality is established based on Kimberlé Williams Crenshaw's (2018) early work (originally published in 1989) whose "focus on the most privileged group members marginalizes those who are multiply burdened, and obscures claims that cannot be understood as resulting from discrete sources of discrimination" (1989, p. 140). In other words, intersectionality is "multi-layered and routinized forms of domination" (Crenshaw, 1990, p. 1245). The complexity of the intersectionality has increased over the years and involves multi-dimensional characteristics of social

C. Bideci (✉)
Business School for the Creative Industries, University for the Creative Arts, Epsom, UK
e-mail: caglar.bideci@uca.ac.uk

© The Author(s), under exclusive license to Springer Nature Switzerland AG 2023
B. S. Nayak (ed.), *Intersectionality and Creative Business Education*,
https://doi.org/10.1007/978-3-031-29952-0_2

inequality in lived experiences (McCall, 2005; Bowleg, 2012; Walby et al., 2012; Harris & Leonardo, 2018; Atewologun, 2018) in certain colour-dominated and particularly gender-dominated cultures that monolithically identified societies (Nash, 2008; Azhar & Gunn, 2021) in which others are forced to be marginalised (Remedios & Snyder, 2015) and discriminated in their lived experience (Collins & Bilge, 2016; Hopkins, 2019; Song, 2020). Eventually, this theory has also been applied broadly to creative education, ensuring inclusivity in learning environments. At the same time, as we become more aware of the diverse backgrounds of our students and colleagues, their sexual orientations, races, disabilities, genders, beliefs, and nationalities, this recognition brings (sometimes multiplies) stigmatisation, stereotypes, and (unintentional) microaggressions (Nadal et al., 2015) or unfavourable labels (Link & Phelan, 2001) to those with differences. As many others develop a non-positive gaze towards these groups, this reaction is not only emerged by age (Brahm, 2019), gender (Brown & Pinel, 2003), weight (Crocker et al., 1993), race and ethnicity (Dovidio et al., 2001; Nadal et al., 2015), physical and mental disabilities (Hebl & King, 2013), sexual orientation (Herek, 2004), religion (Nadal et al., 2015), and socioeconomic status (Link & Phelan, 2001; Twenge & Campbell, 2002) but also self-expression through "tattoos and piercings, dressing too flashily, putting on too much jewellery, too much make-up, too skimpy clothes, too coquettish attire, or too sissy attire; they can all be stigmatized at different times and places" (Sandıkçı & Ger, 2012, p. 111).

The intersectional approaches in the literature acknowledge that there is no homogeneous group within diversity because groups can experience or feel privilege and disadvantage as discrimination against themselves in one place simultaneously because of their sex, race, class, and cultural orientation status (Simien, 2007). Moreover, stigma has no time or context limits. Through interactions, it may develop more strong responses or eliminate the 'undesirable difference' (Goffman, 1963, p. 3), if certain conditions are provided (Sandıkçı & Ger, 2012). For example, according to Verloo (2006, p. 221), as "different inequalities are dissimilar because they are differently framed to be relevant as policy problems", creating a balance between intersectional groups and stigma is an essential point of departure to structure the school environments equally for every person and set up the policies along with the codes of conduct. In this connection, as classrooms are "with all its limitations, remains a location of possibility" (Hooks, 1994, p. 207), it is necessary to develop new and different analytical tools that help to better understand the specific circumstances or conditions (Yuval-Davis, 2006; Hankivsky, 2014) that ensure optimum representation of each identity in theory and practices (Phoenix & Pattynama, 2006). The (self) identity, while signifying the differences, provides space to people for creating a self-concept (including learning skills, understanding, and sharing ideas) in diverse learning experience environments. Or we suppose that it works in this way. However, if students have limited space to express their identity, it draws them back into classes and they become more timid to share their ideas in front of the class or with lecturers and instructors. It also discourages students to develop their self-confidence and self-skills associated with their identities and backgrounds.

According to United Nations Educational, Scientific and Cultural Organization (UNESCO) (2022), inclusivity based on gender and culture is necessary to emerge in creative industries as a primary human right. "Gender diversity and intersectionality are emerging areas of intervention, both contributing to advancing gender equality and fostering more diverse and inclusive cultural and creative sectors" (Planas, 2022, p. 241). Ensuring optimum diversity and inclusivity in the classroom relies on an intersectional approach that promotes participation of underrepresented genders, ethnic minorities, colour, disabilities groups, and underserved communities from different backgrounds. In this connection, it is important to know the degree of vulnerability (Woolf & Wamba, 2019) and "what differences, variations and similarities are considered to exist between and among relevant groups?" (Hankivsky et al., 2012, p. 39).

However, the solution for inclusivity is not solely including the marginalised, labelled, stigmatised, discriminated, stereotyped groups or individuals who suffer from (unintentional) microaggressions in the analytically structured system (Crenshaw, 1989), but by eliminating misconceptions in the existing systems (Loreman et al., 2014) and bringing to surface the invisible (Remedios & Snyder, 2018; Song, 2020) with collective effort (Ainscow & Sandill, 2010) cognitively (Howarth, 2006). To address this, intersectionality must begin to sort out the contradictions that underpin its theory in order to increase its explanatory capacity (Nash, 2008). According to Westfall, inclusivity "cultivates the skills and abilities of its citizens and communities and works towards a goal of equal opportunity and freedom from discrimination" (2010, p. 8), and "is a powerful means to reduce the impact of stigma and discrimination" (Hunting et al., 2015, p. 106), and this also will dismantle the structured powers (Atewologun, 2018). Therefore, it is important to recreate a system that represents all types of groups and multi-dimensional characteristics in unison with the appreciation of differences by exploring their level of capacity for creativity. For this purpose, it is better to understand the relationship between culture and history that shaped the individuals (Whitehead, 2008) and their potential for creativity and identity creation by encouraging them to explore their capacity in knowledge production with authentic reflection (Woolf & Wamba, 2019) and ensuring self-actualisation (Harris & Watson-Vandiver, 2020) in multi-dimensional learning environments with optimum inclusivity with a predictive ability (Adams, 2012).

System Creation, Hierarchy, Control, and Dominance

The system is to create a function which understands associated factors and appreciates differences within the organisation. "At its simplest level, a system is an integrated whole whose essential properties arise from the relationships between its constituent parts" (Hall, 2008, p. 69). With this in mind, systems theories become important elements to not only shape organisations in terms of providing effective management outputs (von Bertalanffy, 1972) but also determine the level of impact and maintain the power of influence according to the position and capacities of the participants (Adams, 2012) to ensure the functionality and effectiveness of the system for all. According to Ackoff (1981), all participants have interrelationships and outputs of these relations can influence the system and one another directly or indirectly. Throughout the interaction, the influence level may change to a certain extent and at a certain point (Fagen & Hall, 1956). In this connection, "a system may be defined as a set of elements standing in interrelation among themselves and with the environment" (von Bertalanffy, 1972, p. 417), which consists of "(1) set of elements; (2) the set of relationships between the elements; and (3) the set of relationships between these elements and the environment" (Hall, 2008, p. 71). Therefore, it is necessary to know participants and more importantly understand the level of influence of these contributors while developing interrelations and interacting with each other in the system.

Since the late 1940s, a wide range of systems approaches has been presented in literature, such as General Systems (von Bertalanffy, 1972); Living Systems (Miller, 1978); Cybernetics (Rosenblueth et al., 1943); and Social Systems (Parsons, 1970) theories. This chapter employs Adams's (2012) system creation model and 'Living Systems Theory' (developed by James Grier Miller in the 1950s and 1960s), which consists of eight interwoven levels and depends on the continuous interrelations in hierarchal interaction, namely (from lower to higher) "cells; organs; organisms; groups; organisations; communities; societies; and supranational system" (Miller & Miller, 1990, p. 158). The aim is to create a systematic approach that is applied to organisational behaviour which describes the behaviour of systems that are alive. The Living Systems Theory has been applied to a wide range of fields, including education, and it has been influential in the development of systems thinking which has influenced the way we think about organisations and the challenges we face. The Living Systems Theory is based on the idea that all living systems, from cells to supranational components, have certain characteristics that allow them to maintain their viability and adapt to their environment while influencing one another and the overall system according to the level of their inputs, throughputs, and outputs. The characteristics of the system include the ability to process and exchange information, adapt, evolve, and self-organise. In this sense, it proposes a learning environment by experience. The relationships between these components are critical to the functioning of the system and this can be understood in terms of their hierarchy of subsystems, each of which has its own interests and influences. This also addresses how the system works in harmony with essential associations. In addition to that Adams's seven grounds for the system are identified as "centrality; contextual; design; goal; information; operational; and viability" (2012, p. 220); these define the relationship between the elements and interaction levels (Laszlo & Krippner, 1998) when the system is in function. These constituent's posit system is self-organising and open for exchanging knowledge between the associated individuals or groups that belong or intend to enter the system (Adams, 2012; Adams et al., 2014). In other words, constituents rely on "acts of perception, interpretation, conceptualization, reflection, contemplation, explanation, articulation, and communication" (Laszlo & Krippner, 1998, p. 23).

However, it should be noted that, due to a lack of awareness towards influence level and lack of information exchange, the system may become of no use, and this increases the complexity of maintaining the relations systematically in collaboration with the functionality of the system. Therefore, the 'centrality' of the system refers to established control mechanisms. 'Contextual' explains the main purpose of the system and 'design' organises the relations and their impact levels while 'goal' defines the optimum outcomes of the actions. To improve the performance of the system, the 'information' brings codes of conduct and knowledge together for associated groups. The 'operational' provides a space to manage the interrelations to activate certain results. The 'viability' tests the operational capacity of the system continuously to ensure the associated groups belong to the proper working ecosystem. To be able to actualise and moderate a working system, the Living System Theory defines the participants of the system. These can be translated according to class and creative education environment into 'students (cell)'; 'administrative staff (organs)'; 'teaching staff (organisms)'; 'governance (groups)'; 'facility managers (organisations)'; 'executives (communities)'; 'the department/s (societies)'; and 'the university (supranational system)'.

Discrimination, Intersectionality, and University Education

Intersectionality posits to dismantle the inequalities in social life. Although the foundation of intersectionality started with coloured women having a lack of fair hearing from the court, it eventually became the sound of all who suffer from inequalities and experience discrimination in society and social institutions. In this chapter, educational aspects of intersectionality and its potential contributions will be taken into account. Fundamentally, intersectionality in creative education aims to reduce inequalities among students and encourages them to have more equal and the best learning experience. However, only knowing the students does not allow this. For example, in the UK, when students start an application to the university, they are faced with identity-reveal questions, including ones to know their sexual orientation, race, and disabilities (if known). Although it is essential to know these differences (Whitehead, 2008), the degree of vulnerability (Woolf & Wamba, 2019), and similarities (Hankivsky et al., 2012) to set up a better creative education system on it, solely including groups or individuals in the structured system does not ensure inclusivity (Crenshaw, 1989). Rather, this may increase the visibility of vulnerability and cause (unintended or systematic) discrimination against them by revealing their identity only. Instead, there should be a system created in which students can express themselves freely while exploring their authentic capacity (Woolf & Wamba, 2019; Harris & Watson-Vandiver, 2020) where optimum inclusivity is ensured (Adams, 2012). In this connection, Miller's Living System Theory can be a good exercise to develop a new system based on participants' influence level. As students are the core value of the system, the university becomes the foundation which will be built on everything that affects the learning experience for different backgrounds. This chapter discusses each participant and their influence level individually and signifies the potential solutions and recommendations by proposing a new system approach.

(a) The university (supranational system)

The role of the university is to create the overall space for the system where the participants can explore their capacities and start interacting with one another. This participant is not related to internal contributors, such as employees and partners, but also the students. Therefore, an inclusive space is necessary to develop and promote collective outcomes according to the power of the institution.

(b) The department/s (societies)

The departments refer to the execution spaces where students and staff can meet. In this connection, the departments have an intermediate role to bring the ideas and policies into practice that create the space for students to explore their capacities and enhance their learning experiences.

(c) Executives (communities)

The executives, mainly, refer to policymakers to ensure quality assurance and provide optimum student experience. Moreover, the executives regulate the capacity of staff to be able to represent the unity of the system and its outcomes.

(d) Facility managers (organisations)

Facility managers are an important group of participants in the system who ensure the quality of creative education and standardised learning experience for the students. They are also important elements that provide optimum technology to execute education.

(e) Governance (groups)

The governance is the management team of the university that enforces the policies, controls the practices, and assesses the outcomes. The main role of governance is to provide constant control over the extent of the learning experience.

(f) Teaching staff (organisms)

Teaching staff are those who have various groups of qualifications and skills to put into practice. They are the ambassadors who interact with students. In this sense, optimum qualifications and better knowledge exchange can bring success to the system in terms of ensuring the best learning experience for the students.

(g) Administrative staff (organs)

The administrative staff is the first group of people whom students meet before starting to explore their learning capacities. In this connection, they are the first representatives of the system. The credibility of the group of participants can affect positively the impression of the students before joining the system.

(h) Students (cell)

Students are the most important components of the system and provide the purpose to run the system. Without students, the system may become dysfunctional, and may end up closing the system with all components. Therefore, students are the most important participants in the overall system. However, whether they are offered a better experience or not is an ongoing discussion. Knowing them well is a crucial starting point to ensure acceptance in the system, minimise misleading their interests, and improve the quality of the learning experience for the students.

With this in mind, the classic hierarchical system approach can be enhanced by reversing it with two-fold structures (Fig. 2.1). This is because hierarchy in classic systems does not allow putting the requirements of students above the policies. In general, policies shape the interests of students. However, in terms of ensuring optimum intersectionality in creative education, knowing the interests and learning capacities of students first and restructuring policies around these levels of interests and learning experience become important practices. As Cousin (2006, p. 5) states, "because it is difficult for teachers to gaze backwards across thresholds, they need to hear what the students' misunderstandings and uncertainties are in order to sympathetically engage with them". This also applies to the whole creative education system provided by the university as the supranational system. In this connection, the position of the university becomes centred on the system to start with it. The university provides a space where different interests and requirements are met. Within this design, each group of participants has their own interests, and they can affect the system at a different level. The suggested system

Fig. 2.1 Two-fold system approach for optimum intersectionality

supports Kolb's (1984) experiential learning structure. This also allows the system to hear students more accurately to structure the threshold which starts with concrete experience (Kolb, 2014). Reflecting the observation experience shapes the policies by providing abstract conceptualisation and finally becomes an active experimentation for all participants in the system. Learn and act are the main thresholds of the suggested system.

To be able to standardise higher (creative) education (Weller, 2015), it is essential to understand all positions of participants and their individual capacities in the system. One of the concrete strategies can be the four-step strategy derived from Brookfield's (2017) four lenses. First, active observation should be centred on each step of the process. Second, there should be an updated discussion of the codes of conduct and practices. Third, administrative and teaching materials should be adjusted proactively according to the needs of students to facilitate the learning experience according to quality assurance requirements. Lastly, constant evaluation with feedback (Stupans et al., 2016) should be provided for each group of participants to assess the implications. However, to ensure effective education (Stefani, 2009), a better understanding of the interests of students not only related to their identity but also their learning capacities and preferences is the fundamental tool to shape the overall quality and inclusivity in the sense of optimum intersectionality. Although policies and executives are important to run the system effectively, 'knowledge-in-action' (Schön, 2017) as part of the stage of learning through the experience (Ghaye, 2011; Swain et al., 2020) becomes the fundamental source of power to ensure quality assurance and inclusive learning opportunities. Korkmaz and Toraman (2020 cited from Siemens, 2004) note that knowledge should "rest in diversity of opinions; connects specialized nodes or information sources; address to see connections between fields, ideas, and concepts is a core skill" (p. 294).

In another respect, the justification of objectives and values for the system and the skills of participants (Denson et al., 2010; Wolfer & Johnson, 2003) are essential components to creating a well-functional system approach. In this sense, as Hativa et al. (2001) state, a system catering to the interests of students is the first practice for providing inclusive learning environments (Coates, 2005). By doing so, the policies and interests of participants can merge in an effective co-creative (Bovill et al., 2011) system with a constructive approach (Brooks & Brooks, 1999) which can encourage more inclusive participatory opportunities in higher (creative) education with integrative intersectionality. To enhance education practices (Smith, 2010) via experiential learning (Kolb & Kolb, 2009, 2018) where optimum inclusivity can be ensured (Dallas et al., 2016; Nijhuis et al., 2005), it is essential to develop advanced learning facilities and effective learning environments in order to build confidence in the learning experience (Fry & Ketteridge, 2008). For this, as Nijhuis et al. (2005) posit, redesigning the overall structure can provide a higher degree of learning and lower misleading. By doing so, this new learning environment can be more functional and explicate the goals of the institution with clear instructions (Nijhuis et al., 2005). This will provide "the ability to draw reasonable conclusions based on evidence, logic, and intellectual honesty" (Rowe et al., 2017, p. 2).

The critical influence comes from professional development based on how the system forms and responds to the positive impact on academic quality standards. Therefore, optimum communication between participants can contribute to enhancing practical implications and better knowledge exchange. To build effective knowledge, according to Brooks and Brooks (1999), understanding the most recent thinking of students along with their capacities would be the practical and wise option to evaluate the expectations and outcomes. In practice, intersectionality is applied to current systems in a number of ways: First, increase diversity, which means having a more diverse group and creating a more inclusive and welcoming environment for all. This helps to provide role models and mentorship for all students but especially for underrepresented groups and can also bring different perspectives and experiences to the educational environment. The second way is to offer a more inclusive curriculum that reflects the experiences of a diverse range of groups. The current systems offer support programmes additional for underrepresented groups to help them succeed in higher (creative) education. The third tool is to provide support for underrepresented students which addresses issues of diversity, equity, and inclusion, and these include things like financial support or counselling services if needed. The fourth strategy is to promote inclusive policies and practices for people who disproportionately impact underrepresented groups, which include gender-neutral restrooms and housing and accommodations for students with disabilities. The fifth approach is to foster a culture of inclusivity and promote an inclusive educational environment climate by promoting diversity and inclusion through events, initiatives, and resources, and by actively addressing incidents of discrimination and bias when they occur. This requires training for faculty and staff on issues related to diversity and inclusion, as well as promoting dialogue and understanding among students.

The above-mentioned strategies are structured before the students join the university. However, as Crenshaw (1989) stated, the solution for inclusivity is not merely to include groups discriminated against or underrepresented in the system. Therefore, there is a need for a new system approach for higher (creative) education institutions which can promote more effective inclusivity to tackle the current problems, act more proactively to address intersectionality, and make sure that they are creating a welcoming and inclusive environment for all. In this connection, there is a need for a space for students to express their own authentic reflection (Woolf & Wamba, 2019) and their level of self-actualisation (Harris & Watson-Vandiver, 2020). In addition to that, providing a better understanding of the degree of vulnerability (Woolf & Wamba, 2019) and differences and similarities among relevant groups (Hankivsky et al., 2012) can help provide more inclusive classes and an optimum learning experience for all. In the two-fold system design, the interests of students become the centre of the learning environment. For this reason, along with the identity, background, and orientation questions, a new topic should be added to explore students' learning capacities and interests while starting the admission process. To create more engaging educational environments it is essential to better understand students' particular subject of interests, expectations, and desires or inclination to do something or to learn more about something.

Although specific subjects allow students to engage according to their interests and act proactively, it is more important to learn their individual interests and more importantly their capacities towards learning in order to restructure policies and standards. For example, there could be an added question of the reason for taking higher (creative) education (specifically in the UK, for instance). There are many different types of learning capacities and experiences, and they can vary from the individual learner to the dynamic of groups they will interact with. One of the learning experiences is formal education, which refers to structured learning that takes place in a classroom or any other educational setting organized and delivered. The other experience is informal creative education, which refers to learning through experience, such as activities like reading or travelling. Online learning is both an old and new term of creative education which addresses self-paced learning or one following a structured schedule; it can be live or recorded content. The collaborative learning experience is one of the types that refer to learning that takes place through interactions with others in order to enhance social skills and critical thinking skills, for example, through group discussions, team projects, or peer feedback. Self-directed learning experience pinpoints learning that is initiated and controlled by the learner. Self-directed learners take an active role in their own learning experience.

Along with the above-stated learning experiences, experiential learning (which also supports the proposed two-fold system approach) refers to learning through hands-on experiences which allow learners to apply knowledge and skills in a practical setting and reflect on not only their experiences but also self-actualisation. For this reason, rather than reminding their identity, race, sexual orientation, who they are, or where they come from by asking multiple questions about them, the admission process should be restructured to explore individual differences and similarities in learning experiences. In the recent era, there are an increasing number of studies which explore differences and similarities in students' learning experiences (see Chen et al., 2014; Poon, 2013; Zerihun et al., 2012). The outcomes of these studies can be applied more constructively along with Kolb's (2014) experiential learning approach and Brookfield's (2017) four lenses. For example, as mentioned previously, active observation should be the centre of the admission process regarding individual learning differences and similarities. Codes of conduct and practices should be updated according to the dynamics and learning capacities of students. Teaching materials should be adjusted according to the needs of students and facilitate the learning experience according to quality assurance requirements along with the administrative implications. Constant evaluation with feedback should be provided to assess the quality of implications throughout the creative education terms. By doing so, the learning experience in higher (creative) education will be more personalised for students and more flexible for educators and providers to facilitate inclusive classes and ensure standard creative education qualities for all. This will dismantle the structured power (Atewologun, 2018) barriers over optimum intersectionality in creative education by providing a better understanding of individual differences and similarities.

To clarify the relationship between the elements and interaction levels (Laszlo & Krippner, 1998) in the two-fold system approach for optimum intersectionality, systems components are situated according to Adams (2012, p. 220) as follows: the centrality of the two-fold system is to explore the interest and capacities of participants along with the identities and the contextual is how the system can provide a better learning experience for all. It also refers to the main aim of the system. The two-fold design dismantles the structured hierarchy and turns it into a more open space for all groups of participants where they can explore their capacities. The goal of the system is to ensure optimum intersectionality with more inclusive engagement. The information is individually influenced by personal capacities and learning experiences. The operational level (as the redesigned system approach) explains the degree of knowledge exchange among groups of participants. The viability ensures that the two-fold system is an open system and welcomes all types of differences and similarities.

Conclusion

This chapter aims to redesign the structured hierarchical system approach in higher (creative) education in order to address optimum intersectionality and effective inclusivity. For this purpose, the chapter discussed intersectionality and broadened the knowledge of the systems approach. As a result, a new system approach has been presented which aligns with education theories (Kolb's experiential learning and Brookfield's four lenses) and contemporary issues. Compared to classic design, this study focused on a two-fold system approach which allows different participants to contribute and have harmony in knowledge exchange. In this connection, Miller's Living Systems Theory has been chosen as a foundational framework to identify the components of the system. In this sense, there are eight participants in the two-fold system and the centre of the system is divided by two folds, with the university as the supranational system. This allows the university to have flexibility in controlling different interests and expectations of participants in the system. The other important contribution of the system is the interest of students; they have their own priorities and need more space to be heard. For this purpose, there is a need for constant interaction among participants and continuous feedback about the implications to ensure the intended outcomes are addressed for the success of the system. However, the existing system approach is limited in terms of information sharing because of the hierarchy. For example, when the admission process comes into practice, students are asked only about demographic characteristics. This may cause unintentional discrimination against underrepresented groups and may end with microaggression. To eliminate this and provide equality among different groups of students, this chapter suggests restructuring the admission process in way of exploring the learning capacities and interests of students first. This will increase self-confidence among students, and compared to (unseen) differentiation according to the demographic features, knowing learning capacities will allow the system to adjust the policies and implications in advance and more effectively.

As mentioned in this chapter, although there are effective solutions to ensure optimum inclusivity, there are still gaps in order to execute the intentions of intersectionality. In this connection, as this chapter proposes, identification questions in the admission processes are needed to be updated in order to provide a better understanding of differences and similarities in learning capacities. For this, the supernatural system (the universities) should collaborate with psychologists and education theorists to redesign the questions of the admission process to build confidence in learning, rather than reminding them who they are and what differences they possess. However, according to Hankivsky et al. (2012), it is also important to know demographic features such as gender, race, or other relevant background features to have a better understanding of differences and similarities, and more importantly the degree of vulnerability (Woolf & Wamba, 2019). Despite the degree of knowledge we develop among students and colleagues, the sole involvement of different groups in the system without understanding them can increase the risk of "multi-layered and routinized forms of domination" (Crenshaw, 1990, p. 1245), as exists in the current systems. Therefore, paying attention to differences with optimum non-structured participation in terms of revealing the capacities and interests can help to readdress the policies in a way of creating a more inclusive learning environment in higher (creative) education. This will ensure unity among different kinds and create classless classes. It is noted that this chapter only focuses on understanding the learning capacities and interests of students and redesigning the existing system approach. In this sense, this chapter has a limitation in representing the overall intersectionality in higher (creative) education. This study refers to one problem in order to fill the gap in the existing literature. Future studies can focus on more indications of intersectionality and apply a methodological approach to test the outcomes.

References

Ackoff, R. L. (1981). On the use of models in corporate planning. *Strategic Management Journal, 2*(4), 353–359.

Adams, K. M. (2012). Systems theory: A formal construct for understanding systems. *International Journal of System of Systems Engineering, 3*(3–4), 209–224.

Adams, K. M., Hester, P. T., Bradley, J. M., Meyers, T. J., & Keating, C. B. (2014). Systems theory as the foundation for understanding systems. *Systems Engineering, 17*(1), 112–123.

Ainscow, M., & Sandill, A. (2010). Developing inclusive education systems: The role of organisational cultures and leadership. *International Journal of Inclusive Education, 14*(4), 401–416.

Atewologun, D. (2018). Intersectionality theory and practice. In *Oxford research encyclopedia of business and management*.

Azhar, S., & Gunn, A. J. (2021). Navigating intersectional stigma: Strategies for coping among cisgender women of color. *Qualitative Health Research, 31*(12), 2194–2210.

Bowleg, L. (2012). The problem with the phrase women and minorities: Intersectionality—An important theoretical framework for public health. *American Journal of Public Health, 102*(7), 1267–1273.

Bovill, C., Cook-Sather, A., & Felten, P. (2011). Students as co-creators of teaching approaches, course design, and curricula: Implications for academic developers. *International Journal for Academic Development, 16*(2), 133–145.

Brahm, G. N. (2019). Intersectionality. *Israel Studies, 24*(2), 157–170.

Brookfield, S. D. (2017). *Becoming a critically reflective teacher*. John Wiley & Sons.

Brooks, J. G. & Brooks, M. G. (1999). *In search of understanding: The case for constructivist classrooms*. Ascd.

Brown, R. P., & Pinel, E. C. (2003). Stigma on my mind: Individual differences in the experience of stereotype threat. *Journal of Experimental Social Psychology, 39*(6), 626–633.

Chen, X., Vorvoreanu, M., & Madhavan, K. (2014). Mining social media data for understanding students' learning experiences. *IEEE Transactions on Learning Technologies, 7*(3), 246–259.

Coates, H. (2005). The value of student engagement for higher education quality assurance. *Quality in Higher Education, 11*(1), 25–36.

Collins, P. H., & Bilge, S. (2016). *Intersectionality*. Polity.

Cousin, G. (2006). An introduction to threshold concepts. *Planet, 17*(1), 4–5.

Crocker, J., Cornwell, B., & Major, B. (1993). The stigma of overweight: Affective consequences of attributional ambiguity. *Journal of Personality and Social Psychology, 64*(1), 60.

Crenshaw, K. (1989). Demarginalizing the intersection of race and sex: A black feminist critique of antidiscrimination doctrine, feminist theory and antiracist politics. In *University of Chicago Legal Forum* (Vol. 1989, p. 1).

Crenshaw, K. (1990). Mapping the margins: Intersectionality, identity politics, and violence against women of color. *Stanford Law Review, 43*(6), 1241–1299.

Crenshaw, K. (2018). Demarginalizing the intersection of race and sex: A black feminist critique of antidiscrimination doctrine, feminist theory, and antiracist politics [1989]. In *Feminist legal theory* (pp. 57–80). Routledge.

Dallas, B. K., McCarthy, A. K., & Long, G. (2016). Examining the educational benefits of and attitudes toward closed captioning among undergraduate students. *Journal of the Scholarship of Teaching and Learning, 16*(2), 50–65.

Denson, N., Loveday, T., & Dalton, H. (2010). Student evaluation of courses: What predicts satisfaction? *Higher Education Research & Development, 29*(4), 339–356.

Dovidio, J. F., Gaertner, S. L., Niemann, Y. F., & Snider, K. (2001). Racial, ethnic, and cultural differences in responding to distinctiveness and discrimination on campus: Stigma and common group identity. *Journal of Social Issues, 57*(1), 167–188.

Fagen, R. E., & Hall, A. D. (1956). Definition of a system general systems. In *Yearbook of the society for the advancement of general systems theory* (pp. 18–28).

Fry, H., & Ketteridge, S. (2008). Enhancing personal practice: Establishing teaching and learning credentials. In *A handbook for teaching and learning in higher education* (pp. 487–502). Routledge.

Hall, C. M. (2008). *Tourism planning: Policies, processes and relationships*. Pearson education.

Hankivsky, O. (2014). Rethinking care ethics: On the promise and potential of an intersectional analysis. *American Political Science Review, 108*(2), 252–264.

Hankivsky, O., Grace, D., Hunting, G., Ferlatte, O., Clark, N., Fridkin, A., & Laviolette, T. (2012). Intersectionality-based policy analysis. In *An intersectionality-based policy analysis framework* (pp. 33–45).

Harris, A., & Leonardo, Z. (2018). Intersectionality, race-gender subordination, and education. *Review of Research in Education, 42*(1), 1–27.

Harris, L., & Watson-Vandiver, M. J. (2020). Decolonizing race and gender intersectionality in education: A collaborative critical autoethnography of hope, healing and justice. *Journal of Cultural Analysis and Social Change, 5*(2), 1–16.

Hativa, N., Barak, R., & Simhi, E. (2001). Exemplary university teachers: Knowledge and beliefs regarding effective teaching dimensions and strategies. *The Journal of Higher Education, 72*(6), 699–729.

Hebl, M. R., & King, E. B. (2013). The social and psychological experience of stigma. In Q. M. Roberson (Ed.), *The Oxford handbook of diversity and work* (pp. 115–131). Oxford University Press.

Herek, G. M. (2004). Beyond "homophobia": Thinking about sexual prejudice and stigma in the twenty-first century. *Sexuality Research & Social Policy, 1*(2), 6–24.

Hooks, B. (1994). *Teaching to transgress: Education as the practice of freedom.* Routledge.

Hopkins, P. (2019). Social geography I: Intersectionality. *Progress in Human Geography, 43*(5), 937–947.

Howarth, C. (2006). Race as stigma: Positioning the stigmatized as agents, not objects. *Journal of Community & Applied Social Psychology, 16*(6), 442–451.

Hunting, G., Grace, D., & Hankivsky, O. (2015). Taking action on stigma and discrimination: An intersectionality-informed model of social inclusion and exclusion. Intersectionalities: A global journal of social work analysis. *Research, Polity, and Practice, 4*(2), 101–125.

Ghaye, T. (2011). *Teaching and learning through reflective practice: A practical guide for positive action.* Routledge.

Goffman, E. (1963). *Stigma: Notes on the management of spoiled identity.* Prentice-Hall.

Kolb, A., & Kolb, D. (2018). Eight important things to know about the experiential learning cycle. *Australian Educational Leader, 40*(3), 8–14.

Kolb, A. Y., & Kolb, D. A. (2009). Experiential learning theory: A dynamic, holistic approach to management learning, education and development. In *The SAGE handbook of management learning, education and development* (Vol. 42, p. 68).

Kolb, D. A. (1984). *Experiential learning: Experience as the source of learning and development*. Prentice-Hall.

Kolb, D. A. (2014). *Experiential learning: Experience as the source of learning and development*. FT Press.

Korkmaz, G., & Toraman, Ç. (2020). Are we ready for the post-COVID-19 educational practice? An investigation into what educators think as to online learning. *International Journal of Technology in Education and Science, 4*(4), 293–309.

Laszlo, A., & Krippner, S. (1998). Systems theories: Their origins, foundations, and development. *Advances in Psychology-Amsterdam, 126*, 47–76.

Loreman, T., Forlin, C., Chambers, D., Sharma, U., & Deppeler, J. (2014). Conceptualising and measuring inclusive education. In *Measuring inclusive education*. Emerald Group Publishing Limited.

Link, B. G., & Phelan, J. C. (2001). Conceptualizing stigma. *Annual Review of Sociology, 27*, 363–385.

McCall, L. (2005). The complexity of intersectionality. *Signs: Journal of Women in Culture and Society, 30*(3), 1771–1800.

Miller, D. (1987). *Material culture and mass consumption* (Vol. 3). Blackwell.

Miller, J. G. (1978). *Living systems*. McGraw Hill.

Miller, J. G., & Miller, J. L. (1990). Introduction: The nature of living systems. *Behavioral Science, 35*(3), 157–163.

Nadal, K. L., Davidoff, K. C., Davis, L. S., Wong, Y., Marshall, D., & McKenzie, V. (2015). Intersectional identities and microaggressions: Influences of race, ethnicity, gender, sexuality, and religion. *Qualitative Psychology, 2*(2), 147–163.

Nash, J. C. (2008). Re-thinking intersectionality. *Feminist Review, 89*(1), 1–15.

Nijhuis, J. F., Segers, M. S., & Gijselaers, W. H. (2005). Influence of redesigning a learning environment on student perceptions and learning strategies. *Learning Environments Research, 8*(1), 67–93.

Parsons, T. (1970). On building social system theory: A personal history. *Daedalus*, 826–881.

Phoenix, A., & Pattynama, P. (2006). Intersectionality. *European Journal of Women's Studies, 13*(3), 187–192.

Planas, V. A. (2022). *Gender equality: One step forward, two steps back*. Re|shaping policies for creativity: Addressing culture as a global public good, UNESCO (No: 64806), pp. 242-261. [online] Accessed Dec 18, 2022, from https://unesdoc.unesco.org/ark:/48223/pf0000380474

Poon, J. (2013). Blended learning: An institutional approach for enhancing students' learning experiences. *Journal of Online Learning and Teaching, 9*(2), 271–288.

Remedios, J. D., & Snyder, S. H. (2015). Where do we go from here? Toward an inclusive and intersectional literature of multiple stigmatization. *Sex Roles, 73*(9), 408–413.

Remedios, J. D., & Snyder, S. H. (2018). Intersectional oppression: Multiple stigmatized identities and perceptions of invisibility, discrimination, and stereotyping. *Journal of Social Issues, 74*(2), 265–281.

Rosenblueth, A., Wiener, N., & Bigelow, J. (1943). Behavior, purpose and teleology. *Philosophy of Science, 10*(1), 18–24.

Rowe, M. P., Gillespie, B. M., Harris, K. R., Koether, S. D., Shannon, L. J. Y., & Rose, L. A. (2017). Redesigning a general education science course to promote critical thinking. *CBE—Life Sciences Education, 14*(3), 1–12.

Sandıkçı, Ö., & Ger, G. (2012). Stigma, consumption and identity. In *The Routledge companion to identity and consumption* (pp. 111–118). Routledge.

Schön, D. A. (2017). *The reflective practitioner: How professionals think in action.* Routledge.

Siemens, G. (2004). *Connectivism: A learning theory for the digital age.*

Simien, E. M. (2007). Doing intersectionality research: From conceptual issues to practical examples. *Politics & Gender, 3*(2), 264–271.

Smith, M. K. (2010). *'David A. Kolb on experiential learning', the encyclopedia of pedagogy and informal education.* [online] Accessed May 01, 2023, from: https://infed.org/mobi/david-a-kolb-on-experiential-learning/

Song, M. (2020). Rethinking minority status and 'visibility'. *Comparative Migration Studies, 8*(1), 1–17.

Stefani, L. (2009). Planning teaching and learning: Curriculum design and development. In *A handbook for teaching and learning in higher education* (pp. 58–75). Routledge.

Stupans, I., McGuren, T., & Babey, A. M. (2016). Student evaluation of teaching: A study exploring student rating instrument free-form text comments. *Innovative Higher Education, 41*(1), 33–42.

Swain, J., Kumlien, K., & Bond, A. (2020). An experiential exercise for teaching theories of work motivation: Using a game to teach equity and expectancy theories. *Organization Management Journal., 17*, 119.

Twenge, J. M., & Campbell, W. K. (2002). Self-esteem and socioeconomic status: A meta-analytic review. *Personality and Social Psychology Review, 6*(1), 59–71.

Verloo, M. (2006). Multiple inequalities, intersectionality and the European Union. *European Journal of Women's Studies, 13*(3), 211–228.

von Bertalanffy, L. (1972). The history and status of general systems theory. *Academy of Management Journal, 15*(4), 407–426.

Walby, S., Armstrong, J., & Strid, S. (2012). Intersectionality: Multiple inequalities in social theory. *Sociology, 46*(2), 224–240.

Weller, S. (2015). *Academic practice: Developing as a professional in higher education.* Sage.

Westfall, R., (2010). Dimensions of social inclusion and exclusion in Yukon.

Whitehead, J. (2008). Using a living theory methodology in improving practice and generating educational knowledge in living theories. *Educational Journal of Living Theories, 1*(1), 103–126.

Wolfer, T. A., & Johnson, M. M. (2003). Re-evaluating student evaluation of teaching: The teaching evaluation form. *Journal of Social Work Education, 39*(1), 111–121.

Woolf, S. B., & Wamba, N. G. (2019). Embracing intersectionality to create a collective living theory of practice. *Action Research, 17*(2), 208–219.

Yuval-Davis, N. (2006). Intersectionality and feminist politics. *European Journal of Women's Studies, 13*(3), 193–209.

United Nations Educational, Scientific and Cultural Organization (UNESCO), (2022). *Re|shaping policies for creativity: addressing culture as a global public good*, UNESCO (No: 64806) [online] Accessed Dec 18, 2022, from https://unesdoc.unesco.org/ark:/48223/pf0000380474

Zerihun, Z., Beishuizen, J., & Van Os, W. (2012). Student learning experience as indicator of teaching quality. *Educational Assessment, Evaluation and Accountability, 24*(2), 99–111.

3

Recognising the Unrecognised: Work-Based Learning Pedagogy as Tempered Radicalism

Anita Walsh, Philip Powell,
and Sara Leal de Matos-Powell

Introduction

Higher education (HE) is considered a potential life-changing activity for people and for society. As Day et al. state, 'The economic, social and cultural case for higher education is compelling. Participation in higher education delivers benefits for individuals and societies. The importance of a highly-skilled, tertiary-educated workforce is recognised as a key driver of a knowledge-based innovative economy. The global labour market increasingly demands a degree as a necessary prerequisite for

A. Walsh
Birkbeck, University of London, London, UK
e-mail: a.walsh@bbk.ac.uk

P. Powell (✉)
Business School for the Creative Industries, University for the Creative Arts, Epsom, UK
e-mail: philip.powell@uca.ac.uk

S. L. de Matos-Powell
University College London, London, UK

B. S. Nayak (ed.), *Intersectionality and Creative Business Education*,
https://doi.org/10.1007/978-3-031-29952-0_3

higher-skilled jobs. Areas with higher levels of graduate-skilled populations are proven to generally have less crime and more social cohesion, with graduates more likely to live longer, healthier lives and with greater civic responsibility.'

While HE can be life-changing, individuals must have the opportunity to participate in order to benefit. Individuals may not be able to participate, or to get full value, for a variety of reasons, many of which relate to disadvantages. While some prospective students will have single issues that will inhibit them, others may present with more issues. Crenshaw's (1989, 1991) identification of 'intersectionality' as a concept represented a call for a move away from considering policies aiming to address disadvantages as single issues, such as those designed solely to address issues relating to gender, race and other characteristics. Rather, she wished to highlight a relational understanding of privilege, power and oppression (Christoffersen & Hankivsky, 2021). From this perspective, intersectionality is about how individual experience is shaped by the range of different factors which interact, often without conscious awareness, to influence life chances.

Intersectionality is a multi-layered and complex process. It is generally understood in terms of race and/or ethnicity or gender, but also includes a range of other factors including disability, age and social class. As Christoffersen and Hankivsky (2021) point out, in a situation where various factors interact, it is not easy to identify which forms of inequality are salient in particular contexts. It has been argued that social class, defined as an aspect of existence grounded in the experience of the economic world with links to culture and society, is a key mediator of life experiences. Yet this has been underutilised as a construct in the context of intersectionality (Block & Corona, 2014). It is, however, a major consideration in terms of widening access to higher education in the UK with a series of approaches designed to facilitate the recruitment of students from socially disadvantaged groups.

The dominance of the market model in higher education, with its emphasis on competition, has adversely affected such activities. Tomlinson (2018, p. 712) points out that equity policies such as widening participation 'largely co-exist alongside a neo-liberal ethic of heightened student market rationality and self interest' in contrast to a culture of higher education as a transformative experience. With such a market model, it is recognised that potential students who have experienced social marginalisation are disadvantaged due to their lack of experience with higher education cultures, meaning that they are less informed and, therefore, less powerful consumers (Rammell, 2016). The requirement for inter-institutional competition based on metrics such as entry qualifications and retention rates has led some higher education institutions (HEIs) to be reluctant to engage fully with widening access, resulting in a persistent attainment gap between different social groupings (Rammell, 2016).

Students from a widening participation background have different needs from higher education given that they frequently come to HE later than the traditional 18-year-old intake for whom university is the logical next step. As Tallantyre argues:

> At the level of equity and diversity, it is essential that higher education support people who wish to continue their learning to higher levels … in whatever context they … find themselves. Since work dominates adult life as the main form of sustainable existence, many will inevitably make their choice in that context. … It has already been proven that workforce development activity is more likely to widen participation by those from lower socio-economic groups than almost any other activity.

All higher education institutions committed to widening access and lifelong learning will have students who are in work while they study, and at the postgraduate level the proportion of students studying part-time in order to enhance their careers is high. More recently, it is likely that members of the 'mainstream' undergraduate student body will have part-time employment due to the lack of grants and loans that fully cover tuition and living expenses.

The introduction in the UK of the Higher Education Qualifications Framework and credit practice into HE, together with modularity, was intended to support the development of a more student-responsive HE system. More recently, the introduction of awards requiring co-operation with employers—for example, Foundation Degrees and the Degree Apprenticeship—has encouraged the recognition of both work-based and academic learning in the higher education curriculum.

Yet this is not an uncontested territory. Higher education with a vocational focus is often defined negatively. It is argued to represent education as either 'investment' or 'consumption' rather than for individual and social emancipation (Coffield, 1999). Responding to employers in the design of programmes is still a contested area—with claims being made relating to 'anticipatory socialisation' prior to labour market entry (Simons & Masschelein, 2008) and learning being a force to produce added value for the employer rather than benefit to the learner (Colley et al., 2003). Much attention has been paid to the extent to which learning in the workplace may be impacted by employers that disadvantage learners by requiring them to acquire learning to meet needs other than their own. Foucault's (1982, 1991) concepts of disciplinary power and the social technology of control outline the extent to which more unobtrusive means of control allow for a more subtle exercise of power through discourse. Discussions critiquing work-based learning refer to Foucault's concept of governmentality, and the extent to which work-based learners are encouraged to self-govern towards conformity, thus reinforcing existing power relations in organisations (Usher & Edwards, 1994). This is contrasted to current arrangements in HE, whereby courses are designed to provide learners with an appropriate academic and developmental learning experience.

Academic staff who practice in the area of work-based learning recognise that such students, who are often mature, bring considerable life and work experience to their studies. From this perspective, using a pedagogic approach which treats students as novices and inducts them into a disciplinary practice which may not be relevant to their life and work experience is inappropriate. However, work-based learning practitioners also recognise the lack of confidence colleagues sometimes have in this approach to academic study (Walsh, 2011).

This chapter next argues that work-based learning offers a potential response to the individual experience of students in the workplace that has been highlighted through intersectionality, using a pedagogic approach based on an epistemology of practice and andragogy, which Knowles (1984) defines as 'the art and science of helping adults learn'. This pedagogic approach recognises that such students bring a wide range of experiences to their studies and that this enables individual personal and professional knowledge to be integrated into academic awards. This move towards student-centred learning, as opposed to discipline-centred learning, contains a challenge to dominant practice for the reasons discussed next. This requires that work-based learning tutors practice 'tempered radicalism'.

Work-Based Learning and the Higher Education Curriculum

As Apple (1993, p. 222) points out, 'The curriculum is never simply a neutral assembly of knowledge. … It is always part of a selective tradition, someone's selection, some group's vision of legitimate knowledge.' In higher education it is the academic disciplines which usually decide the shape of the curriculum.

Academic disciplines are seen by the academy as essential to the maintenance of academic standards through peer review of valid knowledge (Gibbons et al., 1994). This is expressed through the emphasis on research-led teaching, where novice students are exposed to the expert knowledge of academics and are inducted into the practice of a given academic discipline. The majority of students enrol on named awards and enter the discourse of a specific disciplinary practice. Programme structure is approved for its academic coherence by colleagues within the discipline. The strong disciplinary structure and the importance of scholarly values and attainment mean that academia tends to be inward-looking (Jongbloed et al., 2008). It could be argued that many degree programmes are designed to meet the needs of the academy. They are certainly designed to ensure that those who eventually practice within an academic discipline will do so appropriately. But this model may be insufficiently responsive in a context where the majority of students, inexperienced or experienced, do not intend to be academics.

With students entering higher education from a wider range of backgrounds, there is a requirement for a more student-centred response to be integrated into the curriculum, supporting mature students in identifying the professional knowledge they may already possess.

Discussion around this issue may be problematic when disciplinary knowledge is so closely allied to expertise that standards and subject content tend to become conflated, so that 'contextualisation is perceived to be a shortcoming which potentially threatens academic standards' (Walsh, 2007). It has been argued that curriculum change takes place 'at a glacial pace', with relatively minor changes arising from faculty's research interests and the knowledge transmission model still dominant in the academy (Pitt-Watson & Quigley, 2019). Although there are calls in the business education literature for its replacement with a new paradigm, there is limited evidence of attempts to do this.

An emphasis on communities of academic scholars pursuing knowledge for its own sake, rather than engaging with employers and employees to achieve learning perceived to have solely utilitarian value, often implies that the university is sui generis and therefore different to other large organisations. The rhetoric emphasising unequal power relations between employer and employee obscures the degree to which power relations exist within the academy, particularly the power dynamics existing between students and staff. In a context where most students have no wish to pursue an academic career, academic disciplines and the assessment requirements accompanying them could be seen as the exercise of power over learners (Fejes & Nicoll, 2008). Learners must comply with the requirements in order to get their award.

Foucault claims that due to the fluid nature of power dynamics, power is exercised through discourse, and involves both inclusion and exclusion of topics (Knudsen, 2006). Foremost, and therefore most powerful in discursive practices, are assumptions that are taken for granted (Ahl, 2006). An assumption which is embedded in the cognitive approach to learning that is dominant in the academy is the hierarchical ranking of knowledge, with traditional, formal learning taking primacy over informal learning outside the institution (Kennedy, 2015). The emphasis on formal theories leads to a devaluing of other contexts, leading to the assumption that the decontextualised models developed in the university can offer general solutions to particular problems which can be applied in practical situations (Hager & Halliday, 2006). The elevation of knowledge and understandings produced in the university results in a neglect or devaluing of the more tacit and informal aspects of professional practice (Boud & Hager, 2012). When mature work-based learners join the academy, they bring their own expertise which does not fit easily into disciplinary categories and is, usually, uncodified. It is, therefore, frequently assumed that the learning achieved through work is 'weak, ad hoc, concrete and incidental'. The experience and expertise of learners which has developed outside the university can therefore be disregarded. This perspective is rarely challenged since, as Eraut (1994, p. 25) points out: '[P]eople are so accustomed to using the word "knowledge" to refer only to "book knowledge" which is publicly available in codified form, that they have developed only limited awareness of the nature and extent of their personal knowledge'.

The focus on explicit learning of formally presented knowledge fails to recognise that learning is complex, and that several types of knowledge are involved in a performance of any complexity (Eraut, 2000). It is easier to discuss the more codified and explicit aspects of knowledge than to identify and, therefore, discuss tacit personal and professional knowledge. This means that 'informal [workplace] learning is largely invisible, because much of it is either taken for granted or not recognized as learning' (Eraut, 2004, p. 249). This invisibility allows the perpetuation of the dominant paradigm which assumes that the best learning is contained in minds not bodies, and that it can be applied via bodies to change the external world (Beckett & Hager, 2002).

With such an assumption embedded in a cognitive approach to learning which requires a specific context distinct from the 'real world', it is inevitable that practice knowledge would be seen as subordinate. However, there is a considerable literature which challenges the cognitive approach to learning and that emphasises the importance of engagement with practice and active learning.

Wenger (1998) claims that all learning is social, and learning in all settings (whether at work, in the home or on the street) is more similar than different. His claim is that people all learn in a social context through engaging with communities of practice and develop our competence in that context. Such an approach rejects the perspective of cognitive theory, where the 'learning mind' is considered separate from the world and functions best detached from it, and argues that, 'in a theory of situated activity decontextualised learning activity is a contradiction in terms'

(Chaiklin & Lave, 1993, p. 6). The emphasis on the fundamental relationship between activity and learning in this definition draws the boundaries of 'learning' much more widely than in the traditional perspective, which assumes that education is a practice that should be separate from the rest of the society and that learning requires a teacher. This interpretation does not privilege the context provided by an educational institution.

In addition to this challenge to the containment of learning in an institution, Wenger defines 'practice' very specifically. In established usage, practice is often contrasted to theory, and the two are seen as completely distinct. An example of this in the curriculum would be when professional programmes integrate practice placements to expose students to the appropriate workplace. For Wenger (1998, p. 48), however, practice 'does not reflect a dichotomy between the practical and the theoretical, ideals and reality, or talking and doing'—these elements of activity and learning are intrinsically linked and cannot be separated. This means that practice in this model has a much more sophisticated content than that usually attributed to it. Wenger's concept of practice also addresses the theory/practice debate. His interpretation of practice rebalances the relationship between theory and practice, and he draws a relationship between the two that is much more egalitarian. In arguing that, 'Practice is not immune to the influence of theory, but neither is it a mere realization of theory or an incomplete approximation of it', he challenges the long-established dichotomy between the two (Wenger, 1998, p. 48).

A redefining of the relationship between theory and practice provides space in which to recognise the cultural knowledge, which has not been codified, and which may be implicit, plays an important role in most workplaces. Eraut (2000, p. 122) points out, 'Knowledge of contexts and organisations is often acquired through a process of socialization through observation, induction and increasing participation rather than formal enquiry'. Because aspects of organisational culture operate at an informal level, these are not always apparent to those disadvantaged by them. For example, Hodgson (2009) refers to the 'DKDK zone', meaning that individuals do not know what they do not know, including that which is unacknowledged, such as the influence of one's race, gender or class on one's work.

Practice knowledge is knowledge in use, and practising is not the same as learning about practice (Boud, 2016). To adopt such an approach, there needs to be a shift in focus from one on knowledge to one on knowing, that is a shift from an epistemology of possession to an epistemology of practice (Webster-Wright, 2010). In support of the claim for such a shift, Eraut (2004, p. 254) states that 'the research literature on expertise consistently finds that the distinguishing feature of experts is not how much they know but their ability to use their knowledge'. This is the performative aspect of practice knowledge production and application is fundamental to the solution of the immediate problems which arise in practice (Avis, 2003).

Recognition of the validity of knowledge acquired outside the academy impacts the pedagogic approach taken. Laycock, when discussing learner-managed-learning in the workplace, argues that there needs to be a shift from 'didactic to facilitative teaching from dependent to autonomous study, from transmission to interpretation, from the authoritarian to the democratic' (Laycock, 1993, p. 25). This shift is particularly important in the context of mature adult learners who are joining the university from a background of successful workplace practice. They are already operating autonomously in environments of uncertainty and change, since this is what their professional role requires that they do.

As Burns and Costley point out, 'These learners already have intellectual capital, what they seek from HEIs is not so much factual knowledge as ways to research and develop knowledge, reflect and evaluate situations and think autonomously' (Burns & Costley, 2003, p. 45). Therefore, when engaging with such students, rather than being involved in pedagogy (i.e. the transmission model which is based on the teaching of children), academic staff are involved in andragogy—in helping adults learn. In the case of experience-based learning in the workplace, such 'help' involves supporting the learner in 'translating' their prior and current achievements outside the university into a discourse whereby they can be recognised by the academic community. This involves working with the learner on the identification/development of metacognitive skills, and of critical reflection on their own practice. It is through reflection on practice that learning in the workplace can be identified. In much of the debate relating to learning in the workplace, there is an implication that workplace learning is the acquisition of skills, and that theoretical knowledge is not necessary or relevant to the exercise. Such a perspective over-emphasises the importance of context and under-emphasises the agency of individuals. In contrast, reflective practice is focused on identifying learning which is embedded in professional action, and therefore reinforces the fundamental distinction between working and learning. Reflective practice can help demonstrate that, although working and learning can take place at the same time, learning of an appropriate level, which has taken place in the workplace, can be relevant to higher education. As Costley and Portwood (2000) point out, work-based learning draws on professional, academic and experiential learning, using reflection on practice to identify appropriate high-level learning. Through this activity, the academic facilitating the reflection is structuring the learning experience in a way that enhances it, as well as ensuring that the learner meets the standards required for higher education.

However, the pedagogic practice involved in facilitation of reflection on practice is not fully understood in the wider academic community—colleagues who have expertise in reflecting 'out' on theoretical material may have little experience of reflecting 'in' on their own pedagogic approach. The practice of critical reflection is not an intuitive skill, and students who have previously experienced the transmission model find it challenging to structure their own content, rather than being told what is required. Attempts to include reflection in assessment tasks without the appropriate scaffolding result in superficial reflections which have no impact on learning or future practice (Ryan, 2013). In such cases the transformative educational impact that is observed by those colleagues with expert practice in facilitation and whose students are well supported in reflecting is not seen by academic colleagues in the disciplines. Such outcomes reinforce the tendency to disregard learning outside the academy.

It could be argued that academics engaging with workplace learners and developing the more 'radical' approaches to experience-based learning are developing pedagogic responses to the changing student body which can usefully complement those widely used within the academy. However, such responses require a different approach to the learning experience than that adopted when teaching in a conventional discipline.

The recognition of experiential work-based learning offers a challenge to the dominant discourse of higher education, to what counts as a legitimate site of learning, and to what counts as legitimate knowledge (Laycock, 2003). The strongly student-centred perspective adopted by work-based learning practitioners offers a direct contrast to the discipline and tutor-centred perspective expressed in most academic practice. Learning from experience and practice outside the university does not fit into the current disciplinary structure of the academic curriculum and the dominant culture of higher education. The strong link between the academic disciplines and the maintenance of academic standards means that work-based learning practitioners need to demonstrate that their practice is 'academic' enough to be consistently included in the higher education curriculum. Unless they do this, the wider experience that students from non-traditional groupings may bring to their studies will remain unrecognised.

Work-Based Learning Pedagogy and Tempered Radicalism

This discussion suggests that not all students would be able to take advantage of a broadened perspective on academic knowledge. Younger students who come to university directly from school or college may be well suited to programmes which treat them as novices. However, mature students who come from groupings which have been under-represented in higher education often struggle to identify the relevance of traditional programmes to their life and work. The wider integration of experience-based elements into more conventional academic programmes would offer recognition that the students bring something of value to the university, but also enhance individual skills in a way that is directly relevant to individual circumstances.

Work-based learning practitioners have a dual commitment—they recognise the importance of the academic disciplines but are convinced that their particular practice offers a valuable enhancement to the higher education curriculum, providing valid recognition of other forms of knowledge. Propositional knowledge is recognised to be important as a lens through which to analyse and evaluate issues in the real world, but it can 'no longer [be] a plausible standard against which all types of learning [and knowledge] should be judged' (Hager & Halliday, 2006, p. 142). Moving experiential vocational or professional knowledge from the periphery towards equivalence with academic knowledge involves rejection of the established dichotomies between practice and theory but it does not require the rejection of the latter. The different approaches are recognised as complementary rather than conflicting perspectives. Yet to achieve this shift, work-based learning practitioners need to build disciplinary colleagues' confidence in the different pedagogic practices and the nature of the learning their students achieve. There has been some progress in integrating experiential work-based learning into the curriculum but movement generally has been slow and practitioners report that 'there is still much suspicion about experiential learning' (Walsh, 2011 p. 38).

In contrast to transmitting subject expertise in a specific academic discipline, the skills required for facilitating experiential learning are 'skill in learning consultancy, understanding the relationships between work and context, appreciation of transdisciplinarity, facility in fostering enquiry, and knowledge of reflexivity and review' (Boud & Tennant, 2006, p. 303). These are the characteristics which provide for a learner-centred response to experience-based learning, while at the same time addressing the academic requirements of the university. Work-based learning practitioners are committed to the academy and to the value of higher-level learning, but they are also committed to the importance of transdisciplinary work-based learning, whose epistemology could be seen as revolutionary. When working to achieve wider acceptance of this learning, the dual commitments involved in this context could require that they act as 'tempered radicals'.

'Tempered Radicals' are individuals who are committed to the practice and function of their organisations, and are also committed to a cause, community or ideology that is fundamentally different from, even at odds with, the dominant organisational culture (Meyerson & Scully, 1995). The examples cited by the authors are that of a Chief Executive Officer who is a feminist, and a university lecturer who is a radical humanist but lectures on the benefits of capitalism. In some ways tempered radicals are similar to boundary spanners in that they are negotiating and reconciling the discourses of different educational subcultures, but a major difference is that one of the two systems within which they work is seen as threatening by the other. The focus on the link between academic disciplines and standards means that some parts of the academy argue that academic recognition of experiential work-based learning threatens the standards established and maintained by higher education, and changes the nature of the university.

Work-based learning practitioners are aware of the radical nature of their adopted epistemology and pedagogy, and of the discomfort of colleagues with the development of this practice. However, they are aiming not at revolution but at evolution, and the tempering of their radicalism is expressed in their approach to both their own curriculum and that of their colleagues.

Tempered radicals experience tensions between the status quo and alternatives in a way which can stimulate organisational transformation, and in negotiating the interface between their own practice and the academic disciplines, work-based learning practitioners can visualise the opportunity for change. They are 'outsiders within', which means that they have the familiarity with the organisation of the insider, together with the detachment of the outsider, which supports identification of issues or problems (Meyerson & Scully, 1995). The shared values and knowledge of the dominant discourse mean that insider language can be used—engagement with the discourse of the academic discourses and the discourse of experiential learning can help work-based learning practitioners address issues which are seen to be important and problematic in their area.

There is a recognition that, to build confidence in this contrasting approach, concerns need to be explicitly addressed. For example, practitioners report that they 'went quite hard on the learning outcome related to theory', '[are] explicitly including critical analysis/integration of theory' and 'the experience must dialogue with the literature' (Walsh, 2014, p. 117). In the absence of specific disciplinary content, it was recognised to be important to clearly demonstrate that the focus on work-based learning, rather than workplace performance, was appropriately sophisticated and that learners were engaging with a high-level intellectual challenge. The transparency of assessment criteria and learning outcomes, which are often generic to accommodate the individual nature of content, can evidence the need to integrate criticality and reference to theory. Further, assessments based on individual experience cannot be plagiarised in the same way as those using common content.

With regard to the concern with the maintenance of standards, although structuring and supporting workplace learning is a more egalitarian exercise than the conventional teaching of courses, the relationship between university and learner is never an equal one. The learner has to complete an assessment which is deemed appropriate by the university and assessed according to criteria agreed upon within the institution. Thus, although the facility to undertake a 'translation' from one discourse to another allows for wider recognition of learning, it is still the university which decides whether the translation submitted is acceptable or not. Therefore, the maintenance of academic standards remains where it has always been—within the institution.

Discussion and Conclusions

Pedagogic principles underlying the academic recognition of experiential work-based learning offer a contrasting, but complementary, way to support and assess higher-level learning, but awareness and acceptance of such approaches are varied. The integration of experience-based learning into the higher education curriculum offers a challenge to the current academic ordering, emphasising modes of learning and knowledge which have previously been overlooked and undervalued.

Discussions of intersectionality highlight the variety of factors impacting individuals through their life experience and concentrate on sociocultural power orders. Resistance to recognition of experience and learning outside the academy disadvantages mature, work-based learners and is based on a misunderstanding of the nature of the learning gained. Assumptions that work-based learning provides only economic benefit to the organisation overlook the value of higher education to the individual—the student agency, including personal and identity capital, which can be gained through formal and informal experiences of higher education (Tomlinson, 2018).

Graham (2002, p. 2) argues that there is a 'dangerous romanticism in thinking that once upon a time British universities were suitably Newmanesque until the arrival of the utilitarian Philistines'. He further asserts that, although associated closely with the cause for liberal education, Newman claimed that, 'No one can deny that commerce and the professions afford scope for the highest and most diversified powers of the mind' (cited in Graham, 2002, p. 41).

Going further, Beckett and Hager (2002) claim that individuality and the core adult learning principle of self-direction derive from the formative social nature of work, adding that forms of discretionary judgement are involved in all adult work. They argue that the difficulty work-based learning has with fitting the current higher education paradigm has more to do with the problematic nature of the paradigm than with the lack of genuine educational features in practice and informal learning at work (Beckett & Hager, 2002).

With regard to the pedagogy adopted, for Foucault (1982, 1991), the dynamics of power offer possibilities as well as constraints, but for these to be used effectively they have to be recognised. The limits to individual possibilities are a social product which usually operate implicitly and need to be uncovered. Reflection allows a normative 'template of reality' to be made explicit (Kinsella, 2007).

Work-based learning students derive acquaintance with two discourses of power—that of the organisation and that of the academy—and this alerts them to the existence of difference, creating possibilities for individual action (Siebert & Walsh, 2013). When students are given the opportunity to reflect on their beliefs and practices in relation to their own context, they are more likely to see themselves as active change agents in their profession (Ryan, 2013). Learning can, therefore, be used in the service of action, not just for discovery or insight (Beckett & Hager, 2002). The labour market may contain constraints for individuals, but the negotiation of possibilities is strengthened by their work-based learning engagement, whereby the individual and multi-textured experience of each student can be recognised. This proposal for a new paradigm, which is more inclusive of a range of knowledges, is one that offers a corrective to the current paradigm not a replacement of it (Beckett & Hager, 2002).

Boud et al. (2001) claim that work-based learning is one of the few innovations related to teaching and learning in higher education which attempts to engage seriously with the economic, social and educational demands of the current era. The ability to maintain academic standards while recognising knowledge which does not fit into existing academic disciplines can broaden the curriculum to reflect the learning and interests of those who would previously have been excluded from recognition. It cedes some power to students, rather than insisting that, to be valid, learning must occur in forms which have been developed inside the university. Although currently contested, the recognition of experiential work-based learning could offer a more democratic and inclusive paradigm of higher education.

Rammell (2016) points out that, historically, traditional ideas of universities' engagement with 'the public' have meant that established interests with the resources to represent those interests and to influence decision-makers have been those consulted. This means that the shift from elite to mass attendance at university is not reflected in the range of 'publics' with which HEIs engage. The result is that, in terms of a broader social and economic knowledge exchange, 'the notion of democratic accountability of business education and research to public and organizational well-being ... remains largely marginalized' (Syed et al., 2010, p. 79). A changed and more inclusive paradigm of higher education would achieve deeper engagement with a range of individuals and would extend higher-level learning into society.

Change often comes from the margins of an organisation and, although the current scale of work-based learning practice is limited, small innovations can be important, both in terms of evidencing success and of testing the boundaries of capacity for change (Meyerson & Scully, 1995). A tempered approach to achieving change could reassure, and, as Reynolds (1999) points out, the concept of the 'tempered radical' offers a useful strategy which is helpful for colleagues espousing the work-based learning pedagogy who do not wish either their students' knowledge or their own practice to be unrecognised.

References

Ahl, H. (2006). Why research on women entrepreneurs needs new directions. *Entrepreneurship Theory and Practice, 30*(5), 595–621.

Apple, M. W. (1993). The politics of official knowledge: Does a National curriculum make sense? *Teachers College Record, 95*(2), 222–241.

Avis, J. (2003). Re-thinking trust in a performative culture: The case of education. *Journal of Education Policy, 18*(3), 315–332.

Beckett, D., & Hager, P. (2002). *Life, work and learning: Practice in postmodernity*. Routledge.

Block, D., & Corona, V. (2014). Exploring class-based intersectionality. *Language Culture and Curriculum, 27*(1), 27–42.

Boud, D. (2016). Taking professional practice seriously: Implications for deliberate course design. In F. Trede & C. McEwan (Eds.), *Educating the deliberate professional: Preparing practitioners for emergent futures* (pp. 157–173). Springer.

Boud, D., Cohen, R., & Sampson, J. (2001). *Peer learning in higher education: Learning from and with each other*. Kogan Page.

Boud, D., & Hager, P. J. (2012). Re-thinking continuing professional development through changing metaphors and location in professional practices. *Studies in Continuing Education, 34*(1), 17–30.

Boud, D., & Tennant, M. (2006). Putting doctoral education to work: Challenges to academic practice. *Higher Education Research and Development, 25*(3), 293–306.

Burns, G., & Costley, C. (2003). Non-traditional students and 21st century higher education. In D. Hollifield (Ed.), *Knowledge, work and learning: Conference proceedings of the work-based learning network*. Universities Association for Lifelong Learning.

Chaiklin, S., & Lave, J. (1993). *Understanding practice: Perspectives on activity and context*. Cambridge University Press.

Christoffersen, A., & Hankivsky, O. (2021). Responding to inequities in public policy: Is GBA+ the right way to operationalize intersectionality? *Canadian Public Administration, 64*(3), 524–531.

Coffield, F. (1999). *Speaking truth to power: Research and policy on lifelong learning*. Policy Press.

Colley, H., James, D., Diment, K., & Tedder, M. (2003). Learning as becoming in vocational education and training: Class, gender and the role of vocational habitus. *Journal of Vocational Education & Training, 55*(4), 471–498.

Costley, C., & Portwood, D. (2000). *Work based learning and the university: New perspectives and practices*. SEDA.

Crenshaw, K. (1989). Demarginalizing the intersection of race and sex: A black feminist critique of antidiscrimination doctrine, Feminist Theory and Antiracist Politics. *University of Chicago Legal Forum, 1989*(1), 139–168.

Crenshaw, K. (1991). Mapping the margins: Intersectionality, identity politics, and violence against women of colour. *Stanford Law Review, 43*(6), 1241–1299.

Eraut, M. (1994). *Developing professional knowledge and competence.* Falmer Press.

Eraut, M. (2000). Non-formal learning and tacit knowledge in professional work. *British Journal of Educational Psychology, 70*(1), 113–136.

Eraut, M. (2004). Informal learning in the workplace. *Studies in Continuing Education, 26*(2), 247–273.

Fejes, A., & Nicoll, K. (2008). *Foucault and lifelong learning: Governing the subject.* Routledge.

Foucault, M. (1982). The subject and power. *Critical Inquiry, 8*(4), 777–795.

Foucault, M. (1991). *Discipline and punish: The birth of the prison.* Harmondsworth: Penguin.

Gibbons, M., Limoges, C., Nowotny, H., Schwartzman, S., Scott, P., & Trow, M. (1994). *The new production of knowledge: The dynamics of science and research in contemporary societies.* SAGE Publications.

Graham, G. (2002). *Universities: The recovery of an idea.* Imprint Academic.

Hager, P. J., & Halliday, J. (2006). *Recovering informal learning: Wisdom, Judgement and Community.* Springer.

Hodgson, N. (2009). Narrative and social justice from the perspective of governmentality. *Journal of Philosophy of Education, 43*(4), 559–572.

Jongbloed, B., Enders, J., & Salerno, C. (2008). Higher education and its communities: Interconnections, interdependencies and a research agenda. *Higher Education, 56*(3), 303–324.

Kennedy, M. (2015). Knowledge claims and values in higher education. In M. Kennedy, S. Billett, S. Gherardi, & L. Grealish (Eds.), *Practice-based learning in higher education: Jostling cultures* (pp. 31–45). Springer.

Kinsella, E. A. (2007). Embodied reflection and the epistemology of reflective practice. *Journal of Philosophy of Education, 41*(3), 395–409.

Knowles, M. S. (1984). *Andragogy in action: Applying modern principles of adult learning.* Jossey-Bass.

Knudsen, S. (2006). Intersectionality–a theoretical inspiration in the analysis of minority cultures and identities in textbooks. In E. Bruillard, B. Aamotsbakken, S. Knudsen, & M. Horsley (Eds.), *Proceedings of Eighth International Conference on Learning and Educational Media* (pp. 61–76).

Laycock, M. (1993). Enterprise in Higher Education and Learner-Managed-Learning: The use of learning contracts. In N. J. Graves (Ed.), *Learner managed learning: Practice, theory and policy, Leeds: Higher education for capability* (pp. 24–30). Rotuledge.

Laycock, M. (2003). Work-based learning. *Educational Developments, 4*(2), 4–7.

Meyerson, D. E., & Scully, M. A. (1995). Tempered radicalism and the politics of ambivalence and change. *Organization Science, 6*(5), 585–600.

Pitt-Watson, D., & Quigley, E. (2019). *Business school rankings for the 21st century*. United Nations Global Compact.

Rammell, B. (2016). *Protecting the public interest in higher education*. Higher Education Policy Institute.

Reynolds, M. (1999). Critical reflection and management education: Rehabilitating less hierarchical approaches. *Journal of Management Education, 23*(5), 537–553.

Ryan, M. (2013). The pedagogical balancing act: Teaching reflection in higher education. *Teaching in Higher Education, 18*(2), 144–155.

Siebert, S., & Walsh, A. (2013). Reflection in work-based learning: Self-regulation or self-liberation? *Teaching in Higher Education, 18*(2), 167–178.

Simons, M., & Masschelein, J. (2008). The Governmentalization of learning and the assemblage of a learning apparatus. *Educational Theory, 58*(4), 391–415.

Syed, J., Mingers, J., & Murray, P. A. (2010). Beyond rigour and relevance: A critical realist approach to business education. *Management Learning, 41*(1), 71–85.

Tomlinson, M. (2018). Conceptions of the value of higher education in a measured market. *Higher Education, 75*(4), 711–727.

Usher, R., & Edwards, R. (1994). *Postmodernism and education*. Routledge.

Walsh, A. (2007). Engendering debate: Credit recognition of project-based workplace research. *Journal of Workplace Learning, 19*(8), 497–510.

Walsh, A. (2011). Beyond a naturally occurring ethnography: The work-based researcher. *Higher Education, Skills and Work-Based Learning, 1*(1), 38–51.

Walsh, A. (2014). Experiential learning: A new higher education requiring new pedagogic skills. In T. Halttunen, M. Koivisto, & S. Billet (Eds.), *Promoting, assessing, recognizing and certifying lifelong learning* (pp. 109–129). Springer.

Webster-Wright, A. (2010). *Authentic professional learning: Making a difference through learning at work*. Springer.

Wenger, E. (1998). *Communities of practice: Learning, meaning, and identity*. Cambridge University Press.

4

Do #BlackLivesMatter in the Education of Fashion Business Students? A Review of Race and Inclusivity Literature

Julie Blanchard-Emmerson

Introduction

In May 2020, the terrible death of George Floyd, a black man, brutally killed by a white US police officer, provided increased impetus for protests organised as part of the Black Lives Matter (BLM) movement. #BlackLivesMatter, the social media hashtag, was used in helping raise awareness of racist attacks, galvanising protestors and enabling them to organise their activities, spreading worldwide (Bell et al., 2021; Sharma, 2017). At the beginning of June 2020 many fashion companies used their social media channels to post a black square for Blackout Tuesday which, whilst not officially organised by BLM, was about showing solidarity with the movement and black communities (Bakare & Davies, 2020; Dike, 2021). On 3 June, *Women's Wear Daily* reporter Roshitsh's (Roshitsh, 2020) interview with Hannah Stoudemire, co-founder of

J. Blanchard-Emmerson (✉)
Business School for the Creative Industries, University for the Creative Arts, Epsom, UK
e-mail: jblanchard@uca.ac.uk

© The Author(s), under exclusive license to Springer Nature Switzerland AG 2023
B. S. Nayak (ed.), *Intersectionality and Creative Business Education*,
https://doi.org/10.1007/978-3-031-29952-0_4

Fashion for All Foundation, was published. Stoudemire argued that fashion companies were predominately silent about the growing spate of racist attacks and atrocities; though she acknowledged that gradually some sparse comment was appearing (Roshitsh, 2020, p. 10).

By September of that year, I began teaching a unit called 'Fashion Histories and Theories' to Fashion Business Management postgraduate students, based in the Business School at University for the Creative Arts (UCA) in the UK. One of the subjects I wanted to address was the history and theory around race and racialised representation such as preeminent academic Stuart Hall's (2013) work, and to consider these concepts in the context of the fashion industry. The students and I had some interesting discussions around the tokenism of fashion brands posting black squares on social media, whilst black models struggle for work and suffer industry racism (Wissinger, 2012) and Asian women are paid pittance to make fashionable garments (Entwistle, 2015; Clark, 2019).

After the unit, reflecting on my white privilege, and my feelings of embarrassment when addressing the ways in which many white people stereotype, mistreat and abuse people of any racial background besides their own, I decided my allyship needed to go further. I applied for funding to carry out research with students to discuss issues around race, aiming to develop teaching materials that would help enable both teachers and learners to consider the representation of racialised ethnicities, particularly people of colour, both in terms of fashion marketing and levels of fashion industry employment. I hoped that through dialogue, racialised minority students would be able to challenge the ways in which they may be stereotyped and under-represented, whilst white students will be encouraged to question their white privilege and go on to provide allyship to colleagues from racialised minority backgrounds. I used the BLM hashtag in the title of my proposal, both to engage with the debates around racism that inspired the research and as a way of ensuring that once the study was completed, the recommendations could be easily located in keyword searches. Fashion Business education must be vocal about these issues going forward.

Whilst noting fashion's initial glaring silence around issues of race and racism, Stoudemire flagged fashion's growing statements and claims of sustainability, but simultaneously noted that "racism is a sustainability issue; it cuts down on life expectancy. You can't be sustainable and not be anti-racist" (Roshitsh, 2020, p. 10). Indeed, the United Nations, in its Sustainable Development Goals (SDGs), sets out the need for global work to increase inclusive, equitable education (Sengupta et al., 2019, p. 5), reduce inequalities and dramatically improve lives. The UN's initiative, Principles of Responsible Management Education (PRME), aims to encourage business schools to consider these goals in teaching business students to become responsible and sustainable business leaders of the future (PRME Secretariat, 2022).

Business Schools focussing on subjects related to fashion need to engage with these goals around reducing inequality, particularly as the fashion industry is currently far from offering equality or being racially diverse. This inequality is conveyed by many reports in the UK and US, such as the British Fashion Council's (2022) *Diversity and Inclusion in the Fashion Industry,* the British Textiles and Fashion All-Party Parliamentary Group's (2021) *Representation and Inclusion in the Fashion Industry* and the Council of Fashion Designers of America's (2021) *State of Diversity, Equity & Inclusion in Fashion.* For example, the British Fashion Council's (2022) research shows that ethnic diversity is very poor in the fashion industry, particularly in senior roles, with many businesses having solely white people on their boards and executive committees (British Fashion Council & MBS Group, 2022, p. 10). What is also evident from these reports is that there is also an intersection of social identity factors that result in exclusion from key roles, with under-representation also of women, people with a disability and those from socially deprived backgrounds (British Fashion Council & MBS Group, 2022, p. 10; Textiles & Fashion All Parliamentary Party Group, 2021).

My initial academic literature research made clear this interlacing of various subordinated social identities, as scholars discussing the poor wages and working conditions for textile and garment workers highlight that these workers are overwhelmingly women in Asian countries (Clark, 2019; Entwistle, 2015). I argued that new managers entering the fashion industry should be made aware of these issues of inequality. My proposal was that increasing students' knowledge of these ethical problems could strengthen their sense of social responsibility, enabling them to endeavour to improve working conditions for workers and ensure that these workers receive fair pay in the future. Developing professionals who question racial inequalities and fight for equal rights for all is both timely and important, hence my funding applications were successful and PRME and UCA have contributed financially to the research. Whilst intersectionality and the interlocking of social factors to produce subordinated identities is a significant issue, my study aims to focus on race to enable an in-depth exploration of this one axis of subordination (Harris & Leonardo, 2018, p. 7).

In terms of focussing on racial issues, back in 2018, UCA commissioned a manifesto and Inclusive Practice Guide, building on the research carried out on statistics and experiences for "Black, Asian and Minority Ethnic students" (BAME) at the university (UCA, 2018a, 2018b). The Inclusive Practice Guide stated that in 2018/19 the attainment gap between white and BAME students in UCA was such that 21% fewer BAME students received a first- or upper second-class degree than white students (UCA, 2018b, p. 1). Certainly, these figures fit with other more recent research carried out within higher education (HE) in the UK (Arday et al., 2022; Rana et al., 2022).

In the UCA manifesto, amongst the many recommendations to improve attainment, was the need to develop increased opportunities for the co-creation of the curriculum with students (UCA, 2018a, p. 3)—one which my research accords with. White allies and collective resistance to structural and systemic racism are key in developing a more ethnically diverse and inclusive HE, reflective of our multicultural and multi-ethnic society (Arday et al., 2022, p. 20). This same equity needs to be achieved in the fashion industry, where beside ethical reasons, figures show that diverse teams are more profitable (Textiles & Fashion All Parliamentary Party Group, 2021, p. 18) and loss of revenue on sales that could have appealed to diverse spending groups is significant (Textiles & Fashion All Parliamentary Party Group, 2021, p. 36). Linking both, improvements needed in education and business, the Council of Fashion Designers of America (2021) suggest that change might be aided by fashion education incorporating issues of diversity and inclusivity into the curriculum (Council of Fashion Designers of America & PVH Corp, 2021, p. 26). How best to include these issues in fashion history and theory teaching for Fashion Business Management students is the crux of this research project.

The planned study will involve two focus groups of Fashion Business Management postgraduate students debating a set of questions around race, ethnicity, diversity teaching and the fashion industry. Focus groups are group discussions with typically between six and eight participants (Morgan, 1998), and undertaking two focus groups has been shown to be adequate to reveal key themes and ideas for analysis (Guest et al., 2016). I will ask a few questions about the students' experiences with regard to race, what they think educators can do to explore racialised issues and suggestions they have for preparing them for the fashion industry. The idea is that with minimal intervention from the researcher (Gibbs, 1997), participants raise the topics of most relevance to them, generating their own questions and concepts on their own terms (Barbour & Kitzenger, 1999, p. 5). Building on their ideas in a co-construction of knowledge, the aim is to investigate how to develop student engagement and learning in issues relating to racialised minority under-representation, stereotyping and discrimination within the fashion industry. The intended outcome is teaching materials that facilitate good teaching and learning about racialised minority representation in the fashion industry.

As background to the research, a survey of the academic literature is necessary to consider what is already known in relation to another intersection, that where pedagogical literature around race and diversity crosses ways with that about fashion business management teaching. This review of existing scholarship is the focus of this chapter. Firstly, the chapter discusses literature that addresses general pedagogy around increasing inclusive practices and catering for a diverse student body. It will then concentrate on racial diversity, examining language in relation to race to consider the ways educators discuss racial issues. This discussion moves on to exploring the growing social awareness in academia of the need to decolonise the curriculum and how that decolonising can be achieved in relation to fashion education. The next section of the chapter examines literature from the perspective of pedagogy about sustainability and responsibility in business, progressing to teaching about sustainability and responsibility in the fashion business specifically. This final section considers how far this sustainability discussion engages with corporate responsibility around ethnic and racial equality.

Inclusivity in Teaching Practice

Since the turn of the twenty-first century there has been increased academic discussion about creating inclusive learning environments in UK higher education (HE) to support greater social and cultural diversity (Skelton, 2002, pp. 193–194) in an attempt to democratise knowledge (Sengupta et al., 2019; Skelton, 2002). Concurrently there has been a steady rise in the number of international students attending UK HE (Ploner, 2018), resulting in more cultural diversity, if not yet resulting in better satisfaction or outcomes for students from marginalised groups (Mercer-Mapstone et al., 2021). Recommendations around teaching to engage a diverse student body highlight the importance of classrooms to be safe spaces for students to express their own views from their perspectives (Currie, 2007; Dylan, 2012; Sengupta et al., 2019). This safety needs to be a result of the teacher and learner working together to develop the learning environment (Sengupta et al., 2019), which can progress out of an agreement drawn up with the lecturer and students together to create collaborative group norms (Dylan, 2012) and aims to encourage mutual respect.

Dylan (2012) argues that discrimination and inequality, key issues driving this research, must be openly discussed and examined. A teacher should also model good behaviour and communication, for example in reinforcing egalitarianism, ensuring that discriminatory language is corrected "respectfully without censure or derision" (Dylan, 2012, p. 39). Developing mindfulness in both lecturers and students, about the power of words to dominate or deride others, should encourage the acceptance of differences and acknowledgement of our shared humanity. As Johnson et al. (2019) suggest, it is "vital to unpack the nature of language as all terms have an agenda to maintain dominant social structures" (Johnson et al., 2019, p. 86). The power dynamics in the use of language about race and ethnicity is analysed next.

Racial Inclusivity and Language

Whilst BLM was the inspiration for the research, the importance of the lives of people from all racialised minority backgrounds is the focus of my study. Racialised minorities' is a phrase taken from Dr Gabriel (2022), founder and director of Black British Academics, to draw attention to the racialisation of all people of colour and as a critique of whiteness (Gabriel, 2022). Many articles discussing racial diversity and education use the acronym BAME with no rationale for their choice of this term (Arday et al., 2022; Lim, 2022; Rana et al., 2022). UCA (2018a) explains, as seen above, that it stands for Black, Asian and Minority Ethnic students (UCA, 2018a). Whereas Rana et al. (2022) refer to 'Black and minority ethnic' backgrounds (Rana et al., 2022, p. 12) in their abstract and first sentence, but have 'Black Asian and minority ethnic' in their keywords. Universities UK and National Union of Students (2019) report on 'BAME' student attainment acknowledges the challenges of using this type of "homogenising language" (p. 5) and aggregating all racialised ethnic groups. As Gabriel (2022) points out, BAME also reinforces racial inequality by maintaining White as a privileged unnamed identity against which people of colour can only exist as marginal. Gabriel's (2022) suggestion is that, whilst people of colour are also homogenising, it does not use 'minority', a subordinated subject position. Hence this chapter predominately uses the term 'people of colour', and only uses minority when prefaced with racialised, to highlight the invisibility and normalising of white privilege (Dar et al., 2021).

Racial Inclusivity and Teaching Practice

Teaching is political in that power and privilege shape who is taught what and has tended to exacerbate rather than ease inequalities (Johnson et al., 2019; Silva, 2022). As seen earlier, research has uncovered the extent to which educational experiences and achievements at universities are shaped by racial inequalities (Arday et al., 2022). Dar et al. (2021) highlight the colonialist bedrock of capitalism, its continued endemic racism and the rise of white supremacism in the US and the UK, but stress that these issues are not addressed in business schools (Dar et al., 2021). Dar et al. (2021) contend that there are no easy answers to tackling whiteness as a regime of power, replicated in business schools, but call for collective anti-racist scholar-activism whereby academics of colour challenge the white hegemony. Bell et al. (2021) similarly argue for the need to radically challenge the white supremacist nature of business schools. Dar et al. (2021) address their appeal for collective activism to the small number of scholars of colour who exist in academia. This lack of academics of colour is also highlighted by other researchers as part of the reproduction of white privilege to be gatekeepers to types of (white) knowledge (Arday et al., 2021; Mir & Zanoni, 2021). Bell et al. (2021) encourage white female academics to react to and resist anti-blackness, as strongly as they resist gender discrimination (Bell et al., 2021, p. 49); a call to arms that I am rising to in this research, as solving oppression is a job for us all (Mercer-Mapstone et al., 2021).

A sense of belonging is understood to be a key part of retaining and encouraging students of colour, and greater numbers of lecturers from racialised minority backgrounds to act as role models would help (Arday et al., 2022; Bell et al., 2021). Culturally sensitive pastoral tutoring is also considered to play a role in increasing a sense of belonging in students from diverse backgrounds (Rana et al., 2022). These tutorials could be seen to be part of the general notion of academic hospitality, a phrase derived from discussions around welcoming international students, whereby ongoing dialogue of sharing ideas and experiences between staff and students creates hospitable encounters (Ploner, 2018). Academic hospitality could be extended to also think about creating dialogue between *all* students and teachers to help find ways to dissolve estrangement between us, as academics, and them, as students, thereby assisting students to feel at home even at university (Mann, 2001). There are many reasons why students may feel alienated in HE (see Mann, 2001), and Mann (2001) suggests another way to lessen the feelings of alienation for students is also to increase safety, whereby all students feel accepted and respected (Mann, 2001, p. 17).

As suggested earlier, in relation to teaching, safety for all to speak in the classroom needs to be promoted (Currie, 2007; Dylan, 2012; Sengupta et al., 2019). This security can be increased through the willingness of lecturers to share their thoughts about difficult issues such as race (Dylan, 2012). Teachers who never discuss discrimination, oppression and global inequalities lead students to believe that these issues are not important, or that "there is only one view, that promulgated by the dominant culture" (Dylan, 2012, p. 40). Intellectual activism challenges the status quo (Bell et al., 2021; Dar et al., 2021) and promotes social justice (Mir & Zanoni, 2021). To make black lives, and therefore all lives, matter in education, I suggest that academics must view their teaching as a form of intellectual activism. There needs to be constant discussion between university staff and between staff and students about all issues around inequality and what to do about it (Lim, 2022; Rana et al., 2022). Rana et al. (2022) propose that there should be a two-pronged approach to activist teaching: as well as providing a safe space for discussing racism, it also involves tailored curriculum content to reflect a diverse student body, exploring a variety of cultures (Rana et al., 2022, p. 10). This curriculum development is discussed next.

Decolonising the Curriculum

In most of the studies tackling racial inequality and inclusive teaching, one of the frequently cited improvements that could increase student feelings of belonging is a diversification of the curriculum (Arday et al., 2021; Currie, 2007; Phoenix et al., 2020). This broadening of what is taught would aim to increase the range of cultural references and counter white Eurocentrism. Although direct colonial rule no longer exists, the impact of colonialism is still being felt and underpins most institutions, including universities (Arday et al., 2021; Currie, 2007; Phoenix et al., 2020). As already discussed, colonist discourse structures business schools, their pedagogy and their curricula (Bell et al., 2021; Currie, 2007; Dar et al., 2021); hence, the process of critiquing and reforming what is taught within business schools and HE as a whole is usually referred to as decolonisation of the curriculum (Moghli & Kadiwai, 2021).

One of the key components of decolonisation is the inclusion of texts that go beyond the white, patriarchal, Eurocentric canon in subject matter, thereby offering history and examples from a range of cultural backgrounds (Dar et al., 2021; Dylan, 2012). Historically, academics from the Global North/West have universalised their experiences and dominated the scholarly discourse and curricula, so that Global South experiences and knowledge have been erased or silenced (Dar et al., 2021, p. 697). Even within the Global North/West, as seen earlier, the low number of scholars of colour has also created a deficit of research from varied perspectives, unreflective of the multicultural UK population (Arday et al., 2021). Yet, there is existent research that could be used to diversify the viewpoints on offer (Moghli & Kadiwai, 2021). The lack of divergent material is perhaps more related to established, white, male, heterosexual, able-bodied sources of knowledge being presented as objective, benchmark or normative, particularly in business schools, with voices of people of colour sidelined, othered and issues of race considered niche (Dar et al., 2021).

To respond to calls to decolonise the curriculum, UK HE institutions are increasingly (Moghli & Kadiwai, 2021) drawing on a variety of ideas from "feminist researchers, critical race theorists, queer scholars and disability researchers" (Moghli & Kadiwai, 2021, p. 7). This variety of standpoints offers a broadening of ways of looking at the world. However, these initiatives can be seen to be about simply adjusting reading lists and adding to the mainstream, rather than decentring Eurocentric knowledge, or questioning the white, patriarchal canon and the existing power structures of universities (Ahmed, 2012; Arday et al., 2021; Moghli & Kadiwai, 2021). To properly address the inequity of academic power relations, scholars need to unlearn or disrupt knowledge saturated in historical amnesia or informed by colonial histories curated to subjugate and exploit the other (Arday et al., 2021, p. 309). Decolonising the curriculum must not leave the status quo intact; it must address the epistemic violence of colonial knowledge and rewrite these histories (Arday et al., 2021).

It is not just the content of the curriculum that needs to be dismantled, critiqued and re-written but also pedagogy, *how* things are taught (Currie, 2007). As Moghli and Kadiwai (2021) argue, decoloniality in HE is a call to examine the production of knowledge, values, rationality, ways of knowing and being (Moghli & Kadiwai, 2021, p. 4). Rather than working from the starting point of student lack, lecturers could consider more dialogic practice as discussed earlier, learning from students, attempting greater understanding of student's cultural backgrounds and their ways of learning and interaction (Currie, 2007). Arday et al. (2021) propose that it is white scholars who need to act to make these changes, though Swan (2017) counsels that white people should not rush in to act too soon. Hastening to act can deny the agency, and block the actions, of those who are othered and can instead be a form of white self-protection seeking speedy answers to verify their own moral goodness (Swan, 2017, pp. 547–8). Swan's (2017) main proposal is that white academics pause to listen more; this emphasis on listening fits with the recurring notion discussed throughout this chapter of increased dialogue with students, particularly those of colour. Swan (2017) suggests developing encounters and communities with others, in which white people reflect on how knowledge production and space are structured.

Earlier, this section explored critiques of business schools, charged with not listening to the voices of people of colour nor examining the continuing colonial structuring of knowledge. But the business school I work in has developed within a liberal arts university, and the master's degree my research relates to is a *fashion* business management course. Therefore, this chapter turns to fashion scholarship next to consider what reflexive tools the field of fashion education may be offering.

Decolonising the Fashion Curriculum

Decolonising fashion studies has been of recent growing interest to academics, with two key journals in the field, *Fashion Theory* and the *International Journal of Fashion Studies*, having special issues about decolonisation and fashion in 2020 and 2021 respectively. In addition, *Fashion, Style & Popular Culture's* 2021 special issue was titled 'Black Lives Matter: Fashion, Style & Aesthetics', advocating the need for a diversity of voices in fashion scholarship, and tackling issues of social injustice through dialogue around fashion.

The importance of listening, raised in the previous section, is also emphasised at the beginning of Slade and Jansen's (2020) 'Letter from the

Editors' in the Decoloniality and Fashion special issue of *Fashion Theory*. The editors explain how, as a part of a research collective formed a decade ago, they had been experimenting with knowledge-building about fashion through "acknowledging and listening to a diversity of voices across geographies, age, race, gender, and life experiences … to diversify the understandings of fashion" (Slade & Jansen, 2020, p. 810). Despite communicating with members around the world, the editors recognised that most of the collective worked within colonial institutional frameworks on the privileged side, communicating in English, thereby needing to recognise their relationship to privilege (Slade & Jansen, 2020). Also, in an echo of Swan's (2017) injunction, Slade and Jansen (2020) discuss decolonising as the need for those with privilege to take part in painful conversations, and to make way for, and listen to, unprivileged voices (Slade & Jansen, 2020).

Fashion's own history is embedded in a network of colonial institutions and practices; it has come to refer to newness and nowness, and "a system of power and a capitalist industry that was conceived in Europe and exported to the rest of the work through European imperialism and globalization" (Jansen, 2020, p. 815). This system of power and dress, this notion of fashion, is the one that has dominated scholarship in the Global North/West, which concentrated on Euro-American production and consumption of fashion (Taylor, 2013). The system itself was occasionally critiqued by academics such as Wilson (1985) and Phizacklea (1990), who stress that it is an industry predicated on colonialist, misogynist and classist exploitation. There have also been critiques of fashion studies' Eurocentrism ongoing for several decades, for example Craik's (1993) discussion of the ways in which academia repeatedly links fashion exclusively with capitalist societies and notions of civilisation and modernity. Fashion is presented in opposition to the supposedly static, regressive, traditional dress of nations considered less developed (Craik, 1993, p. 7).

Gradually there has been a widening of the places and spaces where fashionable behaviour is recognised as existing, and therefore an increased awareness of the need to internationalise the field (Black et al., 2013; Paulicelli & Clark, 2009). This understanding has prompted the inclusion of research about fashion in a whole range of global contexts into fashion handbooks and edited volumes (Black et al., 2013; Paulicelli & Clark, 2009). But as Jansen (2020) recognises of her own previous work, and that of others, the research of these international contexts is often by scholars from privileged cultural backgrounds working within Eurocentric institutions, bringing with them their colonial bias (Jansen, 2020). For Jansen (2020), that bias was in her definitions of fashionable versus traditional dress, mirroring the classifications foregrounded in Craik's (1993) work, whereby fashion exists only in relationship to imperialist structures and taxonomies. Similarly, this could be said of much work that is added to the canon, as if to supplement the literature is an unproblematic task, a critique explored earlier (Arday et al., 2021; Moghli & Kadiwai, 2021).

One example in the scholarship that relies on the limiting position of fashion's existence only relative to the Western fashion system is research about fashion weeks outside of the Euro-American contexts (Slade & Jansen, 2020). This same intermeshing of problematic power relations exists for professionals working within fashion in the Global South too. For instance, Hughes (2022) argues that on the one hand the creation of Lagos Fashion Week (LGW) enables designers to represent themselves and counter Euro-American global fashion domination. Yet simultaneously, LGW replicated and relied on the "very oppressive power structures they are seeking to overcome" (Hughes, 2022, p. 283), such as the social hierarchy of catwalk shows and seating arrangements, and the promoting of individual designers to the detriment of the skilled craftworkers producing the fabrics.

Peoples from around the world have been finding ways to decolonise fashion in their fashion practice and writing for decades, even centuries (see Cheang et al., 2022). Unfortunately, just as in Hughes (2022) study, "many decolonial efforts reinscribe the very power relations they seek to dismantle as a seemingly inescapable condition of capitalist modernity" (Cheang et al., 2022, pp. 251–252). These contradictions and difficult processes also run through the decolonising of teaching practice. Even in the wish to challenge the existing status quo and to disrupt fashion's colonial history through teaching, Cheang (see Cheang & Suterwalla, 2020) explains her realisation that she had structured her course critiquing fashion history with colonial history and the views of the colonisers first (Cheang & Suterwalla, 2020, p. 884). Despite best intentions, fashion practitioners, academics and teachers find that they are enmeshed in paradoxes and ambiguities. Recognising that there is no pure pre-colonial space or dress to return to, decolonising can be perceived as an ongoing journey, continually unfolding (Barry, 2021; Cheang et al., 2022).

A key proposition moving forward is the importance of positionality, the notion that scholars should be open about their cultural and political standpoint, and reflect on their relationship to power and privilege (Barry, 2021; Cheang & Suterwalla, 2020; Jansen, 2020; Moghli & Kadiwai, 2021; Swan, 2017). However, Swan (2017) advises that white lecturers must be wary of "white-indulgent self-reflexivity that returns white narcissism to the centre" (Swan, 2017, p. 550). Instead, being reflective of their own position and discussing this perspective in their teaching, academics can use their reflexivity to prompt discussion with, and between, students. This dialogue would seek to problematise the notion of the normative, neutral, universal truth and interrogate existing Eurocentric thought, knowledge and power structures (Moghli & Kadiwai, 2021, p. 10). Those in academia should stress the importance of students' right to speak, to draw on their own experiences, to add to the plurality of knowledge that decolonisation should be aiming for (Cheang & Suterwalla, 2020). Yet again Swan (2017) offers a warning, drawing on Ahmed (2002) cited in Swan (2017), p.9, of being aware that in our encounters with others, not all can be spoken, scars and traumas may remain unsaid. Ethical communication remains attentive to what may be unvoiced and accepts unfinished and incomplete knowledge (Swan, 2017, p. 9). This incompleteness is a reminder of the continuous process of communication, learning and decolonising itself, and as Ahmed (2012) argues, of the always unfinished nature of all social action (Ahmed, 2012, p. 11).

Ben Barry (2021) acknowledges this open-endedness of decoloniality and contends that fashion educators' teaching practice should not be for the fashion system that is, "but for the fashion system as it should—and must—be" (Barry, 2021, p. 129). This system must change in relation to a range of social issues, and whilst this chapter has examined criticism around business school education's white supremacist structure, there has been movement in educating about sustainability issues (Perry & Win, 2013). The beginning of this chapter noted that racism and addressing racial inequality should also be part of these sustainability discussions; the next section considers whether there is any sign of this focus emerging in the business pedagogical literature.

Sustainability and Responsibility in Business Education

Sustainability has increasingly become a buzzword in the last few decades, originating in reference to the use of renewable sources without damaging ecosystems, but then proliferating in usage and definitions (Vos, 2007). According to Vos (2007), what the definitions of sustainability generally share is the notion that there is an interlinking between environmental concerns, the economy and society. None of these three interconnected elements should be exploited to the deficit of the others and all should support each other (Vos, 2007, p. 335). International discussions around sustainability and sustainable development, emerging out of decades of global summits and initiatives aiming to cultivate shared plans for peace and prosperity, led to the United Nations creating 17 Sustainable Development Goals (SDGs) in 2015 (United Nations, n.d.). These goals are a call to action for countries to work together to "to improve health and education, reduce inequality, and spur economic growth—all while tackling climate change and working to preserve our oceans and forests" (United Nations, n.d.), demonstrating the linking of society, economy and environment as discussed by Vos (2007).

The UN supported the emergence of Principles for Responsible Management Education (PRME), a global network that encourages business and management HE institutions to engage with the UN SDGs (PRME Secretariat, 2022). Since its inception in 2007, PRME's aim has been to help shape business students into responsible future leaders, who will steer businesses towards responsible development, engaging with these sustainable goals. Currently it has 800 signatories worldwide, all institutions who want their teaching to engage with ideas of sustainability and responsibility in business (PRME Secretariat, 2022). The use of the word "responsible" in relation to sustainability introduces another often-cited concept that frequently goes unexamined but needs unpicking (Hibbert, 2021). As Hibbert (2021) reflects, responsibility can be understood as a moral decision-making, based on shared ideals of societal well-being (Hibbert, 2021, p. 375), under which racial equality could be foregrounded. Hibbert (2021) does note that this definition then leads to further questions about what is considered well-being and the relationship between the individual making the decision and the voices of those with whom they may or may not share the ideals. This last point is important, as in the business education literature the responsibility usually explored is corporate social responsibility (CSR), stressing the idea that the context and culture of the company will be relevant to how people of colour are treated.

Frequently, issues of both sustainability and responsibility are addressed simultaneously, and sometimes inter-changeably. This section now considers how far PRME's objectives, general acknowledgement of sustainability concerns, and issues of corporate social responsibility, translate into teaching practice at HE institutions. Also, it investigates how far this notion of sustainability and responsibility in education engages with ideas of equality, particularly given that notions of morality and well-being are thought integral.

Perry and Win (2013) explain that growing support for PRME has been helped by the understanding that corporate social responsibility should not be a separate activity for businesses but incorporated into the entire business model. They contend this perception is reflected in the way "business ethics, environmental sustainability and social responsibility" (Perry & Win, 2013, p. 50) are all now part of business school curricula. Certainly, Young and Nagpal (2013) describe how in their study there was a move to integrate corporate responsibility, and all its related areas, economic, environmental and social responsibility, into the main Masters of Business Administration curriculum. Young and Nagpal (2013) argue that, to teach sustainability separately suggests that it is not an integral part of business enterprise and runs the risk of "even greater disconnect with the mainstream curriculum and thinking" (Young & Nagpal, 2013, p. 504). This disconnect is likewise noted in Araç and Madran's (2014) research about business schools around the world, as they describe how "corporate responsibility and sustainability issues have entered the current academic environment, but these issues have not yet become embedded in mainstream business school education" (Araç & Madran, 2014, p. 139). They also explain that whilst most business schools make efforts to teach sustainability and responsibility issues, only half of the schools in their study reflect on these issues in their own corporate mission (Araç & Madran, 2014). This lack of universal approach is similarly addressed by Young and Napal (2013), who suggest that sustainability must be embedded holistically throughout the culture, strategy and actions of the university to demonstrate its centrality to all business practice (Young & Nagpal, 2013).

The need to move crucial pedagogical messages from the sideline to the mainstream and emphasise their significance throughout all institutional practices reiterates the decoloniality and anti-racist arguments discussed earlier (Bell et al., 2021; Dar et al., 2021). This dearth of holistic thinking around pedagogy and university culture and practice demonstrates a lack of commitment to change on behalf of institutions. Yet social equity is a key part of sustainable development; as Vos (2007) argues, "[O]ne of the most important, but often overlooked, parameters in definitions of sustainability is equity" (Vos, 2007, p. 5). This relative silence in the sustainability literature and public discussion around people and social equality also exists within the sustainability in business education literature and pedagogy. As Young and Napal (2013) discuss, environmental sustainability has been prioritised at the expense of a greater range of issues (Young & Nagpal, 2013, p. 497). Sharma (2017) suggests that sustainability and responsibility in education must be about developing an ethical, moral stance, but it seems this position is not yet reflected in pedagogical practice in business or management education. How far it enters the fashion business educational discourse is discussed next.

Sustainability and Responsibility in Fashion Business Education

As with the literature around sustainability and business there has been a rise of studies discussing sustainable fashion, for example, Kate Fletcher is an academic who has published widely about sustainability and fashion (Fletcher, 2013; Fletcher & Williams, 2013; Fletcher & Tham, 2016). Fashion education's engagement with sustainability and associated literature is also on the rise (Fletcher & Williams, 2013; Radclyffe-Thomas et al., 2018; Rana & Ha-Brookshire, 2019; Schramme & King, 2019). A key message from this educational research echoes all the urgent calls for behavioural change elsewhere throughout this chapter; ethics and sustainability must be integral core values of fashion management (Schramme & King, 2019, p. 258). Rather than bolted-on, these values must be threaded throughout all practice in education and business (Fletcher & Williams, 2013, p. 81).

Whilst sustainability in fashion education has been increasing, it has mostly focused on design and production, and what has been much less developed in fashion management education is sustainability and social responsibility (Radclyffe-Thomas et al., 2018, p. 91). Johnson et al. (2013), in their survey of research addressing fashion and social responsibility, note the use of the term "social responsibility" as having gained traction since the 1990s (Johnson et al., 2013, p. 147). The authors discuss a key definition of social responsibility (SR) in fashion as referring to balancing the environment, economics and people, through a philosophy informed by ethics and morality. This definition of SR resonates with Sharma's (2017) earlier suggestion that teaching must help students to develop their own moral and ethical code. Johnson et al. (2013) emphasise that responsible industry outcomes must positively affect, or do little harm, to the world and its people, and they also stress issues such as consumer well-being, human rights and health and safety (Johnson et al., 2013). Yet, in the literature that Johnson et al. (2013) survey, they note that whilst fashion and SR research is on the rise, there has been a drop in labour-related research. Labour-related studies could be an area where issues of inequality and racially related labour abuses might be addressed (Johnson et al., 2013).

More recently, Thorisdottir and Johannsdottir (2020) reviewed literature about fashion and the more often used term, CSR, and similarly found an increase in scholarly interest. Yet concurrently the authors explain that the "(fashion) industry is still not taking corporate social responsibility seriously, as few companies have hired CSR experts so far" (Thorisdottir & Johannsdottir, 2020, p. 2), suggesting that issues like racial inequality are still not considered vital concerns in the fashion industry. Thorisdottir and Johannsdottir (2020) propose that future research is needed around workers' rights, welfare and income levels, all of which would add to the knowledge about racial inequality in fashion business. Whilst the fashion industry may not be taking CSR seriously, Radclyffe-Thomas et al. (2018) argue that in fashion sustainability teaching, ethical business practices, such as those relating to CSR, are increasingly a priority for educators. Johnson et al. (2013) found that this interest was not yet fully reflected in the educational literature, a finding that my searches also confirm.

In the research that does exist about fashion, sustainability and CSR pedagogy, an idea that could usefully inform the decolonial, anti-racism curriculum is that of a social conscience framework (Goldberg in Radclyffe-Thomas et al., 2018). In their work at London College of Fashion, Radclyffe-Thomas et al. (2018) refer to developing sustainability literacy through this framework of social conscience. Students are encouraged to identify their values using an interconnected framework: combining their awareness of issues of injustice, their understanding of social structures and their own agency, so that they then can judge their "designation of responsibility and willingness and/or ability for action" (Radclyffe-Thomas et al., 2018, p. 92). It is essential that whilst students are made aware of difficult social issues and learn the skill of critical thinking in order to critique these issues (Rana & Ha-Brookshire, 2019), they are also encouraged to think through ways to move forward so as not to weaken the possibility of being proactive (Dylan, 2012). This social conscience framework was used to harness students' innovation and collaborations as they developed transformative outcomes through analysing case studies of current business practices (Radclyffe-Thomas et al., 2018). To begin to bring this review to a close, active listening is raised as one last fundamental sustainability literacy skill to discuss. Rana and Ha-Brookshire (2019) suggest its value in enabling students to undertake ethical interactions during business negotiation. The impact of active listening reiterates a central message aimed at white educators, raised earlier in this chapter, the significance of listening to people of colour.

Conclusion

This chapter was inspired by the wish to listen to students of colour and to co-construct knowledge with them about how best to develop learning in issues relating to racialised minority under-representation, stereotyping and discrimination within the fashion industry. It reviews a range of literature about inclusive teaching, decolonising the curriculum and pedagogy about sustainability and responsibility in business, to evaluate best practice that may help with addressing racial inequality and inequity in teaching and learning.

Amongst the key ideas raised by the research discussed here is that of safety in the classroom and institution, to make teaching spaces places where students feel able to discuss their experiences and where their individual differences and voices are all respected. Teachers must model good behaviour in their communication, correcting any discriminatory language or ideas respectfully, without censure. Racial inequality and discrimination must be discussed in the classroom and out to demonstrate that these are significant issues, worthy of bringing to account. Staff and students can also work together to critique institutional structures, exploring colonialism in all its forms. As research discussed here shows, institutions too need to play their part; economic, environmental and social concerns must all be embedded throughout their structures.

Safety can also be promoted through using reading and teaching examples that reflect a diversity of perspectives, in subject matter and in terms of who they are, to show that there are more voices than just white patriarchal ones. The diversification and decolonisation of the curriculum should also involve direct critique of the existing canon to demonstrate its bias and position to power. This positionality is a key concept presented in this chapter, whereby academics are also transparent about their position in relation to power. The power dynamics between staff and students, white people and people of colour, between people of colour and academic or business institutions, should be part of a constant dialogue about how to do things differently. This chapter demonstrates that the significant skills needed to be encouraged in students, to increase their sustainability and anti-racist literacy, are critical thinking, ability to reflect on their social conscience and active listening.

What this chapter has not been able to do is discuss the importance of emotions, which was also raised in many sources, and the ways in which these need to be acknowledged in dealing with difficult issues such as discrimination and inequity (Barry, 2021; Cheang & Suterwalla, 2020; Rana & Ha-Brookshire, 2019). This element of human experience could be developed in relation to pedagogical research. Whilst CSR in business education literature has little to offer yet to help with dealing with racial inequality, another further avenue for research might be in terms of the new development of diversity consultants, who are being hired by fashion businesses (Vänskä & Gurova, 2022). This new role might provoke increased discussion in the educational literature.

Swan (2017, p. 548) warns against being a white, middle-class do-gooder, acting and speaking on behalf of the 'other', but instead counsels becoming an active listener. Hopefully, choosing to organise focus groups and allowing students to be in dialogue with each other means that my fundamental role is of a listener. Another significant recommendation is keeping informed about important issues in the field and researching the literature for this chapter has performed that function (Swan, 2017, p. 556). On the other hand, the research is also self-serving, in that this chapter was published out of it and hopefully papers to come. Therefore, to be a scholar-activist, I need, not just to do this research with students, but to think of innovative ways to let the voices and ideas of people of colour be at the forefront in the future.

References

Ahmed, S. (2002). This other and other others. *Economy and Society, 31*(4), 558–572.

Ahmed, S. (2012). *On being included: racism and diversity in institutional life.* Duke University Press.

Araç, S. K., & Madran, C. (2014). Business school as an initiator of the transformation to sustainability: A content analysis for business schools in PRME. *Social Business, 4*(2), 137–152.

Arday, J., Beulluigi, D. Z., & Thomas, D. (2021). Attempting to break the chain: reimaging inclusive pedagogy and decolonising the curriculum within the academy. *Educational Philosophy and Theory, 53*(3), 298–313.

Arday, J., Branchu, C., & Boliver, V. (2022). What do we know about Black and Minority Ethnic (BAME) participation in UK higher education? *Social Policy And Society: A journal of the Social Policy Association, 21*(1), 12–25. https://doi.org/10.1017/S1474746421000579

Bakare, L., & Davies, C. (2020). Blackout tuesday: black squares dominate social media and spark debate. *The Guardian.* Retrieved December 1, 2022, from https://www.theguardian.com/us-news/2020/jun/02/blackout-tuesday-dominates-social-media-millions-show-solidarity-george-floyd

Barbour, R. S., & Kitzenger, J. (1999). *Developing focus group research: politics, theory and practice.* Sage.

Barry, B. (2021). How to transform fashion education: A manifesto for equity, inclusion and decolonization. *International Journal of Fashion Studies, 8*(1), 123–130.

Bell, M. P., Berry, D., & Leopold, J. (2021). Making black lives matter in academia: A black feminist call for collective action against anti-blackness in the academy. *Gender, work, and organization, 28*(S1), 39–57.

Black, S., et al. (2013). Introduction. In S. Black et al. (Eds.), *The handbook of fashion studies* (pp. 23–34). Bloomsbury.

British Fashion Council & MBS Group. (2022). *Diversity and inclusion in the fashion industry.* The MBS Group.

Cheang, S., Rabine, L., & Sandhu, A. (2022). Decolonizing fashion [studies] as process. *International Journal of Fashion Studies, 9*(2), 247–255.

Cheang, S., & Suterwalla, S. (2020). Decolonizing the curriculum? transformation, emotion, and positionality in teaching. *Fashion Theory, 24*(6), 879–900.

Clark, H. (2019). Slow + fashion–women's wisdom. *Fashion Practice, 11*(3), 309–327.

Council of Fashion Designers of America & PVH Corp. (2021). *State of diversity, equity & inclusion in fashion*. Council of Fashion Designers of America & PVH Corp.

Craik, J. (1993). *The face of fashion: cultural studies in fashion*. Routledge.

Currie, G. (2007). "Beyond our imagination" the voice of international students on the MBA. *Management Learning, 38*(5), 539–556.

Dar, S., Liu, H., Martinez, A. D., & Brewis, D. N. (2021). The business school is racist: Act up. *Organization, 28*(4), 695–706.

Dike, J. (2021). Have fashion brands stuck to their black lives matter commitments? *The Popular Times*. Retrieved November 23, 2022, from https://www.thepopulartimes.co/articles/fashion-brands-blm-commitment-gucci-supreme-adidas

Dylan, A. (2012). Safety in the classroom: Safeguarding liberal arts education from the neo-liberal threat. *Canadian Journal of Higher Education, 42*(2), 34–48.

Entwistle, J. (2015). *The fashioned body: Fashion, dress and social theory* (2nd ed.). Polity Press.

Fletcher, K. (2013). *Sustainable fashion and textiles: design journeys*. Taylor and Francis.

Fletcher, K., & Tham, M. (2016). *Routledge handbook of sustainability and fashion*. Routledge.

Fletcher, K., & Williams, D. (2013). Fashion education in sustainability in practice. *Research Journal of Textile and Apparel, 17*(2), 81–88.

Gabriel, D. (2022). *Racial categorisation and terminology*. Retrieved March 15, 2022, from https://blackbritishacademics.co.uk/about/racial-categorisation-and-terminology/

Gibbs, A. (1997). Focus groups, *social research update*, Winter (19).

Guest, G., Namey, E., & McKenna, K. (2016). How many focus groups are enough? building an evidence base for nonprobability sample sizes. *Field Methods, 29*(1), 3–22.

Hall, S. (2013). The spectacle of the other. In S. Hall, J. Evans, & S. Nixon (Eds.), *Representation* (pp. 223–279). Sage.

Harris, A., & Leonardo, Z. (2018). Intersectionality, race-gender subordination, and education. *Review of Research in Education, 42*(1), 1–27.

Hibbert, P. (2021). Responsible management education research: Achievements, risks and opportunities. In PRME (Ed.), *Responsible management education: The PRME Global Movement* (pp. 372–385). Routledge.

Hughes, H. (2022). Performing postcolonial identity: The spectacle of Lagos Fashion Week. *International Journal of Fashion Studies, 9*, 281–298. Decolonizing Fashion as Process.

Jansen, A. M. (2020). Fashion and the Phantasmagoria of modernity: An introduction to decolonial fashion discourse. *Fashion Theory, 24*(6), 815–836.

Johnson, K. K., et al. (2013). Trends in research addressing fashion and social responsibility. *Journal of Global Fashion Marketing, 4*(3), 145–157.

Johnson, P., Houston, B., & Kraglund-Gauthier, W. (2019). Decolonizing the classroom in social justice learning: Perspectives on access and inclusion for participants living with disabilities. In J. Hoffman (Ed.), *Strategies for Fostering Inclusive Classrooms in Higher Education: International Perspectives on Equity and Inclusion* (pp. 83–95). Emerald.

Lim, H. (2022). Case study: Enhancing the learning experiences of BAME students at a university: The university role. *Social Policy and Society, 21*(1), 134–141.

Mann, S. J. (2001). Alternative perspectives on the student experience: Alienation and engagement. *Studies in Higher Education, 26*(1), 7–19.

Mercer-Mapstone, L., Islam, M., & Reid, T. (2021). Are we just engaging "the usual suspects"? Challenges in and practical strategies for supporting equity and diversity in student–staff partnership initiatives. *Teaching in Higher Education, 26*(2), 227–245.

Mir, R., & Zanoni, P. (2021). Black lives matter: Organization recommits to racial justice. *Organization, 28*(1), 3–7.

Moghli, M. A., & Kadiwai, L. (2021). Decolonising the curriculum beyond the surge: Conceptualisation, positionality and conduct. *London Review of Education, 19*(1), 1–16.

Morgan, D. (1998). *The focus group guidebook*. Sage.

Mueller, B. (2021). Decolonising assessment within higher arts education, *Journal of Useful Investigations in Creative Education, (4)*. Retrieved from https://juice-journal.com/2021/11/23/decolonising-assessment-within-higher-arts-education/

Paulicelli, E., & Clark, H. (2009). Introduction. In E. Paulicelli & H. Clark (Eds.), *The fabric of cultures: Fashion, identity, and globalization* (pp. 1–11). Abingdon.

Perry, M., & Win, S. (2013). An evaluation of PRME's contribution to responsibility in higher education. *The Journal of Corporate Citizenship, 2013*(49), 48–70.

Phizacklea, A. (1990). *Unpacking the fashion industry: Gender, racism and class in production*. Routledge.

Phoenix, A., Amesu, A., Naylor, I., & Zafar, K. (2020). Viewpoint: "When black lives matter all lives will matter"-A teacher and three students discuss the BLM movement. *London Review of Education, 18*(3), 519–523.

Ploner, J. (2018). International students' transitions to UK Higher Education–revisiting the concept and practice of academic hospitality. *Journal of Research in International Education, 17*(2), 164–178.

PRME Secretariat. (2022). *About: What is PRME?.* Retrieved December 13, 2022, from https://www.unprme.org/about

Radclyffe-Thomas, N., Varley, R., & Roncha, A. (2018). Balancing the books: Creating a model of responsible fashion business education. *Art, Design & Communication in Higher Education, 17*(1), 89–106.

Rana, K., Bashir, A., Begum, F., & Barlett, H. (2022). Bridging the BAME attainment gap: Student and staff perspectives on tackling academic bias. *Frontiers in Education, 7,* 1–12.

Rana, M. R. I., & Ha-Brookshire, J. (2019). New conceptual framework for fashion business ideation, negotiation, and implementation undergraduate curricula for sustainable development. *International Journal of Fashion Design, Technology and Education, 12*(2), 140–148.

Roshitsh, K. (2020). Dear fashion: Be human, break the silence. *Women's Wear Daily,* 10.

Schramme, A., & King, I. W. (2019). Fashioning a master's degree. *Arts and Humanities in Higher Education, 8*(2–3), 250–268.

Sengupta, E., Blessinger, P., Hoffman, J., & Makhanya, M. (2019). Introduction to strategies for fostering inclusive classrooms in higher education. In J. Hoffman, P. Blessinger, & M. Makhanya (Eds.), *Strategies for fostering inclusive classrooms in higher education: International perspectives on equity and inclusion* (pp. 3–17). Emerald.

Sharma, R. R. (2017). A competency model for management education for sustainability. *Vision, 21*(2), x–xv.

Shealey, A. (2021). #BlackRepresentationsMatter: Viewing digital activism through symbology. *Fashion Style & Popular Culture, 8*(1), 83–96.

Silva, D. (2022). The intersectionality between black lives matter and English language teaching: A raciolinguistic perspective. *TESOL journal, 13*(1).

Skelton, A. (2002). Towards inclusive learning environments in higher education? Reflections on a professional development course for university lecturers. *Teaching in Higher Education, 7*(2), 193–214.

Slade, T., & Jansen, M. A. (2020). Letter from the editors: Decoloniality and fashion. *Fashion Theory, 24*(6), 809–814.

Swan, E. (2017). What are white people to do? listening, challenging ignorance, generous encounters and the "Not Yet" as diversity research praxis. *Gender, Work and Organization, 24*(5), 547–563.

Taylor, L. (2013). Fashion and dress history: Theoretical and methodological approaches. In S. Black et al. (Eds.), *The handbook of fashion studies* (pp. 41–61). Bloomsbury.

Textiles & fashion all parliamentary party group. (2021). *Representation & Inclusion in the Fashion Industry*. Fashion Roundtable.

Thorisdottir, T. S., & Johannsdottir, L. (2020). Corporate social responsibility influencing sustainability within the fashion industry: A systemic review. *Sustainability, 12*(21), 1–64.

UCA. (2018a). *Manifesto for BAME attainment at UCA*. Retrieved March 3, 2022, from https://ucalearningandteaching.files.wordpress.com/2018/12/BAMEManifestoV3.pdf

UCA. (2018b). *Inclusive practice guide: Addressing inequalities experienced by BAME (Black, Asian and Minority Ethnic) students*. Internal UCA guide. Unpublished.

United Nations. (n.d.). *United Nations Department of Economic and Social Affairs Sustainable Development The 17 Goals History*. Retrieved January 11, 2023, from https://sdgs.un.org/goals#history

Universities UK and National Union of Students. (2019). *Black, Asian and minority ethnic student attainment at UK universities: #CLOSINGTHEGAP*. Retrieved April 12, 2022, from https://www.universitiesuk.ac.uk/policy-and-analysis/reports/Documents/2019/bame-student-attainment-uk-universities-closing-the-gap.pdf

Vänskä, A., & Gurova, O. (2022). The fashion scandal: Social media, identity and the globalization of fashion in the twenty-first century. *International Journal of Fashion Studies, 9*(1), 5–27.

Vos, R. O. (2007). Defining sustainability: A conceptual orientation. *Journal of Chemical Technology and Biotechnology, 82*(4), 334–339.

Wilson, E. (1985). *Adorned in dreams: Fashion & modernity*. Virago.

Wissinger, E. (2012). Managing the semiotics of skin tone: Race and aesthetic labor in the fashion modeling industry. *Economic and Industrial Democracy, 33*(1), 125–143.

Woodside, A. G., & Fine, M. B. (2019). Sustainable fashion themes in luxury brand storytelling: The sustainability fashion research grid. *Journal of Global Fashion Marketing, 10*(2), 111–128.

Young, S., & Nagpal, S. (2013). Meeting the growing demand for sustainability-focused management education: a case study of a PRME academic institution. *Higher Education Research & Development, 32*(3), 493–506.

5

How Can We Be Inclusive of Diverse Cultural Perspectives in International Higher Education? Exploring Interculturality

Frank Fitzpatrick

Introduction

The flow of international students to UK higher education continues to grow and becomes ever more diverse as more non-EU students are admitted for university study (HESA, 2022), which highlights the need for higher education institutions and business schools to consider the challenges of a greater diversity of students from a wider range of cultural differences and prior educational experiences in order to create an inclusive and level playing field for academic achievement (de Wit, 2002; Universities, 2021). In order to facilitate this, institutions and their employees require a better understanding of the specific obstacles that international students face in order to adjust to both a new academic context and a new way of life in often unfamiliar cultural surroundings

F. Fitzpatrick (✉)
Business School for the Creative Industries, University for the Creative Arts, Epsom, UK
e-mail: frank.fitzpatrick@uca.ac.uk

© The Author(s), under exclusive license to Springer Nature Switzerland AG 2023
B. S. Nayak (ed.), *Intersectionality and Creative Business Education*,
https://doi.org/10.1007/978-3-031-29952-0_5

and there is evidence that this tends to lag behind expectations (Dervin, 2016).

A better understanding involves an appreciation of what is entailed in the process of cross-cultural adjustment and what kind of practical support can be provided for students engaged in exploring and thriving in a new way of life that may be different to their own. Likewise, better awareness of how to build interculturality and level out the playing field when it comes to ways of learning and approaching academic tasks that may be new and challenging for some is of paramount importance. This chapter explores how higher education institutions can help build a more welcoming and inclusive environment and experience for a growing and increasingly diverse body of international students and enable them to succeed and excel on a level that would demonstrate genuine equity in academic opportunity and achievement.

The Challenges Facing International Students

Relocating for work or study brings a number of well-documented challenges (Fabricius & Preisler, 2015). On the one hand, individuals need to navigate lifestyle changes that come with a new and unfamiliar environment on a range of different levels in their quest to set up a new life in their new location. This involves learning about how life is organised and the way it functions, as well as learning to interpret potentially new patterns of behaviour and verbal and non-verbal communication while navigating unfamiliar contextual dynamics, including the norms and values of a new setting (Cushner & Karim, 2004). On the other hand, in the case of international students, while cultural adjustment is seen as important for academic success (Nasir, 2012), their experience of education may differ considerably from their home environment in how they are expected to engage in learning and assessment, whether at an institutional level or through pedagogical practice (Li & Campbell, 2006). While this is an experience that all students have to confront to some extent, whether home or international students, in that they relocate and abandon their own direct familiar social and support networks, the challenge in this may be considered greater for students from a diverse linguistic background and cultural context.

Culture Shock and Cross-Cultural Adjustment

The oft-quoted model of phased *culture shock*, which sees cross-cultural adjustment as a uniform process regardless of context or individual experience, is now largely seen as inadequate to explain the challenges of relocation (Fitzpatrick, 2017), and a more tailored description of the challenges and stresses of adjustment and convergence have been outlined by more personalised coping and growth models (Kim, 2001; Landis et al., 2004). In these, 'culture shock' is seen as a process of 'adjustment' in which a distinction between *sociocultural* aspects of adjustment, or learning how to live, behave and communicate in a new cultural context, and *psychological* aspects of adjustment, or coping with life changes and the stress of uncertainty and unfamiliarity, is made. To this must be added the challenges relating to weakening *social capital*, and the need to rebuild this, as sojourners move away from familiar and supportive families, communities and personal and professional and friendship networks set in predictable surroundings (Fitzpatrick, 2016).

Such models are indeed more complex and embracing and avoid relegating the personal and difficult challenges of coping with change, or 'acculturative stress' (Berry, 2006), to uniform stages experienced by all in the same way as *culture shock*, although it is also important to be aware of the positive aspects of starting a new life at university or in a new location, which universities can exploit and build upon to enhance the student experience (Sercombe & Young, 2015; Furnham, 2004).

Educational Adjustment

Similarly, a horizon of potential adjustment challenges, or 'learning shock' (Gu & Maley, 2008), can be identified in an unfamiliar learning context. As well as language difficulties and intercultural communication barriers, other challenges identified are unfamiliar patterns of classroom interactions, lack of knowledge of academic norms and conventions and inadequate learning support (Li & Campbell, 2006). The practice of working collaboratively and producing work collectively in groups, for example, or re-wording a published text and presenting it in one's own words, or being asked to think critically and challenge purportedly established academic wisdom, or speak out in front of peers and even challenge or contradict the instructor can create stress and consternation for those not familiar with such techniques or approaches, while confusion about the status and nature of the *independent learner* can have implications for continuance, progression and student experience (McKendry & Boyd, 2012).

In this vein, we must be aware of the how culturally inflected knowledge and pedagogical practice is constructed in different contexts and how this can influence all our modes of perception, expression, learning and communication. In this sense, what can be identified as the '*Enlightenment*-driven disposition' embodied within 'Western' education (Wisker & Robinson, 2014) normalises an objective, neutral, rational and critical approach towards established knowledge constructs, while, in other contexts, the construction and expression of knowledge may not be open to question or, by questioning it, it may be seen to challenge tradition and fundamental social cohesion. Consequently, the very notion of independence may, in itself, be a troublesome challenge for students from societies where individuals are expected to be *interdependent* rather *independent*, framed by tight cultural and community networks that may de-emphasise self-promotion or 'individualism' and focus much more on social cohesion and harmony rather than competitiveness (Triandis, 1995). Contexts that are more *culturally tight*, for example, may create authority structures that are more restrictive for individuals, where deviance or originality are more inhibited than 'looser' contexts (Gelfand, 2018). Some educational practices in higher education, then, may be second nature to some students and not others, and a lack of awareness of alternative perspectives amongst educators can lead to culturally inflected aspects going unrecognised (Wisker & Robinson, 2014). This may result in a tendency to unconsciously commend a certain form of academic engagement that is familiar to us and deride a lack of engagement as failure and in need of 'remedial attention' (Wisker & Robinson, 2014, p. 191) resulting in a far from level playing field.

Understanding Cultural Context

While such variant notions as *cultural tightness* (Gelfand, 2018), *individualism-collectivism* (Hofstede, 2001) or *interdependence* (Triandis, 1995), for example, have become popular clichés within cross-cultural management literature and claim to be able to identify set behavioural characteristics across entire populations that can be comfortably categorised and classified within a frame of distinctive *national cultures*, such an approach to cultural diversity has been consistently challenged as essentialist and over-simplistic (Søderberg, 1999; McSweeney, 2002; Signorini et al., 2009). Furthermore, it is important to contemplate the range of experiences and expectations that students may bring to the educational arena from their own cultural perspective or *cultural context*. Context is not seen, in this sense, as a static notion but as a dynamic behavioural domain to be navigated and influenced by individuals within it through interaction and social construction (Duranti & Goodwin, 1992).

Consequently, context is not just a physical space but also a social and behavioural construct governed by sociocultural conventions and influenced by extra-situational and historical factors. For this reason, Day (2008) contends that what is contextually relevant for people in a particular situation is to be found in the knowledge and orientations of social relationships and their membership of different groups, rather than in the material context itself. A distinction is made, then, between the *proximate context* (see Fig. 5.1), or what is encountered within the *sociocultural* and material space by those unfamiliar with it, and the *distal context*, or what individuals bring to the context in terms of their interpretation of it framed within their cultural perspectives, prior experiences and material resources (Day, 2008). Day (2008) also identifies a *messo* level of context of interaction, at an organisational or institutional level, which, within the university context, can be seen to relate to the higher education sector, together with its values, methods, conventions, regulations and such and how these are framed within a particular university institution and

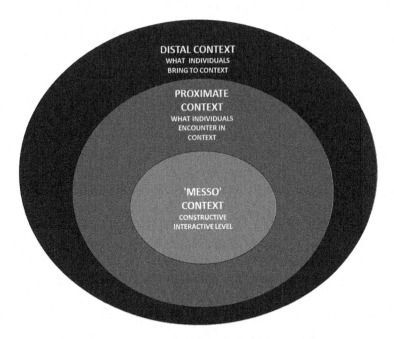

Fig. 5.1   Representation of Day's (2008) 'Messo' context (author)

enacted through the relationships that develop within the praxis of an individual's educational experience.

This, then, creates a dialectic on two levels. First, between the *proximal* factors at the sociocultural level of context, related to features and the dynamics of everyday life within a particular location, which influences *sociocultural adjustment*, and the *distal* elements, related to individual perspectives, identities, resources and expectations drawn upon in the navigation of a new way of life by students on a psychological level. Second, at the 'messo' domain of context, what can be described as 'pedagogical power relations' (Grant, 2010, p. 93) are seen to unfold. This relates to how students interact with the institutional and behavioural framework of university life and hierarchy in order to navigate their particular educational experience, which influences their coping levels and their *psychological adjustment*. Important here are the various social positionings of key academic and administrative gatekeepers that subtly pass judgement on student performance and participation and their sometimes intangible assumptions of conventions and standards of knowledge and behaviour that 'ghost' or stand behind the participants in interaction and which can distort the power balance between students and university authorities (Grant, 2010).

What Universities Can Do to Help Students Adjust

Universities can facilitate the cross-cultural adjustment of students, both within the university context and the wider sociocultural context, in a number of ways. Settling into a new life can involve a number of practical and time-consuming challenges even at a basic or routine level, such as setting up home, learning how everyday life functions and becoming familiar with surroundings and daily routines (Hechanova et al., 2003), but it can also heighten emotional distress and involve a degree of difficulty in forming relationships and networks that can help adjustment. In this sense, the notion of *social support*, or the availability of 'helping relationships' and targeted support mechanisms, has been identified as a way of alleviating elements such as loneliness, stress and depression, which can have a positive impact on both the psychological and sociocultural level (Ong & Ward, 2005). Ong and Ward (2005) identify four functions served by social support:

1. *Emotional support* (displaying understanding, concern, sympathy and caring for others facing challenging circumstances)
2. *Social companionship* (the feeling of social belonging with others across a range of daily activities)
3. *Tangible assistance* (concrete help in terms of material resources, essential services or financial facilitation)
4. *Informational support* (provision of a wide range of information, views and products and services related to becoming familiar with daily life)

Interestingly, the authors conclude that, despite the importance of emotional support at a time of change, it is practical support, together with local social networks, which are the most important for psychological wellbeing, noting that individuals often use their own strategies to create a sense of mastery over their environment and seek support and information from others in order to reduce uncertainty. Building on this, Hechanova et al. (2003) see the provision of institutional support as critical in order to facilitate adjustment, and many universities provide assistance with such key elements as finding accommodation, providing information and bulletins on public services, hosting social events and clubs and, increasingly, wellbeing support and financial flexibility (Baik et al., 2019).

How Universities Can Help Build Awareness and Tolerance of Different Cultural Perspectives and Behaviours

A certain amount of awareness raising and training relating to the issues involved in cross-cultural adjustment amongst staff working at an institutional level has been identified as critical to responding to growing diversity in student populations as universities become more globalised (Leavitt et al., 2017). This is seen as critical not only for students to develop intercultural competence skills in order to facilitate their adaptation to new and diverse environments, but also on a policy and institutional level to facilitate a broader capacity for cultural sensitivity and acceptance (Dervin & Layne, 2013). An example of this is the use and application of the Bennett *Developmental Model of Intercultural Sensitivity (DMIS)* (Landis et al., 2004) in the university environment (Fitzpatrick, 2022: 154–156), which models the journey from *ethnocentrism* (cultural superiority) to *ethnorelativism* (cultural pluralism) in order to develop awareness of and sensitivity to different worldviews held by cultural groups other than one's own.

Likewise, Arasaratnam-Smith and Deardorff (2022) demonstrate the value of exploring individual student narratives related to navigating cultural differences, of self-reflection and of building relationships through intercultural competence in order to engage with issues associated with identity negotiation, stereotyping, cultural difference and communities of support. Such an approach focuses on developing appropriate *Attitudes* (including respect, openness, curiosity, discovery and tolerance for ambiguity), *Knowledge* (including cultural self-awareness, culture specific knowledge, socio-linguistic awareness and a perspective on global issues and trends) and *Skills* (including listening, observing and viewing the world from different perspectives) in order to promote effective and appropriate behaviour and communication in intercultural encounters (Deardorff, 2009). Such work can lead to important insights for educationalists and administrators, who may see their own version of pedagogical and managerial practice as the indisputable and self-evident paradigm of the ideal learning experience and accountability, and can challenge them to accept alternative experiences of learning and social interaction derived from a quite distinct set of cultural assumptions. What might be regarded as conventional wisdom and superior pedagogical methodology by those empowered to induct students into the framework and ethos of genres of knowledge and comportment within one context may be viewed as particularly challenging and uncomfortable from a different point of view or for those with diverse learning experiences and constructs of knowledge (Grant, 2010).

Building Interculturality in Academic Spaces

The notion of *culture* used here is a now well-established, non-essentialist, postmodern concept relating to dynamic, fluid and universal intercultural processes through which identity evolves as a trajectory of experience (Holliday, 2011; Fitzpatrick, 2022), rather than one of a static, bounded and deterministic modernist notion of identity relating to fixed national culture (Hofstede, 2001). *Cultural background* as a way of life and contextual construct is not denied as being influential on sojourners and international students in that they are educated in different languages and hold beliefs, values and views that have been shaped by their upbringing and material experiences and sociocultural filters. Nevertheless, the notion of agency allows individuals to evolve in their cultural perspective and identity as a result of their experiences and social encounters beyond the dynamics of early socialisation, always, however, within the material possibilities available to them. Figure 5.2 shows such a range of influences based on a social constructionist model of culture and cultural identity (Berger & Luckman, 1967; Tajfel, 1982; Benwell & Stokoe, 2006), set within a framework of material conditions (Martin & Nakayama, 2009) which constrain our possibilities and *personal cultural trajectory* (Holliday, 2011).

The process of identity construction is framed by the *cultural resources* at our disposal through the process of *enculturation* in the early stages of our social existence, which influence our understanding of and perspective on our social world, through to a range of *sites of identity construction* (Benwell & Stokoe, 2006) through *socialisation* in which we construct our *social identity* interactively, influenced by many *sociocultural filters* that frame and influence our emerging place in society, while we develop our own *individual cultural identity* through our various personal experiences, encounters, networks and interests (Fitzpatrick, 2020). *Personal identity*, however, continues to evolve and hybridise and the experience of

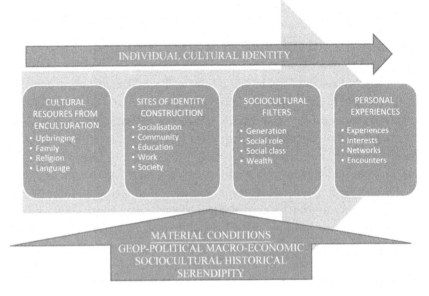

Fig. 5.2 Development of individual cultural identity (author)

being in a new cultural context can enrich this process and trajectory of change substantially.

In this sense, it is important to recognise that the international student, as with all social actors, is much more than their nationality and that it is worth avoiding national or cultural stereotyping that may lead us to place them in the role of the exotic 'other' (*otherisation*) and interpret behaviour as being determined by where they come from (Gu & Maley, 2008). If we focus on students as individuals with diverse abilities, aspirations, expectations, motivations, perspectives and such, that emanate from their own personal trajectory in life, we focus much less on the individual as a product of their environment and more as an agent of their own identity construction through engagement with their social and material environment. The only proviso here, however, is that, as we have seen with reference to Day (2008), it is of value to recognise the challenges of the particular experience of international students who are confronting the dual-pronged process of adjusting to both a new *cultural* environment, or way of life (*proximate context*) and a new *learning* environment and all the challenges that the *messo context* of a UK higher education institution invokes for all involved.

The notion of *interculturality*, then, challenges the largely commonly held assumption that culture resides in a particular location or geography, such as a nation state, which produces predictable interactive outcomes across a given population and considers how individuals from diverse cultural backgrounds interact in a given *context*. It is, thus, derived from the concept of *interstitial* spaces or *third space* (Bhabha, 2004), which can accommodate *cultural hybridity* or the creation of new sociocultural groupings that generate their own particular norms, conventions and relational interactions amongst individuals from different cultural backgrounds. In this sense, it is the shared experiences of studying and working together that can create a shared sense of identity amongst people as a unique and distinct group. This involves building new perspectives, rather than losing existing ones, and indicates how sustained contact with others from diverse cultural backgrounds can help individuals to generate unique outlooks and shared perspectives both within collaborative groups or teams and by developing their own individual cultural trajectory.

In order to facilitate *interculturality*, it is important to ensure that students from different backgrounds have the opportunity to intermingle and participate in sociocultural interaction with each other and with others beyond their immediate in-group. Quite apart from the sociocultural and psychological benefits of building social cohesion amongst students, as well as a sense of belonging and acceptance of diversity, from an educational point of view, there is some evidence that encouraging collaborative learning can enhance academic attainment and that equality of contribution can also help develop intercultural competence (de Hei et al., 2020).

One way of initiating and structuring this is through *cultural mapping*, which includes activities that explore the nature of cultural identity and the influences upon us in our upbringing and our own personal experiences (Fitzpatrick, 2020: 83–85). For example, by conducting a simple mapping activity in which the tutor asks students to individually map out the various influences on their cultural identity (based on Fig. 5.2 above), and then involves them in explaining, comparing, discussing and reflecting on them in small groups, can help them work through issues of identity and adjustment with peers and classmates and give them a platform to share their background and develop an intercultural perspective and a sense of being comfortable with diversity. Such an activity, which can be an introductory icebreaker at any level, can build confidence and pride in students' cultural origins and can also feed into other collaborative group work and discussions in which students then develop their own unique set of relationships and outcomes as discrete *intercultural* groups.

Furthermore, out of the ensuing discussion, it is important to bring out universal features and perspectives in order to focus on 'omnicultural' similarities (Moghaddam, 2012), rather than solely on differences (Nolan et al., 2022). This can include such elements as the commonalities in the way humans live together in groups and societies through social organisation and governance, or the structure of belief and value systems across different cultural contexts, in order to avoid exoticisation and tokenism relating to superficial features of cultural expression, such as dress, rituals, festivals and so on (Fitzpatrick, 2020, p. 262). All in all, by bringing forth notions and discussions of identity and diversity within induction sessions, modules and courses, *interculturality* can be developed as a positive force that enriches the international learning experience and academic attainment more equitably.

Conclusion

Overall, then, by exploring interculturality and cultural diversity in the higher education experience, it is possible to build awareness of and sensitivity to the challenges of studying in an unfamiliar sociocultural and educational environment that is the fate of international students, without necessarily assuming a corrective or remedial stance when dealing with alternative prior learning experiences and approaches. Institutions have a duty of care to provide support for sociocultural and institutional adjustment, rather than simply impose standards of compliance and culturally inflected models of knowledge, if a level playing field is to be the intended and desired outcome of internationalised programmes. Quite apart from this, recognition and appreciation of different perspectives on the learning process can feed back into both pedagogical and administrative practice to the benefit of educational policy and strategy, including staff development and growth. Fostering *interculturality* can enrich the perspective of both the learner and the provider of instruction and governance, as well as deliver an inspiring educational experience that facilitates intercultural development.

References

Arasaratnam-Smith, L. A., & Deardorff, D. K. (2022). *Developing intercultural competence in higher education.* Routledge.

Baik, C., Larcombe, W., & Brooker, A. (2019). How universities can enhance student mental wellbeing: The student perspective. *Higher Education Research & Development, 38*(4), 674–687.

Benwell, B., & Stokoe, E. (2006). *Discourse and identity.* Edinburgh University Press.

Berger, P., & Luckman, T. (1967). *The social construction of reality.* The Penguin Press.

Berry, J. W. (2006). Stress perspectives on acculturation. In D. L. Sam & J. W. Berry (Eds.), *Acculturation psychology* (pp. 43–57). CUP.

Bhabha, H. K. (2004). *The location of culture*. Routledge.

Cushner, K., & Karim, A. (2004). Study abroad at the university level. In D. Landis, J. Bennett, & M. Bennet (Eds.), *Handbook of intercultural training* (3rd ed., pp. 289–308). Sage.

Day, D. (2008). In a bigger, messo, context. *Journal of Pragmatics, 40*(5), 979–996.

de Hei, M., Tabacaru, C., Sjoer, E., Rippe, R., & Walenkamp, J. (2020). Developing intercultural competence through collaborative learning in international higher education. *Journal of Studies in International Education, 24*(2), 190–211.

de Wit, H. (2002). *Internationalization of higher education in The United States of America and Europe*. Greenwood.

Deardorff, D. K. (Ed.). (2009). *The SAGE handbook of intercultural competence*. SAGE.

Dervin, F. (2016). *Interculturality in education*. Palgrave Macmillan.

Dervin, F., & Layne, H. (2013). A guide to interculturality for international and exchange students: An example of hospitality? *Journal of Multicultural Discourses, 8*(1), 1–19.

Duranti, A., & Goodwin, C. (1992). *Rethinking context*. CUP.

Fabricius, A. H., & Preisler, B. (Eds.). (2015). *Transcultural interaction and linguistic diversity in higher education: The student experience*. Palgrave Macmillan.

Fitzpatrick, F. (2016). *Voices from Cuba: Redefining culture shock*. Lambert.

Fitzpatrick, F. (2017). Taking the 'culture' out of 'culture shock': A critical review of literature on cross-cultural adjustment in international relocation. *Critical Perspectives on International Business, 13*(4), 278–296.

Fitzpatrick, F. (2020). *Understanding intercultural interaction: An analysis of key concepts*. Emerald Publishing.

Fitzpatrick, F. (2022). Towards interculturality in international creative business management in higher education. In P. Powell & B. S. Nayak (Eds.), *Contours of creative business education*. Palgrave Macmillan.

Furnham, A. (2004). Foreign students' education and culture shock. *The Psychologist, 17*(1), 16–19.

Gelfand, M. (2018). *Rule makers, rule breakers: How tight and loose cultures wire our world*. Scribner.

Grant, B. M. (2010). Negotiating the layered relations of supervision. In M. Walker & P. Thompson (Eds.), *The Routledge doctoral supervisor's companion: Supporting effective research in education and the social sciences*. Routledge.

Gu, Q., & Maley, A. (2008). Changing places: A study of Chinese students in the UK. *Language and Intercultural Communication, 8*(4), 224–245.

Hechanova, R., Beehr, T. A., & Christiansen, N. D. (2003). Antecedents and consequences of employees' adjustment to overseas assignment: A meta-analytical review. *Applied Psychology, 52*(2), 213–236.

HESA. (2022). *Higher education student statistics: UK, 2020/21–where students come from and go to study*. Retrieved July 08, 2022, from https://www.hesa.ac.uk/news/25-01-2022/sb262-higher-education-student-statistics/location

Hofstede, G. (2001). *Culture's consequences*. Sage.

Holliday, A. (2011). *Intercultural communication and ideology*. Sage.

Kim, Y. Y. (2001). *Becoming intercultural: An integrative theory of communication and cross-cultural adaptation*. Sage Publications.

Landis, D., Bennett, J. M., & Bennett, M. J. (2004). *Handbook of intercultural training*. Sage Publications.

Leavitt, L., Wisdom, S., & Leavitt, K. (2017). *Cultural awareness and competency development in higher education*. IGI Global

Li, M., & Campbell, J. (2006). *Cultural adaptation: A case study of Asian students' learning experiences at a New Zealand university*. EDU-COM International Conference. Retrieved December 15, 2022, from https://ro.ecu.edu.au/ceducom/86

Martin, J., & Nakayama, T. (2009). *Intercultural communication in contexts*. McGraw-Hill Education.

McKendry, S., & Boyd, V. (2012). Defining the "independent learner" in UK higher education: Staff and students' understanding of the concept. *International Journal of Teaching and Learning in Higher Education, 24*(2), 209–220.

McSweeney, B. (2002). Hofstede's model of national cultural differences and their consequences: A triumph of faith–A failure of analysis. *Human Relations, 55*(1), 89–118.

Moghaddam, F. M. (2012). The omnicultural imperative. *Culture and psychology, 18*(3), 304–330.

Nasir, M. (2012). Effects of cultural adjustment on academic achievement of international students. *Journal of Elementary Education, 22*, 95–103.

Nolan, E., Héliot, Y. F., & Rienties, B. (2022). Encouraging intercultural interaction by cultural specific learning design. *Journal of Studies in International Education*. Retrieved December 20, 2022, from https://doi.org/10.1177/10283153221145083.

Ong, A. S. J., & Ward, C. (2005). The construction and validation of a social support measure for sojourners. *Journal of Cross-Cultural Psychology, 36*(6), 637–661.

Sercombe, P., & Young, T. (2015). Student adjustment: Diversity and uniformity of experience. In A. H. Fabricius et al. (Eds.), *Transcultural interaction and linguistic diversity in higher education*. Palgrave Macmillan.

Signorini, P., Wiesemes, R., & Murphy, R. (2009). Developing alternative frameworks for exploring intercultural learning: A critique of Hofstede's cultural difference model. *Teaching in Higher Education, 14*(3), 253–264.

Søderberg, A.-M. (1999). Do national cultures always make a difference? In T. Vestergaard (Ed.), *Language, culture and identity*. Aarhus University.

Tajfel, H. (1982). *Social identity and intergroup relations* (Vol. 33, p. 1). CUP.

Triandis, H. C. (1995). *Individualism and collectivism*. Westview Press.

Universities UK. (2021). *Black, Asian and Minority Ethnic student attainment at UK universities: Closing the gap report*. Retrieved March 08, 2022, from https://www.universitiesuk.ac.uk/sites/default/files/field/downloads/2021-07/bame-student-attainment.pdf

Wisker, G., & Robinson, G. (2014). Examiner practices and culturally inflected doctoral theses. *Discourse: Studies in the Cultural Politics of Education, 35*(2), 190–205.

6

How Do We Build Intercultural Understanding and Awareness into Teaching to Develop a More Inclusive and Professional Practice?

Kathleen Hinwood and Laura Holme

Difference is the essence of humanity. Difference is an accident of birth and it should therefore never be the source of hatred or conflict. The answer to difference is to respect it. Therein lies a most fundamental principle of peace: respect for diversity.
John Hume

Introduction

The landscape of higher education has in recent years undergone "seismic changes" (Staley & Trinkle, 2011) in terms of student body demographic, delivery-mode and increasing competition as the number and range of institutions have expanded across the globe. In the UK, such reverberations have been felt profoundly, where there has been a dramatic increase in the number of domestic students attending university (Deeks, 2020) whilst also grappling with radical changes to the way that higher

K. Hinwood • L. Holme (✉)
Business School for the Creative Industries, University for the Creative Arts, Epsom, UK
e-mail: Kathleen.Hinwood@uca.ac.uk; Laura.Holme@uca.ac.uk

© The Author(s), under exclusive license to Springer Nature Switzerland AG 2023
B. S. Nayak (ed.), *Intersectionality and Creative Business Education*,
https://doi.org/10.1007/978-3-031-29952-0_6

education has been funded since 2012 (Walsh, 2022). As a consequence of this, there has been a growing incentive for institutions to generate income from international students, which they have become particularly reliant on. Additionally, there have been demands from students who wish to study abroad, particularly those from emerging markets where the standard of living has increased and globalisation in the industry and education has become a key driver. The commoditisation of higher education has generated an industry of recruitment to fulfil and propagate such demand.

According to Ryan, the globalisation of education, particularly in the postgraduate sector, has led to "large classes and time constraints [which are the] real issues in the massification of higher education" (2011). Such practicalities are contrary to the resounding acknowledgement that student-centred learning is beneficial for the student, the cohort and the facilitator alike. Therefore, despite the funding model which promotes the notion of international students as *cash cows*, "universities need to focus on developing an environment where everyone can see themselves reflected, and where they feel they belong" (Keyes, 1986).

In recognition of the changing nature of higher education it is important to build intercultural understanding and awareness into teaching practice, to develop a more inclusive and professional educational experience. In our courses, we need to demonstrate ways in which academics can design curricula, teach and assess in ways in which students are heard, listened to, understood and can thrive; ways in which we can create the spaces for students regardless of background or history (Vorster, 2017).

Why Do We Have Internationalisation in Our Universities?

Beyond the precarious nature of the current funding model for higher education, there is a continuing trend for international students to study in the UK, Australia and the US, which is reflective of the global workforce and a desire to develop a world view. The demand for "cross-border"

(Youssef, 2014) qualifications for students from emerging markets provides them with the opportunity for a qualification that may be more highly valued when they return home, giving them the requisite skills needed for contemporary careers, or an opportunity to work in the UK, for example. It also "provides a way of distinguishing oneself" (Deeks, 2020), particularly "If [students] come from a non-English-speaking country, studying abroad in an institution or country where English is spoken […] while also building English skills" (Deeks, 2020). International students contributed approximately £20.4bn to the UK economy in 2018 (MAS, 2018), which signifies their ongoing importance in the economics of not only universities but also the communities that benefit from this influx. Therefore, there needs to be an acknowledgement of the significance of internationalisation within our institutions as a concept and on an individual level in terms of student-centred learning with "unconditional positive regard" (Rogers, 1995).

There is a danger that there are not necessarily the appropriate resources in place for the volume of international students that are attending certain institutions within the UK, which puts pressure on existing resources, particularly in relation to housing. Many students, and in particular, international students have been found to be *sofa surfing,* temporarily homeless or living too far from campus to be able to be a productive and engaged student (Hall, 2022). The housing crisis is expected to be exacerbated by "rapidly expanding universities and international students returning amid the easing of the Covid pandemic." "[The situation has already] deteriorate[d] in January when a new intake arrived, and again [pressure will mount] in September 2023, which is expected to be another record university recruitment round" (Hall, 2022). Alongside pressures on infrastructure, there is a threat to the quality of educational delivery, and the overall student experience as a shopping cart approach to higher education is continuing to evolve.

Despite the COVID-19 pandemic that impacted several industries and countries adversely, universities to some extent were unimpeded—even with lockdowns and remote learning becoming the norm for the best part of two years. According to the Migration Observatory at the University of Oxford, international students enrolled in UK higher education institutions (HEIs) in 2020/21 made up to 22% of all HE students, with over 600,000 students enrolled (Walsh, 2022). International students are often charged a fee that provides the university with a premium over and above the cost of providing the education, (Deeks, 2020) that allows for home-domiciled students to be subsidised to a large degree (Walsh, 2022). Additionally, student recruitment has expanded beyond Europe now as "was particularly evident post-Brexit where applications from prospective students from EU fell by approximately 50%, from 2020 to 2022" (Walsh, 2022). This trend is supported by the evidence of tuition fees from non-EU students, which has grown substantially from 2000/1 to 2021—making up 17% of universities' total income with 80% of the revenue coming from non-EU backgrounds (Walsh, 2022).

Over-reliance on a singular culture leaves institutions vulnerable to global crises such as the COVID-19 pandemic which impacted some institutions, particularly those reliant on students from China due to their tight lockdown restrictions. In terms of consumption, this avenue of income can be lost overnight. However, it is not just a fiscal risk but also has the potential to jeopardise the student experience. Having the exchange of cultural reference benefits students greatly with information and new ways of seeing that they have never thought before, contributing to social learning. Therefore, a cultural mix benefits large international cohorts so there is not a single culture dominating the experience, or excluding others through customs and language. This has been observed first-hand where an individual Chinese student was in a course with home-domiciled students—leading to isolation and inability for the student to participate fully. This was seen to be alleviated when in a cross-taught unit, the student was able to converse with three or four other Chinese students, enabling them to share thoughts, ideas and have a break from speaking English (Trenkic & Warmington, 2019), providing a counterpoint to the argument that monocultures are always a detriment to the learning experience. However, such segregated experiences can take away from the learning experience and the development of a community of practice if individuals are excluded.

This notion is supported by international students, who have also argued that one of the reasons for enrolling in a master's degree in the UK is to have the opportunity to mix with different students from different countries and cultures. The anticipation of such an experience may not occur as the aforementioned reliance on students from particular regions means that the cohorts may be less "diverse than expected". According to one student, "Apart from the group of other Nigerian students, it is mainly South Asians—I was expecting there to be more different nationalities like Chinese". The lack of diversity within cohort can also lead to communication difficulties as the same student remarked:

I have tried to include Indian students in group discussions but often it is difficult to have these conversations. Even though we are friends we try to carry them along but when we are having conversations before we know it, they are totally lost or when they're having conversations in their native language, we are so totally lost. Did they even get to understand like what we say sometimes? Working in seminar groups is such a nice experience for the people that can speak the language.

Such problems with communication and understanding can also lead to a lack of transferable knowledge and the opportunity for socialisation. It has been observed that language barriers and cultural differences can lead to the loss of educational efficiency so appropriate frameworks and interventions need to be developed to support the student experience.

Cultural Variation, Interculturality, Cultural Bias and the Classroom

In terms of cultural identity, UK institutions suffer from a sense of "cultural superiority that is rife in English language education systems." However, part of the attraction for an international student may be the enrichment of their own intercultural awareness through understanding of local values and cultures. Bell and Kipar (2016)

There is a prevailing assumption that immersion in culture and education will eradicate all problems associated with intercultural differences which also absolves to a degree, the responsibility of governments and universities. Such assumptions also pre-determine a cultural bias, failing to acknowledge individuals within a culture group and their prior educational experiences. The path to interculturality is also often clouded by the assumption that the home institution has the correct approach to learning and that immediately puts others at a disadvantage. Failing to acknowledge individuals within a culture group leads to cultural bias and fails to understand "the transition to a different system of teaching and learning, and of integration with peers and communication with tutors, which lead to a "study and social shock"" (Sovic, 2008).

Such assumptions and cultural biases need to be acknowledged from the researchers, as non-participant or even participating observers, that there is potential "effects of possible observer bias [that] should be anticipated in the design of ethnographic research" (Roller & Lavrakas, 2015). Furthermore, as with any issue of inclusivity, developing a culturally proactive role in understanding cultural variation and becoming culturally inclusive will help mitigate our own cultural biases. It is imperative that assumptions are not made and individuals are not stereotyped due to cultural or educational backgrounds, where presumptions about behaviour and attitudes are made before knowledge.

To illustrate this point, a student from China recently did a presentation about her experiences and life before university. She revealed that she had travelled extensively throughout Europe and had been an exchange student in Latvia and speaks the language fluently. This surprised her tutor, who assumed that as a student from a collectivist society, with little confidence in English that she had not travelled beyond China before. Such stereotyping or unconscious bias therefore prevails unless there is active engagement with the students, bringing the individual into the equation by

asking questions and listening to the answers [which] allows you to check out assumptions and generalisations and to increase your cultural awareness. (Carroll, 2006)

When asked, experienced academics almost always say that the most important way to improve your teaching of international students is to get to know them as people and to get to know something about their life before University. (Carroll, 2006)

Lecturers need to be sensitive to students' previous academic and cultural backgrounds, fostering a culturally pro-active mindset by developing knowledge and awareness of cultural variation in student expectations and of UK higher education requirements. Content should be culturally inclusive—Eurocentric materials or culturally laden language, such as idioms may reduce accessibility for international students. Acronyms and business jargon can also obfuscate meaning so it's important to ensure that both industry-specific words and academic language are clearly defined. Carroll believes that "every single change we make to help international students also helps all students" (Carroll, 2006).

However, due to the changing dynamics of student demographics, there is a danger that in "treating all students equally," the facilitator may involve inadvertent discrimination by assuming that international students are of a lower calibre than the home-domiciled students, who are somehow superior, particularly if those in a position of power are unaware of cross-cultural variation in expectations and behaviour norms (Bell & Kipar, 2016).

In creating a paradigm such as this demonstrates a lack of understanding of interculturality which has until this point manifested in lower marks generally for international students. Although this may be in part due to difficulties in studying in a second language, it also reflects a level of demotivation from international cohorts, due to different teaching and learning approaches than those the students have previously experienced (Trenkic & Warmington, 2019).

Research suggests that institutions do not offer enough transitional support to international students, nor do they offer "individuals equal opportunities to learn, using flexible approaches that can be customized and adjusted for individual needs" (Ryan, 2012). For successful interculturality to occur, it needs to be embedded into the curriculum so both students and lecturers treat it as a priority (Bell & Kipar, 2016). Such an inclusive approach would account for not just ethnic and cultural diversity but also neurodiversity, physical and mental health issues, as well as the actual space for learning. It would therefore be, comprehensive in its meaning, scope and interpretation. As part of that inclusion, respect, tolerance and positive reinforcement are to be encouraged in the classroom (Aubrey & Riley, 2016).

According to social constructivists, learning can be influenced by social factors which include environmental, cultural as well as interaction with others. By engaging with others, learners create a framework for discourse, building social relations and reflective learning within an environment conducive to learning. Those who need more help, according to Vygotsky, can benefit from "scaffolding," where a more capable other is aware "of the individual [...] abilities and [are] responsive to their needs" (Aubrey & Riley, 2016). The idea of scaffolding is a consequence of Vygotsky's notion of Zone of Proximal Development (ZPD) which reflects the gap between what one knows and what one can know. This is reflected in higher education, which is particularly focused on student-centred learning. Many of the activities undertaken are dependent on oral communication which can preclude students from various cultural backgrounds. Generally, in UK institutions, students who speak up in class are perceived to be active participants, engaged in the class, whereas the quieter students risk the accusation of being 'less able' (Ryan, 2012). However, many international students may struggle to engage because of cultural or linguistic experiences.

To enable an intercultural environment that offers inclusivity and cultural exchange, there needs to be a provision of clear guidance and instructions, setting clear ground rules at the beginning, modelling and scaffolding. Interculturality is a complex concept and therefore requires a number of different approaches. Skinner's notion of positive reinforcement and operant conditioning can benefit students in preparation for the professional workplace where reliability, participation and repetitive activity may be appropriate (Aubrey & Riley, 2016) whilst also providing international students with a roadmap to follow.

Despite the accusation that universities are happy to take money and not support international students adequately is not entirely true. Sometimes, the difficulty lies in students accessing the support services that are available to them. According to Thi et al., many international students perceive support services as nothing more than a way to fix learning problems, rather than an active, and engaged network that enables development and progress for the student. Students are less likely to engage with those services when negative assumptions prevail. There may also be cultural reasons why they are not seeking these services. Support also often falls outside of the regular classroom activity so students are less engaged with it. It is up to the lecturer or class facilitator to understand why students may not be using the services and help them to access them. Again, if it becomes an embedded part of a programme, with an intended learning outcome. Then the motivation on behalf of both the student and the lecturer changes (Tran, 2013).

> The notion of "independent learning" in Western institutions can be misunderstood by newly enrolled Asian international students and linked to the need to learn by oneself rather than asking questions and relying on the teacher, support service and peers for help. (Tran, 2013)

Motivation is the driver for learning. So many factors contribute to a positive and constructive learning experience and without motivation the learning experience is minimal. Interculturality adds another complexity to the learning experience, as well as enhancing the experience by stimulating and cultivating new ways of thinking, therefore a singular approach is not going to be as fruitful as using a diverse approach mirroring the diversity of any cohort. In creating a curriculum that combines theories, activities and outcomes from a range of disciplines creates a community of practice that have interculturality at the heart of it.

Interculturality and Community of Practice

It has been argued that "feeling part of a community of learners has been shown to foster students' engagement and sense of belonging, leading to higher retention and achievement of learning outcomes" (Prodgers et al., 2022). It is evident that developing such an identity is key to the success of interculturality; therefore, it makes sense that communities of practice are developed and promoted. Communities of Practice provides students with "a shared way of doing and approaching things" via social interaction. It is a useful tool to bring cohesion to a group and also codifies individual cohorts allowing them a sense of professional identity and practice in a learning environment. A former student from China commented on the fact that at the beginning of the course that as they are all strangers, and don't know one another that they need to create a culture of a community, to get to know one another and then they can further build the community themselves.

The notion of communities of practice extolled by theorists, Lave and Wenger, focused on shared activities with an exclusive purpose of both work-based learning and also in-classroom learning. Known as socially situated learning, learning takes place within the framework of a community's shared experience (Aubrey & Riley, 2016). According to UNESCO (2005), "Interculturality: refers to the existence and equitable interaction of diverse cultures and the possibility of generating shared cultural expressions through dialogue and mutual respect." Developing "cultural synergy" (Adler, 1980) is key to communities of practice, where knowledge and skills are seen as being shared acquisitions, with an emphasis on fostering relationships and a focus on a shared purpose. Joint enterprise and shared repertoire enables a sense of community to be established. "This sharing starts a learning conversation which [-] is 'awesomely democratic'" (hooks, 2012).

There are also clear links between the work of Carl Rogers on person-centred education and the Community of Inquiry (CoI) framework which posits a model of supports for social collaborative learning. Findings suggest significant links between the Rogerian constructs of the level of regard and empathy and the CoI concept of teaching presence.

As persons are empathically heard, it becomes possible for them to listen more accurately to the flow of inner experiences. But as a person understands and prizes self, the self becomes more congruent with the experiences. The person thus becomes more real, more genuine. These tendencies, […] enable the person to be a more effective growth-enhancer for himself or herself. There is a greater freedom to be the true, whole person (Rogers, 1995)

Inclusive Teaching Practice and Induction Process

Warwick in his Ten Tips for Teaching International Students,

> advocates getting to know your students and acknowledge and celebrate the diversity of the class, as well as the encouragement of speaking in class.

He says that "these first few class contributions are very important for the class dynamics as the module develops". (Warwick, 2019)

Induction programmes should be designed expressly to focus on the students and their cohort. One suggestion is to create a space for the students to introduce themselves, perhaps by telling a story, or describing themselves through 'three words.' This would allow them to feel present and listened to and understood, and to feel free to develop social relationships, before formal academic learning.

> The induction programme was good when there were activities to get to know one another. The Language Club allowed me to get to know people based on interests. If there was a Fresher's Fair, people could connect based on interest, rather than their course or country or language.

The next activity could be a group-based task, a project designed where intercultural skills are an asset. This would be preceded by a seminar on 'how to work in groups' establishing the norms, and involving students in setting clear guidelines for good participation. By implementing a group covenant that includes respect for each other, and their opinions and feelings, listening and not talking when someone else is presenting an idea, including ideas and concepts from across the globe, and by providing a supportive and encouraging environment.

Presentations from the groups would be followed by peer feedback sessions, demonstrating that the power doesn't lie with the teacher and that learning comes from within, and from their peers.

At this stage, reflective practice could be introduced and a self-reflective report could be written about the experience of their learning journey, the group work and peer feedback sessions.

A successful induction process should start to establish a healthy and nurturing foundation, focused on the students as individuals enabling a more real and accepting cohort, free and willing to engage and form a community.

Inclusive Teaching Approaches

Moving into formal academic learning, "Online lecture classes are really counter-productive because there's zero opportunity for interaction with the lecturers, and among the students" and

> I would suggest the seminars are the best thing to do. You know, the lecture sessions should always be followed by the seminars. You get a chance to speak and you are being appreciated for your point. So you get that confidence that, you know, whatever I'm thinking that is being accepted and acknowledged.

It is crucial to continue to create an inclusive classroom climate where all students are encouraged to participate, by learning about students' backgrounds and tailoring approaches accordingly, establishing ground rules for discussing controversial issues, and developing (and helping students develop) deeper racial and socio-economic awareness. (Yale. edu, 2010)

Group work in its simplest form enables students to interact, share knowledge and experiences and build confidence to express their views. Therefore, using group work as a platform on which to build intercultural relationships and to help students recognise the value of diversity seems a logical progression. However, in order for this to be beneficial in the long term, activities with specific multicultural facets within curricula need to be fostered. (Ryan, 2012)

Developing group work in this way engenders inclusivity and interculturality. By embedding the work into the framework of the course, it aligns it constructively with the intended learning outcomes, making it clear what the expected learning from such activity would be. Not only does this kind of learning adhere to Bigg's principle of constructive alignment, but it also favours Dewey's Approach to learner-centred pedagogy within an experiential framework. On that basis, scaffolding becomes part of the building blocks of the activity. Firstly, the student may need to understand how to be an active participant in a group, and secondly through the interaction with the other participants, where their learning is scaffolded by a "More Knowledgeable Other" within the group (Aubrey & Riley, 2016).

Such an experiment was undertaken at the University of Bath with group work, which is so fundamental to academic learning in the UK. It can be difficult for international students who have never worked in this way and they can be reluctant to work with peers whose first language is different from their own. Although it is not just international students but home students too, will tend to form groups of monocultures, when left to their own devices. When students are chosen randomly to form a group, they tend to be more successful in overcoming cultural barriers.

What the study at Bath University discovered is that many international students do not know how to behave in a group. They do not understand their role within the group and therefore integrating them is not always successful. For this purpose, they therefore decided to have an induction at the beginning of term, building skills for team work, rather than just setting students a task and splitting them into teams, talking about what the objectives of the team work were and what the roles within a team might look like (Ryan, 2012).

Often in group work, some members find it more difficult to participate due to a lack of familiarity or knowledge of the topic, language barriers or lack of confidence. One focus of the activity was to support students in developing strategies to encourage all students to participate by assigning them different roles of responsibility within each multicultural team. By focusing on the skills aspect, it enabled both the international students, and the less confident students to express their ideas. The activity encouraged them to discuss their prior experience related to the project thereby facilitating a deeper understanding of different cultures, and enhancing interculturality within the classroom.

Embedding the group work into the curriculum meant that it had to be assessed and therefore meet set criteria, which included improvement of intercultural communication as an intended learning outcome, which ensured improved intercultural competency as well as the development of other skills. As part of this exercise, the students were also asked to write an account of their group work, which reflected on their skill development, ability to communicate, manage challenges and be more aware of their peers' needs and different working methods.

My group members were from Nigeria, India, Bangladesh and Nepal and we managed to be cohesive through regular Zoom calls and sharing ideas and allocating roles. That was a very good experience.

Oral presentations have been shown to be extremely successful with respect to improving learners' L2 skills, and increasing their autonomy. For example, Girard et al. found that using oral presentations in their classroom led to greater class interaction and participation, an increased interest in learning, and noticeable improvements in their students' communication and presentation skills.

King adds that oral presentations have been shown to help bridge the gap between language study and language use; that presentations require students to use all four language skills in a naturally integrated way; and that presentations have been shown to encourage students to become active and autonomous learners (Brooks & Wilson, 2015).

One of the main benefits of using presentations in the classroom is that oral presentations are student-centred. When students are asked to give an oral presentation, it is one of the few times in the language classroom that the students themselves have direct control of both the content and the flow of the classroom (Brooks & Wilson, 2015).

When we do group presentations, you've got an opportunity to learn together. Focused on an assignment seems to be a great way to make people feel more confident and comfortable in smaller groups.

Oral presentations also provide students with a process-driven activity that requires them to use English, not just while they are giving the presentation itself but also while they are preparing to present. One good example of this is group presentations. Group presentations require students to work together to plan and prepare for their presentation. During group work students can be encouraged to use English to negotiate meaning with the other members of their group and to work together, in English, to plan how they will present their ideas to the other members of the class. As with the Bath University experiment, it enabled students to also have a greater understanding through multicultural discussions.

Incorporating Diverse Perspectives

Hearing diverse perspectives can enrich student learning by exposing everyone to stimulating discussion, expanding approaches to traditional and contemporary issues and situating learning within students' own contexts while exploring those contexts. Students are more motivated to take control of their learning in classroom climates that recognise them, draw relevant connections to their lives, and respond to their unique concerns.

Inclusive teaching builds upon an instructor's basic instinct to ensure all voices are heard and that all students have a chance to participate fully in the learning process, by digging a little deeper into why participation imbalances exist. To develop this complex climate, instructors must practice a mixture of intrapersonal and interpersonal awareness, regular curriculum review and knowledge of inclusive practices.

To teach inclusively, it is important to look at the reading lists and other resources whether that be case studies, articles, videos and all material upon which lectures and workshops are based, then we can look through the lens with which these are being created. Are they inclusive? Are they diverse? Are they intercultural?

One student expressed:

> I think for me in Nigeria, most of the books we use are authors in Nigeria, or Africa. They're actually British or American. I don't find as a problem. But I think when I went to the library, and I saw something about like, African fashion, that featured Nigerian artists and designers, I was like, wow, this is amazing.

In article "Challenging the Graveyard," Jayne Batch says that "many libraries can feel like a graveyard filled with dead, white men, and that we need to curate collections that reflect a diversity of experience and ideas—and the diversity of our students" (40,475,275, 2019).

Goldsmith's College introduced an initiative "Liberate the Library" with the aim to "diversify our collections, to de-centre Whiteness, to challenge non-inclusive structures in knowledge management and their impact on library collections, users, and services. We will take an intersectional approach to our liberation work to encompass the many parts of a person's identity" ("Closing the Gap,", 2019, p. 48).

The goal of a curriculum with diverse perspectives is to ensure students feel included, and not alienated.

> When those who have the power to name and to socially construct reality choose not to see you or hear you, whether you are dark-skinned, old, disabled, female, or speak with a different accent or dialect than theirs, when someone with the authority of a teacher, say, describes the world and you are not in it, there is a moment of psychic disequilibrium, as if you looked into a mirror and saw nothing. (Keyes, 1986)

Conclusion

Much sentiment has prevailed upon the notion that higher education is "[a] place for learning by the whole person, with feelings and ideas merged. […] bringing together cognitive learning, which has always been needed, and affective-experiential learning, which is so underplayed in education today". In order to concretise this view, it is imperative that there is an acknowledgement across HEIs, particularly in the UK, that if the current fiscal model of HEIs continues, then internationalism of UK HEIs will continue to flourish. With the backdrop of an increasing number of students seeking cross-border education, we have seen a dramatic and continuous increase in the number of international students at UK HEIs, particularly from emerging markets. As such, international students form a fundamental and necessary part of HEIs.

As contributors to the education of not only themselves, but also home-domiciled students, it is imperative that international students are seen; that the value of their diversity and their cultural experience contributes to the educational experience of everyone. Therefore, there is an increasing need for interculturality in the classroom, whereby designing and developing curricula that meets the needs of a diverse classroom through recognition of the other in discourse and learning experiences develops a community of learners.

The commoditisation of education has led to students been referred to as "customers" and as such it is important that they are given the "unconditional regard" from the top of the institution down. Considerations need to be made to embed interculturality throughout the student experience, from induction to formal academic learning, inclusive of all staff, both academic and administrative. It needs to be a university-wide mission with a widening set of principles and unified framework to ensure that the source of our teaching and the students' learning is truly reflective of interculturality.

Interculturality provides a positive student experience for both international and home students, ensuring that the needs of individuals are met within a diverse and engaging framework that enables a community of practice to evolve. There is an expectation that developing such a learning experience will improve the attainment levels of international students, leading to student satisfaction which will benefit HEIs in the long term by building the number of applications, improving reputational standing on league tables, making interculturality a viable and sustainable proposition.

References

Adler, N. J. (1980). *Cultural synergy: The management of cross-cultural organizations* (pp. 163–184). McGill University.

Aubrey, K., & Riley, A. (2016). *Understanding & using educational theories.* Sage.

Bell J & Kipar N., (2016) *Section C: Supporting student groups: How can lecturers and students in higher education improve their intercultural awareness, and in the process create a more inclusive international teaching and learning environment? Equality and diversity in learning and teaching in higher education.* Heriot-Watt University.

Brooks, G., & Wilson, J. (2015). Using oral presentations to improve students' English language skills. In *Kwansei Gakuin University Humanities Review* (Vol. 19, pp. 199–212).

Carroll, J. (2006). Teaching international students. Edited by Jude Carroll & Janette Ryan. *British Journal of Educational Technology, 37*(6), 987–987.

"Closing the Gap". (2019). https://Www.Universitiesuk.Ac.Uk/Policy-And-Analysis/Reports/Documents/2019/Bame-Student-Attainment-Uk-Universities-Case-Studies.Pdf, www.universitiesuk.ac.uk/policy-and-analysis/reports/Documents/2019/bame-student-attainment-uk-universities-case-studies.pdf

Deeks, A. J. (2020). *Drivers of globalisation of higher education over the last 70 years editors: Hilligje van't land, Andreas Corcoran, Diana-Camelia Iancu, the promise of higher education, essays in honour of 70 years of IAU.* Springer.

Hall, R. (2022., December 26). *UK student housing reaching 'crisis point' as bad as 1970s, charity warns growing numbers of students are experiencing hidden homelessness or accepting poor accommodation.* The Guardian.

hooks, B. (2012). *Teaching critical thinking.* Review by Samantha Warren.

Keyes, C. (1986). *The aesthetics of power: The poetry of Adrienne rich.* University Of Georgia Press.

Migration Advisory Committee (MAS). (2018, September). *Impact of international students in the UK.* https://www.gov.uk/government/organisations/migration-advisory-committee © Crown copyright.

Prodgers L. , Travis E. & Pownall M. (2022) *"It's hard to feel a part of something when you've never met people": Defining "learning community"* in an online era Accepted: 12 June 2022 © The Author(s).

Rogers, C. (1995). *A way of being.* [edition unavailable]. Houghton Mifflin Harcourt. Accessed Jan 5, 2023, from https://www.perlego.com/book/2450068/a-way-of-being-pdf

Roller, M. & Lavrakas, P. (2015). *Ethnography: Mitigating observer bias applied qualitative research design: A Total quality framework approach* (pp. 207–212).

Ryan, J. (2012). *Cross cultural teaching and learning for home and international students: Internationalisation, pedagogy and curriculum in higher education.* Routledge.

Ryan, M. (2011). Improving reflective writing in higher education: A social semiotic perspective. *Teaching in Higher Education, 16*(1), 99–111. https://doi.org/10.1080/13562517.2010.507311

Sovic, S. (2008). Coping with stress: The perspective of international students., Queen Mary, University of London. *Art, Design & Communication in Higher Education, 6*(3), 145–158. https://doi.org/10.1386/adch.6.3.145_1

Staley, D., & Trinkle, D. (2011). *The changing landscape of higher education.* Educaus E- review.

Tran, L. T. (2013). *Teaching international students in vocational education: New pedagogical approaches.* ACER Press.

Trenkic, D., & Warmington, M. (2019). Language and literacy skills of home and international university students: How different are they, and does it matter? *Bilingualism: Language and Cognition.*, Cambridge University Press, *22*(2), 349–365.

UNESCO. (2005). *"Interculturality" Article 4.8 of the convention on the protection and promotion of the diversity of cultural expressions.*

Vorster, J.-A. (2017). The "decolonial turn": What does it mean for academic staff development? *Education as Change, 21*(1), 31–49.

Walsh, P. (2022). *Student migration to the UK briefing, the migration Observatory at the University of Oxford.* Accessed Dec 20, 2022, from https://migrationobservatory.ox.ac.uk/resources/briefings/student-migration-to-the-uk/

Warwick, P. (2019). *Ten tips for teaching international students | advance HE.* [online] Advance-he.ac.uk. Accessed Nov 21, 2019, from https://www.advance-he.ac.uk/knowledge-hub/ten-tips-teaching-international-students

Yale.edu. (2010). *Inclusive teaching strategies | Poorvu Center for teaching and learning.* [online] Available at: https://poorvucenter.yale.edu/Inclusive TeachingStrategies

Youssef, L. (2014). Globalisation and higher education: From within-border to cross-border. *Open Learning: The Journal of Open, Distance and e-Learning, 29*(2), 100–115. https://doi.org/10.1080/02680513.2014.932686

7

Understanding Knowledge-Hiding and Its Role in Intersectional Academia

Imran Hameed, Shajara Ul-Durar,
and Ghulam Ali Arain

Introduction

In organisations, knowledge embodies information, suggestions, ideas, and expertise relevant to jobs performed by employees (Connelly et al., 2012). Knowledge is considered a source of success and competitive advantage in modern-day organisations (Curado & Vieira, 2019). Resultantly, knowledge management has emerged as a vital speciality for practitioners and academics, evident through an ever-increasing number of research publications and the latest tools applied in organisations, such as intra-organisational wikis and learning portals (Kiniti & Standing,

I. Hameed
Faculty of Business Administration, Lahore School of Economics,
Lahore, Pakistan

S. Ul-Durar (✉)
Business School for the Creative Industries, University for the Creative Arts,
Epsom, UK
e-mail: Shajara.ul-durar@sunderland.ac.uk

G. A. Arain
United Arab Emirates University, Al Ain, UAE

B. S. Nayak (ed.), *Intersectionality and Creative Business Education*,
https://doi.org/10.1007/978-3-031-29952-0_7

129

2013). Practitioners and academics focus on designing knowledge management initiatives and methods for enhancing knowledge-sharing among organisational members (Webster et al., 2008). However, despite the efforts, most knowledge management initiatives fail even if employees are encouraged and rewarded (Bock et al., 2005). Akhavan et al. (2005) noted that about 50% to 70% of knowledge management projects face failures.

The researchers have attributed this high failure rate to resistance from employees to accept organisational initiatives (Li et al., 2016). This assertion emphasises two important notions: (1) most knowledge within organisations is controlled (i.e., created, used, and owned) at the individual level, and (2) for effective knowledge-sharing, employees' willingness is critical (Ipe, 2003; Kelloway & Barling, 2000). Considering these reasons, Webster et al. (2008) raised the question that organisations need to know why employees are not always willing to share their knowledge with others. However, knowledge-hiding was scantly discussed within existing management literature (Davenport & Prusak, 1998; Greenberg et al., 2007; Schein, 2004), and Webster et al. (2008). They defined it as "an intentional attempt to withhold or conceal knowledge requested by another individual" (p. 4).

Later, Connelly et al. (2012) introduced a multidimensional construct of knowledge-hiding comprising evasive hiding (i.e., when knowingly, the hider provides incorrect or incomplete information or falsely commits to provide requested information later), playing dumb (i.e., when the hider pretends not to possess the requested knowledge), and rationalised hiding (i.e., when hider tries to justify the knowledge-hiding, e.g., by saying that it is a secret). Connelly et al. (2012) further used interdependence theory (Kelley & Thibaut, 1978) to explain the role of perceived context and anticipated future consequences while choosing among these specific knowledge-hiding behaviours (i.e., evasive hiding, rationalised hiding, and playing dumb). For instance, evasive hiding might be opted for by an employee when the context is perceived as highly competitive, and the victim is perceived to reciprocate negatively. Rationalised hiding would be a preferred strategy in a cooperative context, and the hider would aim to avoid the victim's adverse reciprocal reactions (Connelly & Zweig, 2015).

To fully understand the concept of knowledge-hiding, it is essential to differentiate knowledge-hiding from other similar constructs, such as knowledge-sharing and knowledge-hoarding.

Overlapping Concepts of Knowledge Management

Knowledge management literature has identified multiple knowledge-related behaviours which may affect the outcomes of organisational knowledge management initiatives, such as knowledge-sharing (Ipe, 2003), knowledge-hiding (Connelly et al., 2012), and knowledge-hoarding (Hislop, 2003). For readers' clarity, in this section, we present the critical differences between knowledge-hiding and these overlapping concepts so that the later assertions can be made without confusion.

Knowledge-sharing refers to making knowledge available to others (Ipe, 2003). Knowledge-sharing has multiple positive outcomes for organisations, such as creativity (Kremer et al., 2019), firm performance (Nguyen et al., 2018), and reduced turnover intentions (Lakshman et al., 2021). However, the literature highlights that employees should be motivated and rewarded to share their knowledge with others, which is acknowledged to be a difficult task (Wittenbaum et al., 2004). To overcome this challenge, researchers explored multiple methods and interventions for encouraging knowledge-sharing. Such as linking sharing with status and reputation (Moghavvemi et al., 2017), nurturing relationships for reciprocal acts like knowledge-sharing (Chen et al., 2014), and creating awareness of the positive outcomes of sharing norms for employee behaviours (Ko et al., 2005). In addition, some researchers focused on the power of incentives (Lyu & Zhang, 2017), fairness (Hameed et al., 2019), and climate (Park & Kim, 2018) in encouraging employee knowledge-sharing in organisations. Further, as knowledge-sharing is an interpersonal exchange, relying on social exchange theory (Blau, 1964), several researchers emphasised trust among organisational members as an essential antecedent of knowledge-sharing for capturing the complexity of this relationship (Bhatti et al., 2021; Le & Lei, 2018).

Generally, it is believed that knowledge-sharing and knowledge-hiding are antonyms, where the absence of knowledge sharing means knowledge-hiding and vice versa (Gagné et al., 2019), which is untrue. Yes, there is some overlap, but these two are distinct constructs, and at the same time, there is no apparent dichotomy (i.e., employees can either share or hide knowledge) between the two (Webster et al., 2008). Knowledge-sharing is a positive behaviour through which employees' knowledge is absorbed and used by other employees in organisations, resulting in positive organisational outcomes (e.g., economic and competitive value) (Ipe, 2003). In contrast, knowledge-hiding is a counterproductive behaviour resulting in weak interpersonal relationships and decreased economic and competitive value (Connelly et al., 2019).

From the social dilemma perspective, knowledge-hiding and knowledge-sharing can co-occur (Gagné et al., 2019). For example, an employee may decide to hide the knowledge that is unique and salient for their job security while, at the same time, sharing the other knowledge that is less salient or linked to rewards and incentives placed for knowledge-sharing (Fang, 2017; Gagné et al., 2019). Hadjielias et al. (2021) argued that knowledge-hiding and sharing have a negative relationship, where knowledge-hiding focuses on maintaining power through unique knowledge retention resulting in reduced knowledge-sharing. In conclusion, knowledge-sharing and hiding have a similar relationship as described for counterproductive behaviour and organisational citizenship behaviour, being unique with a capacity to co-occur (Connelly & Zweig, 2015).

Knowledge-hoarding refers to knowledge accumulation that may or may not be shared in the future (Hislop, 2003); more importantly, it is the knowledge that others have not requested. For example, maintaining the secrecy of personal information and concealing information that could be distressing if revealed to others, but this act is not targeted at some specific person (Lane & Wegner, 1995). In addition, knowledge-hoarding is not necessarily attributed to malevolent intentions or divergent interests of employees from the organisation (Webster et al., 2008). It is argued that employees hoarding knowledge might have positive intentions, such as trying to honour their social commitments to clients, colleagues, or organisations (Sitkin & Brodt, 2006).

Both knowledge-hiding and knowledge-hoarding are broadly categorised under knowledge withholding (Webster et al., 2008). However, in contrast to knowledge-hoarding, knowledge-hiding refers to the active involvement of two parties where one party requests the knowledge and the other party hides that requested knowledge. Like knowledge-hoarding, knowledge-hiding may be motivated by self-interest or pro-social intentions, but hiding in response to an explicit request from another person categorises this act as deviant behaviour. In other words, the requester perceives this act of concealing knowledge as deviant behaviour, and at the same time, the concealer might see it as preserving confidentiality (Webster et al., 2008).

Knowledge-Hiding in Organisations

Knowledge-hiding, as defined earlier, refers to an intentional act of concealing knowledge from the person who has requested it (Connelly et al., 2012). The hider might choose from different hiding tactics, for example, evasive hiding, playing dumb, and rationalised hiding, as per situational demands and knowledge-hiding objectives. The extant knowledge-hiding literature has identified several antecedents and outcomes of knowledge-hiding. The first and most recently published meta-analysis on the nomological network of knowledge-hiding (i.e., Arain et al., 2022a, 2022b) has categorised knowledge-hiding antecedents into four groups, that is, individual, interpersonal, contextual, and knowledge characteristics. The individual antecedents include dark personality traits (Pan et al., 2018), negative affective states (Fang, 2017), and territoriality (Singh, 2019). Interpersonal antecedents include perceived competition (Semerci, 2019) and task interdependence (Rhee et al., 2017). The contextual antecedents include factors such as abusive supervision (Jahanzeb et al., 2019), job pressure (Riaz et al., 2019), and workplace mistreatment (Yao et al., 2020). Knowledge characteristics include knowledge complexity (Chen, 2020) and knowledge-based psychological ownership (Wang et al., 2019).

Arain et al. (2022a, 2022b) have categorised knowledge-hiding outcomes into two groups, that is, performance outcomes and attitudinal and interpersonal outcomes. According to their findings, knowledge-hiding negatively impacts performance outcomes, including creative and innovative performance (Černe et al., 2017), extra-role performance (Arain et al., 2020b), and task performance (Singh, 2019). The attitudinal and interpersonal outcomes include job satisfaction (Peng, 2013), turnover intention (Offergelt et al., 2018), distrust (Arain et al., 2020a), and reciprocal knowledge-hiding (Connelly & Zweig, 2015).

Horizontal and Vertical Knowledge-Hiding

The knowledge-hiding literature further differentiates between two levels of knowledge-hiding, that is, horizontal and vertical knowledge-hiding. Horizontal knowledge-hiding is among peers (Connelly et al., 2012). Vertical knowledge-hiding, also called "top-down" knowledge-hiding, refers to a supervisor's knowledge-hiding from a supervisee (Arain et al., 2018). Much of the existing knowledge-hiding literature has focused on the antecedents and outcomes of horizontal knowledge-hiding and highlighted its detrimental consequences for organisational performance, that is, an annual loss of approximately $31.5 billion was attributed to employee knowledge-hiding in Fortune 500 companies (Babcock, 2004).

Webster et al. (2008) and Connelly et al. (2012) have yet to differentiate between horizontal and vertical knowledge-hiding, as was later highlighted by Arain et al. (2018), where they focused on the detrimental effect of top-down knowledge-hiding. However, an increasing number of studies have suggested that vertical knowledge-hiding has much more damaging consequences at the workplace than its counterpart, horizontal knowledge-hiding (Arain et al., 2019, 2020b). Specifically, more recently published studies have exhibited that knowledge-hiding by a supervisor reduces the supervisor-directed Organizational Citizenship Behavior (OCB), employees' innovative work behaviour, supervisor-based trust, and self-efficacy, while it intensifies silence, moral disengagement, and team interpersonal deviance (Arain et al., 2020b, 2021, 2022a, 2022b).

Supervisor knowledge-hiding (SKH) from subordinates is categorised as unethical supervisory behaviour where the supervisor either provides wrong information, that is, deceives the subordinate (evasive hiding), pretends not to possess the information (playing dumb), or blames others for not sharing the required knowledge (rationalised hiding) (Arain et al., 2020a). First, by acting unethically, supervisors nourish a culture of deception in the workplace through their role modelling act. Secondly, knowledge management literature identifies the supervisor's role as a facilitator of knowledge-sharing; however, by acting deceitfully, supervisors tarnish the foundations of social exchange at the workplace. As a result, subordinates reciprocate by lowering their positive behaviours (Arain et al., 2020a) and hiding knowledge from their coworker.

Knowledge-Hiding in Academia

The existing literature mainly discusses knowledge management in the context of corporate organisations; however, it is crucial to consider that knowledge plays a vital role in higher education institutions (Al-Kurdi et al., 2018). Higher educational institutions have a primary objective of knowledge creation and dissemination (Basu & Sengupta, 2007). Knowledge is generally divided into two streams, that is, tacit knowledge and explicit knowledge. According to the dynamic theory of organisational knowledge creation (Nonaka, 1994), explicit knowledge is easily expressed and transferred. In contrast, tacit knowledge is difficult to share as it is often rooted in culture, artefacts, and individual identities (Zutshi et al., 2021). For example, some people and processes-related knowledge in universities are deep (i.e., political interactions and database systems). On the other hand, some knowledge is visible at the surface (policies, research outputs, and biographies) (Nonaka & Toyama, 2015). The knowledge status also changes with time, as what is hidden today may be shared openly in the future (Zutshi et al., 2021).

In academia, explicit knowledge is easily shared as compared to tacit knowledge. In higher education institutions, explicit knowledge can comprise calls for research grants and dissemination of scholarly events information. However, tacit knowledge can incorporate innovative research ideas or new conceptual models, which is a competitive advantage. Such tacit knowledge is only shared when academics have high trust (Nadeem et al., 2020). Similarly, knowledge-hiding is an issue faced by postgraduate students. Garg et al. (2021) argued that students often indulge in rationalised hiding by perceiving that the obtained knowledge is exclusively for them.

Although knowledge-hiding has received extensive limelight in the management literature during the past decade, only a handful of studies have explored this phenomenon in academia (Xiong et al., 2019; Zhao et al., 2016). Higher education institutions are, without any bias, the best platform for knowledge dissemination (Al-Kurdi et al., 2018). However, Fauzi (2022) has argued that this is different because academics are required to achieve scholarship and status, such as grant accomplishments and publications, leading towards a comparison of achievements. This effect has made academics treat knowledge as an asset and use it for competitive advantage. Similarly, this phenomenon is true for students, as their grades are linked with financial assistance and employment (Fauzi, 2022). This suggests that although higher education institutions are the best place for knowledge creation and dissemination, not all academics and scholars are willing to share their knowledge.

Wang et al. (2014) argued that academics evaluate the trade-off between the pros and cons of a specific situation and decide whether to engage in knowledge-sharing or hiding. Although multiple theories have been applied to explain knowledge-hiding in academia, for example, psychological owner theory and theory of reasoned action, the most widely used theory is the social exchange theory (Blau, 1964). The central tenant of social exchange theory is that social relationships comprise reciprocal benefits; in this case, the people expect reciprocal knowledge-sharing in exchange for shared knowledge (Serenko & Bontis, 2016). Usually, people will be open to entertaining knowledge requests from others when they see possible rewards of such sharing, for example, recognition, reciprocal knowledge-sharing, support, or other rewards. In contrast, they will choose to hide knowledge if they see nothing in return for them.

Social exchange theory also explains how individuals choose between three forms of knowledge-hiding (i.e., evasive hiding, playing dumb, and rationalised hiding) according to their situations (Bari et al., 2019). For example, when the requester holds significant power and the knowledge holder feels that evasive hiding or playing dumb can have an adverse reciprocal reaction from the requester, they may choose to use rationalised hiding by justifying their action of hiding knowledge (Connelly et al., 2012). Social exchange theory also helps us understand that knowledge-hiding and sharing can co-occur. Academics have quite a liberty to choose whether they want to cooperate with someone or not (Niedergassel & Leker, 2011), which means that they can choose to hide knowledge selectively (Hernaus et al., 2019). Usually, such decisions to cooperate are based on trust between the two parties. In untrustworthy relationships, insignificant information is shared with the requester, and essential or vital information is withheld (Fong et al., 2018).

Moving further in understanding knowledge-hiding in academia, in the next section, we present a discussion on knowledge-hiding by two main stakeholders, that is, academics and students, of the academic ecosystem (Fauzi, 2022).

Knowledge-Hiding by Academics

Acknowledging the fact that knowledge-hiding exists in academia, as highlighted in prior research studies, makes us curious to understand why academics indulge in this damaging behaviour. This knowledge is essential to ensure the implementation of successful knowledge management practices so that the very objective of higher educational institutions, that is, stimulation of creativity and innovation, problem-solving (referred to as knowledge creation), and teaching (i.e., knowledge dissemination) could be performed most effectively (Fauzi, 2022). To do so, many researchers have identified different antecedents of knowledge-hiding by academics. For example, Samdani et al. (2019) identified perceived supervisory support as a factor of knowledge-hiding in academics in the Pakistani context. In the Chinese context, Ghani et al. (2020b) highlighted interactional justice and professional commitment as essential predictors of knowledge-hiding in an academic context. In the past few years, some review studies have also been conducted to synthesise and highlight the determinants of knowledge-hiding for academics; most significant include Zutshi et al. (2021) and Fauzi (2022). However, for a comprehensive understanding of the factors, it is essential first to understand the inherent tension in academic roles that might affect knowledge-hiding.

Academic Role Dimensions

Zutshi et al. (2021) have identified three distinct role dimensions for academics (in higher education), namely, research, teaching, and leadership-administration (i.e., service). It is argued that these roles involve knowledge-rich activities which require both knowledge dissemination and production and interaction with multiple parties (i.e., students, subordinates, peers, and external parties). Therefore, while performing these roles, academics feel many tensions related to each of these roles.

The teaching role mainly relates to knowledge-sharing/dissemination. Usually, knowledge withholding in teaching occurs when it is believed that complex knowledge is of a higher level and does not suit the learner's requirements. Such information is supposed to be shared when the learner achieves a specific level of competency, which might be a prerequisite (Zutshi et al., 2021). The adult learning principles suggest that no information may be hidden from the seeker (Friberg & McKinney, 2019). It is argued that the learner may not understand complex knowledge at this time, but providing advanced information can allow the learner to learn through repeated interactions, thus discouraging knowledge-hiding (Zutshi et al., 2021). However, some specific learning environments, such as simulated or structured learning, may need knowledge-hiding, revealing some information at different levels or specific junctures (Zutshi et al., 2021). Zutshi et al. (2021) explained around 33 different tensions faced by academics while performing their teaching role, for example, getting high evaluations and teaching awards, knowing what students need, students may need to be handheld, and seeking public acceptance. These tensions can cause academics to exhibit knowledge-hiding behaviour in this role.

Research role is another key performance indicator for assessing academics. Academic research can be divided into two types: (1) incremental growth of the established field and (2) discovery of new knowledge. Both types of research aim to unearth hidden knowledge, where discovery involves working in unchartered territory, and incremental growth of a field requires working through known knowledge pathways (Zutshi et al., 2021). Research academics working in teams may need to hide knowledge because of some ethical concerns, for example, the requirement of ethical approval, data security, confidentiality, and personal risk, because of the belief that these issues can potentially harm the planning, execution, and dissemination of the intended research (Michaelidou et al., 2021). Zutshi et al. (2021) have again listed 33 tensions of academics while performing research roles. For instance, pushing for grant money and research awards, good research endures and boosting career, and knowing which research direction to follow, can threaten established power brokers; innovation is expected.

Leadership administration (or service) is a third critical role of academics in higher education institutions. This role is generally expressed through committees and specialist roles within or across departments. Participation in external academic committees, for example, thesis examinations, the peer-review process, and editorial board membership, is also considered necessary for this role (Zutshi et al., 2021). Zutshi et al. (2021) argued that working in silos, political territories, and pressure from different forces such as university administration, student unions, and lobby groups can hinder knowledge-sharing and encourage knowledge-hiding. Zutshi et al. (2021) again listed 33 tensions for academics while performing this role, for example, can do too much for no gain, profitability may diminish, lobby groups may divert from required strategic focus and committee work undermines individual autonomy.

Determinants of Knowledge-Hiding by Academics

Academic institutions should be agile by developing strategic flexibility and efficiency to meet the challenges of the dynamic business environment (Debellis et al., 2021). These attributes help educational institutions develop a creditable scholarship cycle, reassessing and readapting supportive activities in a cycle with difficulties of the digital environment (Fauzi, 2022). Understanding the determinants of knowledge-hiding in academia is vital for applying knowledge management practice in higher education institutions exhibiting a country's intellectual contribution.

The knowledge-hiding literature of higher education institutions has categorised the determinants of knowledge-hiding into different categories, such as organisational and contextual factors by Zutshi et al. (2021), whereas Fauzi (2022) has categorised these into individual, organisational, technological, and cultural factors. Therefore, we are relying on these studies for discussing the categories for a detailed presentation of determinants of knowledge-hiding in academia.

Individual and interpersonal factors are essential because for someone to share their knowledge with others, they must first be willing to share the knowledge. Individual behavioural factors like attitude, competitiveness, privacy, trust, and self-efficacy significantly impact one's tendency to hide or share knowledge (Nadeem et al., 2020; Wang et al., 2014). Such as in the case of highly competitive individuals, the literature highlights that they usually indulge in knowledge-hiding behaviour because of the fear of losing competitive advantage and recognition (Hernaus et al., 2019). Further, a sense of personal ownership of knowledge (acquired after long academic service) is also linked with knowledge-hiding. Such individuals feel that knowledge is their prized possession and should not be shared with others (Demirkasimoglu, 2016). People low in self-efficacy hide knowledge because sometimes they are not confident about the accuracy of their knowledge and want to save themselves from embarrassment and shame; therefore, they tend to hide knowledge (Anand et al., 2020; Garg et al., 2021). Al-Kurdi et al. (2018) have shown that academics hide knowledge from individuals they do not trust. They relied on social exchange theory to explain this effect that reciprocal exchange relationship does not hold in case of low trust among parties.

Research has also identified other intrinsic factors that affect an individual's knowledge-hiding behaviour. These factors include envy towards coworkers and idea implementation. Weng et al. (2020) argued that when academics envy their coworkers, they hide knowledge from them because they do not want them to succeed. Li et al. (2020) argued that employees hide knowledge from their coworkers because of the fear that this could harm the process of their idea implementation. Individual personality traits are also reported to impact their knowledge-hiding behaviours. The literature suggests that dark personality traits, that is, Machiavellianism, narcissism, and psychopathy (Wang et al., 2014), and big five personality model, that is, extroversion, agreeableness, neuroticism, openness, and conscientiousness (Karim, 2020), provide essential insights in understanding individual's psychological processes underlying knowledge-hiding behaviour.

Organisational factors are also exhibited by literature to impact academic knowledge-hiding behaviour. These factors include organisational justice, distributive, interactional, procedural justice, leader-member exchange, team outcome, and shared goals. The studies primarily highlighted that positive leadership, that is, leader-member exchange, discourages knowledge-hiding (Weng et al., 2020). In contrast, negative leadership styles, such as abusive supervision, encourage knowledge-hiding (Ghani et al., 2020a). Li et al. (2020) have identified team territorial climate, Bari et al. (2019) have identified team creativity, and Huo et al. (2016) identified team task dependency as a vital antecedent of knowledge-hiding. Supervisory support is also crucial in determining knowledge-hiding in academics (Samdani et al., 2019).

Contextual factors can include the nature of knowledge, job characteristics, and the request. Research has shown that knowledge is more prevalent in the case of tacit knowledge as compared to explicit knowledge. Hernaus et al. (2019) have argued that creative insights and personal information are usually hidden from others as they are part of tacit knowledge. On the other hand, the call for grants is a form of explicit knowledge, which is usually open to scrutiny and sharing. However, this knowledge can be converted to tacit knowledge when someone applies for that grant and might be hidden (Bari et al., 2020). Further, Yang and Ribiere (2020) have argued that tacit knowledge is difficult to share; therefore, sharing takes time and effort, resulting in knowledge-hiding bias, as academics want to invest less effort into the process.

Hernaus et al. (2019) have argued that the nature of the job also affects the knowledge-hiding behaviour of academics. They specifically argued that if the job is designed to seek support and input from colleagues and requires information sharing related to vital resources, knowledge-hiding is reduced in such cases. Another important factor is related to the nature of the knowledge request and the requester's attributes. For example, Demirkasimoglu (2016) exhibited that usually, knowledge hider uses rational hiding when the knowledge request comes from a colleague. On the contrary, the hider can probably use the playing dumb strategy when the supervisor requests knowledge (Huo et al., 2016).

Cultural factors include national culture (Zutshi et al., 2021) and organisational culture (Fauzi, 2022). Although research on the impact of national culture on knowledge-hiding is inconclusive, research shows that developing countries emphasise collaborative performance over individualism (Arain et al., 2020a). Furthermore, prior research has also asserted that Chinese academics indulge in knowledge-hiding to some extent, whereas Turkish academics do not exhibit this behaviour (Demirkasimoglu, 2016). There is much room for future research to dig into this domain of knowledge-hiding research.

Furthermore, there is extensive discussion in the literature on the role of organisational culture in academic knowledge-hiding, where siloed departmental culture is argued to encourage knowledge-hiding in academics (Fullwood et al., 2013). The competitive culture, where individualised rewards are focused on instead of collective rewards, also encourages knowledge-hiding (Wang & Noe, 2010). A pressured work environment in academia, such as pressure for publications and funding, also urges the need for secrecy and knowledge-hiding among academics (Walsh & Hong, 2003).

Other factors are technological factors and gender, which may impact academics' knowledge-hiding behaviour. The literature suggests that female academics indulge more in knowledge-hiding behaviour as compared to their male counterparts because of their uncertain feelings about their colleague (Yang & Ribiere, 2020). Other demographic factors of individuals, such as age, and official rank, can also affect the individuals' knowledge-hiding behaviour (Anand et al., 2020), which warrants additional inquiry in future research. Some studies have also explored the impact of technology-related factors on academics' knowledge-hiding behaviour (Zhai et al., 2020). For example, Zhai et al. (2020) argued that because of cloud and digital storage, knowledge is at risk of cyber-attacks, a concern of privacy and hacking, and academics' novel ideas and work is perceived to be at threat. Therefore, it results in knowledge-hiding because of these concerns.

Evasive Hiding, Playing Dumb, and Rationalised Hiding

Although it is known through the seminal work of Connelly et al. (2012) that the situation and their motives guide individuals' choice for specific knowledge-hiding behaviours, there is still limited research discussing the dimensional-level knowledge-hiding in academia (Hernaus et al., 2019). Specifically, evasive hiding refers to when the academic shares incorrect information with the requester. Playing dumb refers to answering that I do not possess the requested knowledge, and rationalised hiding refers to justifying not sharing the requested information (e.g., saying that this information is secret).

The knowledge in academia is complex because of the nature of academic work, where knowledge is continuously evolving, and novel problems must be solved. The limited available research evidence in academia suggests that academics indulge in evasive hiding (Demirkasimoglu, 2016) rather than playing dumb and rationalised hiding because of two main reasons. Firstly, the playing dumb strategy may not be suitable because saying I do not possess the required knowledge can lead to embarrassment. Secondly, they may need to be able to provide a reasonable excuse (i.e., rationalised hiding) for not sharing the requested information (Hernaus et al., 2019) because of clear rules and policies. Hernaus et al. (2019) have identified personal competitiveness as a significant predictor of evasive hiding. They argued that people have varying tendencies to react favourably (i.e., collaborative manner) or unfavourably (i.e., selfish manner) to others' requests, depending on personal competitiveness. However, there is still a need for future research to explore the most dominantly used knowledge-hiding strategy in academia and the motives behind selecting a particular strategy.

Knowledge-Hiding by Students

The problem of knowledge-hiding is also witnessed among students, as observed in the case of academics. A few studies explore knowledge-hiding in academia; even smaller numbers have focused on students' knowledge-hiding (Fauzi, 2022). However, the available literature differentiates between the knowledge-seeking of undergraduate and postgraduate students. Postgraduate students are supposed to be self-reliant and independent in knowledge-seeking, whereas undergraduate students face competition and challenges among peers during their years in higher education institutions (Fauzi, 2022). In academic institutions, students are oriented, trained, and encouraged to comprehend knowledge through exchange, negotiation, and expression. Usually, undergraduate students hide knowledge because of competition for grades and job opportunities. In contrast, postgraduate students (i.e., PhD and master's students) hide knowledge because they perceive that their knowledge is exclusive to their possession and mostly choose rationalised hiding (Garg et al., 2021).

The literature suggests that knowledge-hiding by students can result in multiple adverse outcomes, such as weakening of interpersonal relationships (Gillies, 2014), lowering team creativity (Bari et al., 2019), increase in loneliness, and weak institutional commitment (Garg & Anand, 2020). The studies have also shown that, like academics, students' knowledge-hiding is also affected by trust in interpersonal relationships (Nadeem et al., 2020). A recent study by Garg et al. (2021) has identified that a sense of relatedness among students negatively relates to student knowledge-hiding. They further highlighted that performance motivation (academic outcome orientation) and territoriality (creating, communicating, preserving and re-establishing territories) positively related to student knowledge-hiding. While explaining these effects, Garg et al. (2021) relied on the theory of reasoned action (Fishbein & Ajzen, 1977).

Using the stimulus organism response paradigm, Zhai et al. (2020) have argued that social networking sites, such as WeChat, Facebook, QQ, and WhatsApp, are believed to reduce the distance between people and increase interaction. However, nowadays, these social networking tools are also used for learning purposes, and learners should take advantage of these tools for knowledge-sharing. Still, the research shows that the expected potential use of these social networking tools for knowledge-sharing has yet to be fully reaped, and some issues have been identified in the case of students (Zhai et al., 2020). Fang (2017) conducted initial research in this domain and identified some antecedents of knowledge-hiding in the case of social networking tools (e.g., guilt and fear). They used online collaborative learning as the organism's response, arguing that the use of social media enhances collaborative learning. Moving further in this area, Zhai et al. (2020) used stimulus (referred to as privacy concern in terms of limited control over information exchange transactions). They argued that students might hide knowledge because they fear that others can have unauthorised access to shared information and misuse it. However, the student will opt for knowledge-hiding because of the attached fears.

Some studies have also discussed boundary conditions that help lower students' knowledge-hiding behaviour. For example, Garg et al. (2021) argued that students' academic self-efficacy is a significant moderator. Specifically, students high in academic self-efficacy exhibit a weak relationship between knowledge-hiding and academic performance, whereas students low in academic self-efficacy exhibit a strong relationship. In addition, Zhai et al. (2020) identified supervisory support as a boundary condition of privacy concerns and student knowledge-hiding. They referred to supervisory support as the instructor's role in encouraging the use of social networking tools for knowledge dissemination, appreciating the students' contributions, and providing quick feedback. Zhai et al. (2020) argued that supervisory support weakens privacy concerns and knowledge-hiding relationships. These findings are essential for enhancing collaborative learning through online learning tools where support from instructors, lecturers, and advisors can strengthen the knowledge-sharing climate among students. Further, instructors can help build students' academic self-efficacy through positive reinforcements and create a trust culture (i.e., favourable reciprocal relationships) among students, potentially reducing students' knowledge-hiding.

Individual Demographies and Knowledge-Hiding

Although different antecedents of knowledge-hiding are discussed previously, it is important to highlight in detail the individuals' demographics and personal characteristics related to knowledge-hiding due to two main reasons. First, individual demographics and characteristics are enduring attributes (i.e., unchangeable); hence no interventions can be designed to correct those (e.g., individuals' personality traits or gender cannot be changed). Secondly, individual understanding characteristics can serve as the first line of defence. These individuals with a high tendency to exhibit knowledge-hiding could be screened out during the hiring/selection or promotion process. In line with these reasons, in the present section, we try synthesising existing literature where such characteristics are discussed with knowledge-hiding. In addition, although only a handful of studies have used such individual factors as direct antecedents of knowledge-hiding, we try to look for research papers that have used such characteristics as moderators or boundary conditions of knowledge-hiding.

Pan et al. (2018) explored the effect of the dark personality triad on knowledge-hiding, and in addition, they have also identified the moderating effect of employee gender on this relationship. This is a significant study because it has tried to triangulate two individual characteristics in understanding their knowledge-hiding behaviour. First, they hypothesised the negative relationship between Machiavellianism, narcissism, and psychopathy by arguing that such people do not believe in norms of reciprocity, are externally motivated, and are cold; therefore, they have a high tendency to exhibit knowledge-hiding. Secondly, they explored the difference in knowledge-hiding these personalities for different gender. Although they could not find any direct effect of gender difference in knowledge-hiding, the moderation of gender for the indirect effect of the dark personality triad (i.e., for psychopathy and narcissism except Machiavellianism) through transactional psychological contract was significant. These results highlighted that narcissism and psychopathy had a more substantial effect on knowledge-hiding for men than women.

Irum et al. (2020) theorised that employees facing incivility react by withholding from sharing the requested knowledge. While doing this, they proposed that this relationship varies with the gender of the victimised employees. They have argued that men will be more reactive to incivility and are more likely to engage in all forms of knowledge-hiding than women. Hernaus et al. (2019), through bivariate correlation results, showed that knowledge-hiding was negatively correlated with respondents' age and academic rank and positively correlated with job tenure. This suggested that knowledge-hiding decreases with age and academic rank, whereas job tenure generally increases knowledge-hiding. These results were not supported through the model testing phase; therefore, it is suggested that future studies should theorise and test such effects to enhance the understanding of academics and practitioners for designing targeted knowledge management interventions.

Another interesting stream of research has highlighted the role of employee status (in terms of local vs foreigner/expatriate) on knowledge-hiding behaviour and the reactions of those employees if they are the victims of knowledge-hiding (Arain et al., 2019, 2020a). These studies specifically argued that foreign workers usually enjoy less favourable exchange at their workplaces, for example, limited duration work visas, limited voice opportunities in the face of supervisory abuse, and limited job security. Relying on this general perception of foreign workers, they proposed that in response to top-down knowledge-hiding (i.e., vertical knowledge-hiding), foreign workers tend to show higher distrust in supervisors. On the other hand, foreign workers are less expressive in their behaviour, as they exhibit less reduction in OCB directed towards supervisors (compared to local nationals) because of limited job security (Arain et al., 2020b).

Further, interestingly, the study of Arain et al. (2019) explored two different situations (1) when both the knowledge holder and requester have the same nationality and (2) when the knowledge holder and requester have different nationalities. Initially, they argued that local nationals would show a stronger reaction to supervisor knowledge-hiding (SKH) than foreign nationals. Further, they have proposed that while facing SKH, when both supervisor and supervisee are local nationals, the effect of SKH on the supervisee's innovative work behaviour will be much stronger than when the supervisor is a local national and supervisee is an expatriate (Arain et al., 2019).

Social role theory (Eagly & Wood, 1999) can also guide us in future research on how employees might react to SKH depending on whether the supervisor is male or female. This theory focuses on gender role differences and similarities in societies. Gender role stereotypes suggest that women are expected to be nurturing, kind, and helpful, and men are supposed to be achievement-oriented and aggressive. Therefore, in future research alongside other attributes, it is recommended that social role beliefs be incorporated while exploring the impact of knowledge-hiding on employee behavioural reactions. This line of research will help understand the specific nature of knowledge management interventions required in a given situation.

In addition, *intersectionality* refers to the interaction between gender, race, and other categories that differentiate an individual's life, cultural ideologies, and institutional arrangements from others and how these interactions result in outcomes in terms of power (Davis, 2008). Usually, the term intersectionality is used to explain how women of colour are sidelined based on gender and race (Crenshaw, 1991). Recently, management scholars used intersectionality to explain how these interconnections of gender, sexuality, and race impact organisational processes (Acker, 2006). Similarly, the management literature has called for more intersectional research on organisational processes, which are considered regular but develop relations of privilege and inequality (Holvino, 2010). In a recent study related to knowledge management, Harris (2017) explained (in an academic setting) "how a seemingly neutral academic concept— organisational knowledge—is only neutral if whiteness, masculinity, and heterosexuality are considered the norm" (page 18). The findings of this study highlight that knowledge-hiding literature needs to explore intersectionality's role in identifying varying knowledge-hiding tendencies towards different intersections at the workplace.

According to Tefera et al. (2018), although intersectionality initially appeared as a method to observe marginalisation, it has also been a source to evaluate marginalisation and compare it with privilege. Academics can use it to understand group actions in classes as their study reveals how white monolingual and monocultural students might get some advantages over marginalised students who might affect their voice. It can then be considered a reason for hiding knowledge because they notice how some other students could be privileged. Language has also been proven as a cause of being privileged. They further suggested that intersectional perspectives often exist as a conceptual aspiration rather than a comprehensive framework which makes it vague in practical terms. There is a need for a more codified body of knowledge which demands continuous research to be carried out in academic institutions so that challenges can be embraced.

Nunez (2014) tried to fill this gap by developing a multilevel model to employ intersectionality in educational research, which assists in finding relationships between social categories to create better learning opportunities for all students. The model can highlight the intersecting processes within the power system while considering socio-economic background. During the study, Nunez (2014) noticed that marginalised students do not feel like part of the institution and prefer hiding their emotions rather than sharing their experiences with the concerned bodies. By creating an inclusive environment, they can feel an improved connection with the institution and perform better.

Education must be socially just and address intersectionality at all levels of education by considering it a way to design and conduct educational research. There is a need for conceptual acuity, which can guide better understanding to conduct research to its fullest expression. Focusing on macroeconomic sectors might also be helpful by taking intersectoral and micro- and macro-level analyses. It will examine the connection between social group identities and social issues which might affect behaviour towards knowledge-hiding and knowledge-sharing (Agosto & Roland, 2018). Besic (2020) suggests that further research on intersectionality might result in reducing discrimination in the educational sector so that inclusive education may give better access to broader educational and social opportunities for all students regards of their age, gender, race, disability region, religion, belief, social class, marital status or sexual orientations. Focusing on one factor and ignoring others would make the analysis more complex. Instead would increase complexities as these factors are interrelated. There is a need to "thinking intersectionally" so that appropriate policies can be created and implemented to promote inclusive education and avoid discrimination against all learners. To resolve the issues, there should not be just a focus on differences among student groups but also within them so that students facing difficulties because of intersectionality might not become invisible.

Thus, there is a need for changes in attitudes and practices, which also require understanding cultural legacies, specifically when globalisation has increased diversity drastically. The academics can apply intersectional pedagogy to design inclusive curricula to address the needs of all students while reducing social issues arising from intersectionality and relevant context, which might or might not influence knowledge-hiding tendencies depending on personal experiences.

Conclusion

This chapter has highlighted that knowledge management practices usually fail because of the unwillingness of employees to share knowledge, as, in reality, they are the ones who possess, use, and share that knowledge. Therefore, organisations need to understand why employees hide knowledge. After developing some insights about tacit and explicit knowledge, we synthesised the literature explaining different antecedents of knowledge-hiding in organisations and the detrimental outcomes of this behaviour. First, the theoretical distinctions are drawn between knowledge-hiding, sharing, and hoarding, and then two different forms of knowledge-hiding (i.e., horizontal and vertical knowledge-hiding). The contemporary knowledge management literature acknowledges that top-down knowledge-hiding (i.e., supervisor knowledge-hiding from subordinates) is much more detrimental for the knowledge requester and organisation than horizontal knowledge-hiding (i.e., knowledge-hiding from coworkers).

A detailed discussion is presented related to knowledge-hiding in academia, where three crucial role dimensions of academics and examples of tensions while performing these roles are synthesised. Understanding these roles and inherent tensions helped us explore the reasons behind knowledge hidden by academics. Different categories of knowledge-hiding antecedents are presented, using evidence of published research work, which are helpful while designing knowledge management interventions in academic work settings. However, academics are only one of the players in the higher education institutions' ecosystem. Therefore, we explored the knowledge-hiding antecedents and motives of students. While doing this, a distinction between undergraduate and postgraduate students and their different knowledge-seeking behaviours is drawn. While discussing these factors, important future research areas and gaps in existing literature are presented.

Finally, an in-depth discussion is done on the role of individual demographics in knowledge-hiding (both in the role of hider and requester of knowledge). The main reason for this discussion was that individual demographics are enduring attributes; therefore, no interventions can be designed to change those. Therefore, this understanding can help us design better hiring/selection or promotion processes. In this section, we identified two novel theoretical approaches for future research in knowledge-hiding literature: social role theory and intersectionality.

References

Acker, J. (2006). Inequality regimes: Gender, class, and race in organisations. *Gender & Society, 20*(4), 441–464.

Agosto, V., & Roland, E. (2018). Intersectionality and educational leadership: A critical review. *Review of Research in Education., 42*(1), 255–285.

Akhavan, P., Jafari, M., & Fathian, M. (2005). Exploring the failure factors of implementing knowledge management system in organisations. *Journal of Knowledge Management Practice, 6*, 1–8.

Al-Kurdi, O., El-Haddadeh, R., & Eldabi, T. (2018). Knowledge sharing in higher education institutions: A systematic review. *Journal of Enterprise Information Management., 31*, 226.

Anand, A., Centobelli, P., & Cerchione, R. J. J. (2020). Why should I share knowledge with others? A review-based framework on events leading to knowledge hiding. *Journal of Organizational Change Management, 33*, 2.

Arain, G. A., Bhatti, Z. A., Ashraf, N., & Fang, Y.-H. (2018). Top-down knowledge hiding in Organisations: An empirical study of the consequences of supervisor knowledge hiding among local and foreign Workers in the Middle East. *Journal of Business Ethics, 168*, 1–15.

Arain, G. A., Bhatti, Z., Hameed, I., & Fang, Y.-H. (2019). Top-down knowledge hiding and innovative work behaviour (IWB): A three-way moderated-mediation analysis of self-efficacy and local/foreign status. *Journal of Knowledge Management, 24*, 127.

Arain, G. A., Bhatti, Z. A., Ashraf, N., & Fang, Y.-H. (2020a). Top-down knowledge hiding in Organisations: An empirical study of the consequences of supervisor knowledge hiding among local and foreign Workers in the Middle East. *Journal of Business Ethics, 164*(3), 611–625. https://doi.org/10.1007/s10551-018-4056-2

Arain, G. A., Hameed, I., Khan, A. K., Umrani, W. A., & Sheikh, A. Z. (2020b). Consequences of supervisor knowledge hiding in Organisations: A multilevel mediation analysis. *Applied Psychology, 70*(3), 1242–1266.

Arain, G. A., Strologo, A. D., & Dhir, A. (2021). How and when do employees hide knowledge from coworkers? *Journal of Knowledge Management., 26*(7), 1789–1806. https://doi.org/10.1108/JKM-03-2021-0185

Arain, G. A., Bhatti, Z., Hameed, I., Khan, A. K., & Rudolph, C. (2022a). A meta-analysis of the nomological network of knowledge hiding in organisations. *Personnel Psychology, 00*, 1–32. Advance online publication. https://doi.org/10.1111/peps.12562

Arain, G. A., Hameed, I., Khan, A. K., Nicolau, J. L., & Dhir, A. (2022b). How and when does leader knowledge hiding trickle down the organisational hierarchy in the tourism context? A team-level analysis. *Tourism Management, 91*, 104486.

Babcock, P. (2004). Shedding light on knowledge management. *HR Magazine, 49*(5), 46–51.

Bari, M. W., Abrar, M., Shaheen, S., Bashir, M., & Fanchen, M. J. S. O. (2019). Knowledge hiding behaviours and team creativity: The contingent role of perceived mastery motivational climate. *SAGE Open, 9*(3), 2158244019876297.

Bari, M. W., Ghaffar, M., & Ahmad, B. J. J. (2020). Knowledge-hiding behaviours and employees' silence: Mediating role of psychological contract breach. *Journal of Knowledge Management, 24*(9), 2171.

Basu, B., & Sengupta, K. (2007). Assessing success factors of knowledge management initiatives of academic institutions â€" a case of an Indian business school. *Electronic Journal of Knowledge Management, 5*(3), 273–282.

Besic, E. (2020). Intersectionality: A pathway towards inclusive education? *Prospects, 49*, 111–122.

Bhatti, S. H., Kiyani, S. K., Dust, S. B., & Zakariya, R. (2021). The impact of ethical leadership on project success: The mediating role of trust and knowledge sharing. *International Journal of Managing Projects in Business., 14*, 982.

Blau, P. M. (1964). *Exchange and power in social life.* Wiley.

Bock, G.-W., Zmud, R. W., Kim, Y.-G., & Lee, J.-N. (2005). Behavioural intention formation in knowledge sharing: Examining the roles of extrinsic motivators, social-psychological forces, and organisational climate. *MIS Quarterly, 29*, 87–111.

Černe, M., Hernaus, T., Dysvik, A., & Škerlavaj, M. (2017). The role of multi-level synergistic interplay among team mastery climate, knowledge hiding, and job characteristics in stimulating innovative work behaviour. *Human Resource Management Journal, 27*(2), 281–299.

Chen, C. (2020). The effect of leader knowledge hiding on employee voice behaviour—The role of leader-member exchange and knowledge distance. *Open Journal of Social Sciences, 8*(04), 69.

Chen, Y.-H., Lin, T.-P., & Yen, D. C. (2014). How to facilitate inter-organisational knowledge sharing: The impact of trust. *Information and Management, 51*(5), 568–578.

Connelly, C. E., & Zweig, D. (2015). How perpetrators and targets construe knowledge hiding in organisations. *European Journal of Work and Organizational Psychology, 24*(3), 479–489.

Connelly, C. E., Zweig, D., Webster, J., & Trougakos, J. P. (2012). Knowledge hiding in organisations. *Journal of Organizational Behaviour, 33*(1), 64–88.

Connelly, C. E., Černe, M., Dysvik, A., & Škerlavaj, M. (2019). Understanding knowledge hiding in organisations. *Journal of Organizational Behaviour, 40*, 779.

Crenshaw, K. (1991). Mapping the margins: Intersectionality, identity politics, and violence against women of color. *Stanford Law Review, 43*(6), 1241–1299.

Curado, C., & Vieira, S. (2019). Trust, knowledge sharing and organisational commitment in SMEs. *Personnel Review, 48*(6), 1449–1468.

Davenport, T. H., & Prusak, L. (1998). *Working knowledge: How organisations manage what they know.* Harvard Business Press.

Davis, K. (2008). Intersectionality as buzzword: A sociology of science perspective on what makes a feminist theory successful. *Feminist Theory, 9*(1), 67–85.

Debellis, F., De Massis, A., Petruzzelli, A. M., Frattini, F., & Del Giudice, M. (2021). Strategic agility and international joint ventures: The willingness-ability paradox of family firms. *Journal of International Management, 27*(1), 100739.

Demirkasimoglu, N. (2016). Knowledge hiding in academia: Is personality a key factor? *International Journal of Higher Education, 5*(1), 128–140.

Eagly, A. H., & Wood, W. (1999). The origins of sex differences in human behaviour: Evolved dispositions versus social roles. *American Psychologist, 54*(6), 408.

Fang, Y. H. (2017). Coping with fear and guilt using mobile social networking applications: Knowledge hiding, loafing, and sharing. *Telematics and Informatics, 34*(5), 779–797.

Fauzi, M. A. (2022). Knowledge hiding behaviour in higher education institutions: A scientometric analysis and systematic literature review approach. *Journal of Knowledge Management, 27*(2), 302–327.

Fishbein, M., & Ajzen, I. (1977). Belief, attitude, intention, and behaviour: An introduction to theory and research. *Philosophy and Rhetoric, 10*(2).

Fong, P. S., Men, C., Luo, J., & Jia, R. (2018). Knowledge hiding and team creativity: The contingent role of task interdependence. *Management Decision, 56*(2), 329–343.

Friberg, J., & McKinney, K. (2019). *Applying the scholarship of teaching and learning beyond the individual classroom.* Indiana University Press.

Fullwood, R., Rowley, J., & Delbridge, R. (2013). Knowledge sharing amongst academics in UK universities. *Journal of Knowledge Management, 17*, 123.

Gagné, M., Tian, A. W., Soo, C., Zhang, B., Ho, K. S. B., & Hosszu, K. (2019). Different motivations for knowledge sharing and hiding: The role of motivating work design. *Journal of Organizational Behaviour, 40*(7), 783–799.

Garg, N., & Anand, P. (2020). Knowledge hiding, conscientiousness, loneliness and affective commitment: A moderated mediation model. *International Journal of Educational Management, 34*, 1417.

Garg, N., Talukdar, A., Ganguly, A., & Kumar, C. (2021). Knowledge hiding in academia: An empirical study of Indian higher education students. *Journal of Knowledge Management, 25,* 2196.

Ghani, U., Teo, T., Li, Y., Usman, M., Islam, Z. U., Gul, H., Naeem, R. M., Bahadar, H., Yuan, J., & Zhai, X. (2020a). Tit for tat: Abusive supervision and knowledge hiding-the role of psychological contract breach and psychological ownership. *International Journal of Environmental Research and Public Health, 17*(4), 1240.

Ghani, U., Zhai, X., Spector, J. M., Chen, N.-S., Lin, L., Ding, D., & Usman, M. J. H. E. (2020b). Knowledge hiding in higher education: Role of interactional justice and professional commitment. *Higher Education, 79*(2), 325–344.

Gillies, R. M. (2014). Cooperative learning: Developments in research. *International Journal of Educational Psychology, 3*(2), 125–140.

Greenberg, J., Brinsfield, C., & Edwards, M. (2007). *Silence as deviant work behaviour: The peril of words unspoken.* Symposium presented at the annual meeting of the Society for Industrial and Organizational Psychology, New York, NY.

Hadjielias, E., Christofi, M., & Tarba, S. (2021). Knowledge hiding and knowledge sharing in small family farms: A stewardship view. *Journal of Business Research, 137,* 279–292.

Hameed, Z., Khan, I. U., Sheikh, Z., Islam, T., Rasheed, M. I., & Naeem, R. M. (2019). Organisational justice and knowledge sharing behaviour: The role of psychological ownership and perceived organisational support. *Personnel Review, 48,* 748.

Harris, K. L. (2017). Re-situating organisational knowledge: Violence, intersectionality and the privilege of partial perspective. *Human Relations, 70*(3), 263–285.

Hernaus, T., Cerne, M., Connelly, C., Poloski Vokic, N., & Škerlavaj, M. (2019). Evasive knowledge hiding in academia: When competitive individuals are asked to collaborate. *Journal of Knowledge Management, 23*(4), 597–618.

Hislop, D. (2003). Linking human resource management and knowledge management via commitment: A review and research agenda. *Employee Relations, 25*(2), 182–202.

Holvino, E. (2010). Intersections: The simultaneity of race, gender and class in organisation studies. *Gender, Work and Organisation, 17*(3), 248–277.

Huo, W., Cai, Z., Luo, J., Men, C., & Jia, R. (2016). Antecedents and intervention mechanisms: A multi-level study of R&D team's knowledge hiding behaviour. *Journal of Knowledge Management, 20*(5), 880–897.

Ipe, M. (2003). Knowledge sharing in organisations: A conceptual framework. *Human Resource Development Review, 2*(4), 337–359.

Irum, A., Ghosh, K., & Pandey, A. (2020). Workplace incivility and knowledge hiding: a research agenda. *Benchmarking: An International Journal, 27,* 958–980.

Jahanzeb, S., Fatima, T., Bouckenooghe, D., & Bashir, F. (2019). The knowledge hiding link: A moderated mediation model of how abusive supervision affects employee creativity. *European Journal of Work and Organizational Psychology, 28*(6), 810–819.

Karim, D. N. (2020). Effect of dark personalities on knowledge hiding behaviour at higher education institutions. *Journal of Information and Knowledge Management, 19*(04), 2050031.

Kelley, H. H., & Thibaut, J. W. (1978). *Interpersonal relations: A theory of interdependence.* Wiley.

Kelloway, E. K., & Barling, J. (2000). Knowledge work as organisational behaviour. *International Journal of Management Reviews, 2*(3), 287–304.

Kiniti, S., & Standing, C. (2013). Wikis as knowledge management systems: Issues and challenges. *Journal of Systems and Information Technology, 15,* 189.

Ko, D.-G., Kirsch, L. J., & King, W. R. (2005). Antecedents of knowledge transfer from consultants to clients in enterprise system implementations. *MIS Quarterly, 29,* 59–85.

Kremer, H., Villamor, I., & Aguinis, H. (2019). Innovation leadership: Best-practice recommendations for promoting employee creativity, voice, and knowledge sharing. *Business Horizons, 62*(1), 65–74.

Lakshman, C., Rai, S., & Lakshman, S. (2021). Knowledge sharing, organisational commitment and turnover intention among knowledge workers: A knowledge-based perspective. *Journal of Asia Business Studies, 16*(5), 768–785.

Lane, J. D., & Wegner, D. M. (1995). The cognitive consequences of secrecy. *Journal of Personality and Social Psychology, 69*(2), 237.

Le, P. B., & Lei, H. (2018). The mediating role of trust in stimulating the relationship between transformational leadership and knowledge-sharing processes. *Journal of Knowledge Management., 22,* 521.

Li, J., Liu, M., & Liu, X. (2016). Why do employees resist knowledge management systems? An empirical study from the status quo bias and inertia perspectives. *Computers in Human Behaviour, 65,* 189–200.

Li, X., Wei, W. X., Huo, W., Huang, Y., Zheng, M., & Yan, J. (2020). You reap what you sow: Knowledge hiding, territorial and idea implementation. *International Journal of Emerging Markets, 16*(8), 1583–1603.

Lyu, H., & Zhang, Z. (2017). Incentives for knowledge sharing: Impact of organisational culture and information technology. *Enterprise Information Systems, 11*(9), 1416–1435.

Michaelidou, N., Micevski, M., & Cadogan, J. W. (2021). Users' ethical perceptions of social media research: Conceptualisation and measurement. *Journal of Business Research, 124*, 684–694.

Moghavvemi, S., Sharabati, M., Paramanathan, T., & Rahin, N. M. (2017). The impact of perceived enjoyment, perceived reciprocal benefits, and knowledge power on students' knowledge sharing through Facebook. *The International Journal of Management Education, 15*(1), 1–12.

Nadeem, M. A., Liu, Z., Ghani, U., Younis, A., & Xu, Y. (2020). Impact of shared goals on knowledge hiding behaviour: The moderating role of trust. *Management decision, 59*(6), 1312–1332.

Nguyen, N. P., Ngo, L. V., Bucic, T., & Phong, N. D. (2018). Cross-functional knowledge sharing, coordination and firm performance: The role of cross-functional competition. *Industrial Marketing Management, 71*, 123–134.

Niedergassel, B., & Leker, J. (2011). Different dimensions of knowledge in cooperative R&D projects of university scientists. *Technovation, 31*(4), 142–150.

Nonaka, I. (1994). A dynamic theory of organisational knowledge creation. *Organisation Science, 5*(1), 14–37.

Nonaka, I., & Toyama, R. (2015). The knowledge-creating theory revisited: Knowledge creation as a synthesising process. In *The essentials of knowledge management* (pp. 95–110). Springer.

Nunez, A. M. (2014). Employing multilevel intersectionality in educational research: Latino identities, contexts, and college access. *Educational Research, 43*(2), 85.

Offergelt, F., Spörrle, M., Moser, K., & Shaw, J. D. (2018). Leader-signaled knowledge hiding: Effects on employees' job attitudes and empowerment. *Journal of Organizational Behaviour, 40*(7), 819. https://doi.org/10.1002/job.2343

Pan, W., Zhang, Q., Teo, T. S., & Lim, V. K. (2018). The dark triad and knowledge hiding. *International Journal of Information Management, 42*, 36–48.

Park, S., & Kim, E.-J. (2018). Fostering organisational learning through leadership and knowledge sharing. *Journal of Knowledge Management, 22*, 1408.

Peng, H. (2013). Why and when do people hide knowledge? *Journal of Knowledge Management, 17*(3), 398–415.

Rhee, Y. W., Choi, J. N. J. J., & o. O. B. (2017). Knowledge management behaviour and individual creativity: Goal orientations as antecedents and in-group social status as moderating contingency. *Journal of Organizational Behavior, 38*(6), 813–832.

Riaz, S., Xu, Y., & Hussain, S. (2019). Workplace ostracism and knowledge hiding: The mediating role of job tension. *Sustainability, 11*(20), 5547.

Samdani, H., Ali, B., & Kamal, N. (2019). Knowledge hiding and creativity in higher education institutes: Understanding the contingent role of perceived supervisory support. *Global Social Sciences Review, 4*(4), 341–349.

Schein, E. H. (2004). *Organisational culture and leadership* (3rd ed.). Lossey-Bass.

Semerci, A. B. (2019). Examination of knowledge hiding with conflict, competition and personal values. *International Journal of Conflict Management, 30*, 111.

Serenko, A., & Bontis, N. (2016). Negotiate, reciprocate, or cooperate? The impact of exchange modes on inter-employee knowledge sharing. *Journal of Knowledge Management, 20*(4), 687–712.

Singh, S. K. (2019). Territoriality, task performance, and workplace deviance: Empirical evidence on role of knowledge hiding. *Journal of Business Research, 97*, 10–19.

Sitkin, S., & Brodt, S. (2006). *Coping with the paradox of secrecy norms in organisations. Working paper*, Duke University, Durham, NC, USA.

Tefera, A. A., Powers, J. M., & Fischman, G. E. (2018). Intersectionality in education: A conceptual aspiration and research imperative. *Review of Research in Education, 42*(1), vii–xvii.

Walsh, J. P., & Hong, W. (2003). Secrecy is increasing in step with competition. *Nature, 422*(6934), 801–802.

Wang, S., & Noe, R. A. (2010). Knowledge sharing: A review and directions for future research. *Human Resource Management Review, 20*(2), 115–131.

Wang, Y.-S., Lin, H.-H., Li, C.-R., & Lin, S.-J. (2014). What drives students' knowledge-withholding intention in management education? An empirical study in Taiwan. *Academy of Management Learning and Education, 13*(4), 547–568.

Wang, Y., Han, M. S., Xiang, D., & Hampson, D. P. (2019). The double-edged effects of perceived knowledge hiding: Empirical evidence from the sales context. *Journal of Knowledge Management, 23*, 279.

Webster, J., Brown, G., Zweig, D., Connelly, C. E., Brodt, S., & Sitkin, S. (2008). Beyond knowledge sharing: Withholding knowledge at work. In *Research in personnel and human resources management* (pp. 1–37). Emerald Group.

Weng, Q., Latif, K., Khan, A. K., Tariq, H., Butt, H. P., Obaid, A., & Sarwar, N. (2020). Loaded with knowledge, yet green with envy: Leader–member exchange comparison and coworkers-directed knowledge hiding behaviour. *Journal of Knowledge Management, 24,* 1653.

Wittenbaum, G. M., Hollingshead, A. B., & Botero, I. C. (2004). From cooperative to motivated information sharing in groups: Moving beyond the hidden profile paradigm. *Communication Monographs, 71*(3), 286–310.

Xiong, C., Chang, V., Scuotto, V., Shi, Y., & Paoloni, N. (2019). The social-psychological approach in understanding knowledge hiding within international R&D teams: An inductive analysis. *Journal of Business Research, 128,* 799–811.

Yang, K., & Ribiere, V. (2020). Drivers of knowledge hiding in the university context. *Online Journal of Applied Knowledge Management (OJAKM), 8*(1), 99–116.

Yao, Z., Zhang, X., Luo, J., & Huang, H. (2020). Offense is the best defense: The impact of workplace bullying on knowledge hiding. *Journal of Knowledge Management, 24,* 675.

Zhai, X., Wang, M., & Ghani, U. (2020). The SOR (stimulus-organism-response) paradigm in online learning: An empirical study of students' knowledge hiding perceptions. *Interactive Learning Environments, 28*(5), 586–601.

Zhao, H., Xia, Q., He, P., Sheard, G., & Wan, P. (2016). Workplace ostracism and knowledge hiding in service organisations. *International Journal of Hospitality Management, 59,* 84–94.

Zutshi, A., Creed, A., Bhattacharya, A., Bavik, A., Sohal, A., & Bavik, Y. L. (2021). Demystifying knowledge hiding in academic roles in higher education. *Journal of Business Research, 137,* 206–221.

8

Working with Dementia: Applying Creative Education to Interdisciplinary and Cross-Organisational Practice

Mark Brill

Introduction

The examples presented here demonstrate how approaches to research, creative thinking and education can bring a direct impact on real-world practice, and in turn, how that practice can inform creative business pedagogy. As such, it exemplifies an interdisciplinarity that is fundamental to the development of these projects. It illustrates the way that creative approaches and techniques can be applied to community-based practice to help develop effective solutions.

In the context of the case studies, there are questions of intersectionality is one of inclusivity and diversity in older adults, particularly those living with dementia. This chapter, therefore, identifies challenges in ageism, disability and inequality for those living with age-related diseases (Centre for Better Ageing, 2020). In particular, the projects described

M. Brill (✉)
Business School for the Creative Industries, University for the Creative Arts, Epsom, UK
e-mail: MBrill@uca.ac.uk

here have utilised digital media to deliver creatively directed tools, such as music or visual arts, that alleviate the impact of dementia in older adults living with the disease. Leveraging such tools through digital applications brings the potential to broaden access to therapies and well-being. These, in turn, bring opportunities to help address inequalities associated with ageing, which include gender, ethnicity and cultural diversity. Throughout the projects discussed here, there is a through-line of creativity, often in the context of enterprise that extends to address questions and societal problems.

Memory Tracks: Connecting Music and Dementia; Case Study 1

This project demonstrates how creative pedagogy was instrumental in identifying a tool that utilised music to support dementia care. It also shows how academic research can not only validate concepts but also support enterprise initiatives. In this example, academic research led to collaborations with a community organisation and a small technology business. Subsequently, the cross-sectoral research offered validation for the development of a commercially available digital health application, Memory Tracks (Cunningham et al., 2019).

Whilst the connection between dementia, music and memory has been widely understood (Simmons-Stern et al., 2012), Anderson (2016) proposed a particular relationship in which memorable songs could be used to trigger reminders for people living with dementia to undertake daily tasks. In support of this thesis, research interviews were carried out that included the author of this chapter. In the interview, cited in the thesis, a smartphone application was proposed, to enable musical triggers connected to daily activities for people living with dementia. The author also identified the potential to use sensors in the home or care home environment as behavioural prompts for these musical triggers.

In 2017, the author attended a research workshop by the Consortium for Research Excellence, Support and Training, now called GuildHE. The two-day event utilised the Sandpit approach to interdisciplinary and cross-sectoral research that considered industrial or societal challenges (The Sandpit, n.d.). It was here that the author proposed research to further test the hypothesis of a connection between music, memory and daily activities for people with dementia. It led to the formation of an interdisciplinary academic team that included music, user experience design, computing and audio computing. Further cross-sectoral partners were subsequently invited to join the research team that included an independent care home group, Pendine Park Organisation in North Wales (Pendine Park, n.d.) and health technology SME, Memory Tracks (Memory Tracks, n.d.). To further underline the interdisciplinary nature of the project, the co-researchers at Pendine Park were the Artist-in-Residence at Wrexham, and at Carnarvon, the Musician-in-Residence.

The term 'song-task association' was proposed by the research team to describe the relationship between music, memory and activities. From this concept, an initial study was designed that considered how music could be used as a trigger to undertake daily tasks, such as getting up, washing, taking medication or eating meals. To enable these tasks to be studied, a prototype app was built for Android tablet devices, and a cohort of 14 participants were identified from residents at Pendine Park's Wrexham and Carnarvon care homes. The original thesis (Anderson, 2016) proposed support for those with early stages of dementia at home, triggered by the subject or close family member. However, the study cohort for this research typically showed more advanced stages of dementia. As a result, the task songs were triggered by care staff. The choice of the Android platform was informed by the ease of development, coding and the cost of providing tablet devices for use by the care home staff.

Underpinning the approach to the research was an understanding that music, from earliest years, between the ages of four and seven, is retained in the memory even after the onset of dementia (Simmons-Stern et al., 2012). The initial objective was to identify music that was memorable to each participant living with dementia, in order to offer an appropriate trigger for specific activities. A 'music recognition scale' was first proposed, to identify the most appropriate songs to use. The researchers or carers would observe visual or audible cues in the person living with dementia and identify how they responded to songs. Whilst this approach may have proven effective, as the research progressed, it became clear that a simpler means of identifying music was more expedient. As song-task association considered memory, rather than reminiscence, the objective was to find music that was well-known to the person living with dementia, but not necessarily ones that elicited an emotional response. This was achieved by mapping the year of the subject's birth to the most popular songs, based on published charts, to when they were between the ages of four and seven years.

Consideration was given to the app user experience (UX), as it was intended to be used in a care home context, where staff were focussed on the delivery of care and did not generally use digital technologies in this setting. This utilised approaches taught in creative education, through the broad principles of UX (Norman, 2013). The chosen UX used a tile-based format with large icons and accompanying text descriptions, such as 'get dressed', 'wash' or 'take medication'. This allowed for easy and rapid identification by the care team, who would be delivering the song-task association to the people with dementia. There was one tablet device for each resident taking part in the study. Each was pre-populated with the most common tasks carried out in this setting and songs relevant to the age of the person with dementia. These could be edited to address specific challenges for the individual or to amend the associated songs for recognition or preference.

In addition to the Android tablets loaded with the app, a printed survey sheet was used to record the individual responses to song-task association. Six measurements were taken, that combined the Self-Assessment Manikin scale (arousal, valence, and dominance), and three Quality of Life in Alzheimer's disease measures (physical health, memory, and life as a whole). There was a two-week base line study, followed by a four-week period using music associated to tasks. The study was carried out consecutively at the two care homes in Wrexham and Carnarvon. Prior to each study, care staff were shown how to use the app and reporting sheets. The care home team also helped select the residents for the study cohort and suggested relevant activities for each person's song-task association.

The role of the artist and musician in residence at the two care homes was significant in ensuring that the study was effective. Both staff members understood the relevance of music in this context and were able to communicate this to the care team who were working with the residents. They also took a practical role to make the Android tablets and survey sheets available for each resident. It demonstrates the benefits of cross-organisational research, as the academic team members were not in daily contact with the care staff and could not build the necessary relationships for the most effective study. There were, however, challenges in delivering the survey on the ground. In some instances, the tablet batteries were not charged, and the carers were unable to use them. There were further issues with using individual, personalised music in communal areas, such as dining or sitting rooms. This was resolved by staggering the playing of songs for each individual.

Study Results

The quantitative results suggested a beneficial impact in the use of music associated to specific tasks, but given the cohort size and length of study, it was not conclusive. The qualitative study, however, showed a clearer benefit of the use of personalised music in dementia care. A thematic analysis was developed from structured interviews with 26 care home professionals about the impact of the use of song-task association. The responses were either positive or neutral. On the theme of 'ability', example responses were:

(i) 'I know [participant name] loves it, downstairs, she likes the memory of it'.
(ii) 'When she tells me she needs the toilet she grabs the tablet as if to tell me "let's go"'.

A positive connection was made with music and memory with comments such as: 'He said a couple of times 'Oh I knew this song when I was a boy'. The study was not able to identify a clear link between memorable music and specific activities, or song-task association. However, as an initial study, it considered the effectiveness of the approach that has led members of the academic team to seek further research funding in this field.

Memory Tracks is a support tool for people living with dementia and as such it is neither clinical nor therapeutic. However, in the field of older adult care, an understanding of the impact is important; the initial research, led by an academic team, helped to support the subsequent development of the publicly available app that was released in the app store. As well as adding a level of evidence, the study also offered an informal co-design approach. During the interviews, a carer commented that using music to achieve tasks was even more effective when she sang along to it. That resulted in the addition of sing-along songs that included lyrics, which were built into the commercial release of the app.

Whilst the research demonstrated benefits and potential cost savings from using the app, there were a number of barriers to the adoption of song-task association. The first was the adoption of technology in care homes. These challenges include availability of suitable tablet devices, management of these devices in the care home and restrictions on how they may be used by staff. Further challenges to scaling Memory Tracks were business related. In the care home environment where costs are tightly managed, additional spending on this type of technology can be seen as something of a luxury. The research was able to demonstrate a clear benefit of the app; however, it was not possible to consider any cost-benefits within the scope of the initial research. Furthermore, with the closure of care homes to visitors during the pandemic further exacerbated the challenges for uptake of the app. A key learning from this was that academic research can help bring validity, but in itself does not provide a sufficient incentive for use. The Memory Tracks team see the future possibilities as using song-task association within other care apps, especially those that are already embedded in care homes. This business proposition offers a further opportunity for study by academic or student researchers within creative business education.

Memory Matters: Digitising Cognitive Stimulation Therapy; Case Study 2

This case study relates to an ongoing cross-organisational project that includes the author as a member of the Memory Tracks team, working in partnership with a Community Interest Company (CIC), Memory Matters. As a larger undertaking than the first case study, there are many interdisciplinary objectives in which creative business education can take a role in understanding a range of challenges and methods to identify solutions. It also exemplifies the relevance of academic research to impact solutions that support ageing and age-related disabilities. Through interdisciplinary and cross-organisational practice, the project discussed here will result in the development of a digital platform centred on an iPad app that will Cognitive Stimulation Therapy (CST). CST is an evidence-based treatment for people with mild to moderate dementia. Following a series of studies by the team at University College London, CST has been recommended by the UK government's National Institute for Health and Care Excellence (NICE, 2018). Group CST treatment is usually provided for groups of six participants over 14 core sessions of themed activities, followed by further top-up sessions. The therapy aims to actively stimulate and engage with people with dementia, which also bring the social benefits of group interaction. CST is particularly effective with comprehension and language, which has been shown to reduce the impact of dementia and to increase the quality of life (QOL).

During the pandemic, restrictions on gatherings meant that CST sessions were moved online, delivered by trained CST facilitators via Zoom and similar video conferencing platforms. This was a simple adaptation from the face-to-face sessions that utilised analogue materials, such as flip charts or written cards shown on camera during the calls. The Memory Tracks team, including the author, worked in partnership with Memory

Matters, who have been delivering CST sessions in Devon and Cornwall area since 2012 (Memory Matters, n.d.). As the pandemic demonstrated the potential to deliver online sessions effectively, the two organisations successfully applied for funding from the UK Research and Innovation Healthy Ageing strand to develop a digital version of the therapy that could be delivered entirely through a mobile or tablet-based application (UKRI, n.d.).

A study of virtual CST programmes during the pandemic brought further insight for the development of this project (Perkins et al., 2022). It suggested that Zoom-based CST sessions can engage people with dementia, however, they have not shown the same level of effectiveness as face-to-face sessions. Challenges such as connectivity, latency and audio quality were highlighted in the study. It proposed that digital CST was harder to deliver for ensemble activities or those that required more complex instructions. Conversely, creative or physical activities showed more effectiveness, although some of those tasks required materials to be sent to the participants before the session. The Memory Matters team believed that an app specifically designed to deliver virtual CST sessions may be able to address these challenges more effectively, with activities tailored to the digital medium. Additionally, online sessions offer several additional benefits, such as removing the need for the participants to travel (Betts et al., 2019). This is especially advantageous in remote areas or for participants with limited mobility or who are physically vulnerable.

One question that was considered early in the development of the app was whether older adults had access to and felt able to use the technology utilised in virtual CST. Although there has been a lack of research in this area there is a common perception that older adults often lack devices or sufficient knowledge of the technology (Betts et al., 2019). As a result, the author looked to understand these issues within the context of a virtual CST app. During the co-design process of the app, the Memory Matters team formed a research cohort. This included CST participants and facilitators largely recruited through an active Facebook Group. In the first phase of this research, CST participants (n = 44) were asked about their use of digital technologies. Eighty per cent stated that they regularly use a smartphone and 73.3% use a tablet, such as an iPad, with 86.7% of those using their devices to make video calls. The survey also pointed to a degree of digital literacy, with 56.3% stating that they were able to 'work out the technology themselves' and 31.5% responding that they 'needed help to get started' but did not require ongoing support. It suggests that contrary to some perceptions there was sufficient confidence in using technology.

It has been observed that digital technologies offer an opportunity for older adults to be more socially connected, which in turn plays an important role in maintaining health and well-being (Czaja & Lee, 2014). A peer support network for older women called The Zoomettes (DEEP: The UK Network of Dementia Voices, n.d.) also pointed to positive benefits of virtual groups for people with dementia. The approach of this group showed that older adults were both willing to engage with the technologies proposed for the CST app. It also suggested that the more confident users would be able to support those who may feel anxious about using the technology. A Zoomette's 2019 report found that 'in terms of using ZOOM itself, there had been some teething problems, but most participants had found it easy to use' (DEEP: The UK Network of Dementia Voices, n.d.). This was supported by a guide made by one of the Zoomette members that offered a clear, empathetic approach to technical help (Isaacs, 2019). One theme in the group's feedback was the suggestion that online sessions for people with dementia can bring a more open discussion as participants will tend to be more relaxed in their own homes: 'facilitators noted that there was much more open and honest conversation than in face to face, mixed groups we have worked with'. For the development of the Memory Matters app, it suggests that, given an appropriate environment, digitally delivered CST may offer greater benefits of active participation than in face-to-face groups.

Comparisons in technology usage tend to be made with young adults, especially with higher education where it is widely used within the learning environment. As with older adults, there are common, though contrary, perceptions that there is a high degree of understanding and confidence with digital technologies in young adults. The term 'digital native' is one that has often been applied to a generation that has grown up with connected technologies (Prenksy, 2001). Although it offers a convenient description, it may be seen as somewhat misleading, as digital usage is not homogenous (Selwyn, 2009). There appears to be a spectrum of knowledge and engagement with technology that is influenced by a variety of factors including socioeconomic background, education, or access in which intersectionality plays a part (Golding, 2000). Furthermore, the concept of the 'digital native' is also problematic in the context of older adults, who conversely have been labelled as 'digital immigrants', a label that suggests a lack of competence on their part. It has resulted in the Memory Matters research cohort identified a usage in older adults that tended towards utility and core communications, such as video calling with family members. In contrast, younger users tend to use technology more broadly that includes games or passive consumption of content such as social media or video (Crook and Harrison, 2008). There are further questions to consider around that of peer support in the adoption of technologies. Whilst often informal, peer support may take place invisibly with those who are socialising the most, such as school or higher education students. For older adults, social networks tend to be smaller and less frequent. It may be this feature, as much as lack of familiarity with digital technologies that may present a barrier to technology adoption.

Developing Digital CST

CST was initially developed as a face-to-face activity, so creating an entirely digital version presented several challenges. During the pandemic, groups typically moved online, convening via video conferencing tools, such as Zoom. In a second survey of the research cohort with CST facilitators ($n = 16$), appropriate session plans (50%) and activity prompts (66.7%) pointed to a need to include guidance through the CST sessions. As a result, the importance of providing appropriate activities for virtual CST, as well as offering a range of options for facilitators, became a focus for the app development.

The team at Memory Matters brought extensive knowledge of CST and working with people with dementia. However, they did not have previous experience in developing digital tools or advanced mobile or tablet applications. The partnership with the Memory Tracks team was important to transition CST effectively to a digital platform. Co-design was also at the core of this project, as functionality was just one part of the app. It was fundamental that older adults, carers and facilitators were able to access the app easily, participating effectively CST without the 'distraction' of managing unfamiliar technology tools.

The technology-delivering team, Memory Tracks, therefore brought a set of objectives to the development and co-design process (such as?). A Design Thinking () approach was one that the Memory Tracks team had previously experienced and identified as one that would be appropriate for this delivery. As a member of this team, the author had utilised this approach in creative education (Luka, 2014), and in particular, two approaches in the earlier stages of the project, Problem Framing (Carlgren, 2016) and Empathy Mapping (Gasparini, 2015).

As the teams were based in Devon, Cornwall and London, the initial development work, a discovery phase, was undertaken through Zoom-based meetings. To enable the Design Thinking process, a digital collaboration platform, Miro, was used, and a series of templates were created for the techniques to be utilised. There were some benefits, such as asynchronous collaboration and functions to export frames in pdf format. As a UK Research and Innovation (UKRI)-funded project, it was necessary to produce quarterly reports and the Miro pdfs formed a good basis for this. The methodology was also able to draw out information and understanding that had not been previously identified. During the Problem Framing exercise, it became clear that there were challenges in setting up face-to-face CST sessions that included facilitator training, access to appropriate materials for running activities, as well as transportation for participants to attend sessions. Travel was an important issue for communities in Cornwall, which tend to be rural with fewer public transport options. In addition to convenience, the cost of travel was also a factor that could be alleviated by using digital solutions. The Problem Framing also helped to identify another key challenge for the team, which was the perception of CST as a non-pharmacological therapy. Despite the wealth of research to the contrary, the CST practitioners at Memory Matters found it difficult to convince health authorities of the benefits.

The Digital CST Structure

Central to creating an effective CST programme is the structured approach across and within each session. The format is centred on an introduction, main activity and closing summary over 45 minutes to 1 hour. The introduction is in the form of a reality orientation (RO) that gives prompts, written on a board, that connect the group with the day, date, season and weather (Spector et al., 2000). Within this introductory section, there is also a group song, which is a popular piece of music that is agreed within the group at the start of a series of sessions.

The RO board is followed by a main activity—each of these 14 sessions is designed to develop different areas of cognitive ability such as childhood, food, using money, categorising objects or being creative (Cognitive Stimulation Therapy, n.d.). The app development team undertook a series of workshops to understand how activities could be best delivered for a digital platform. The design process began with a list that included 140 appropriate activities within the CST framework. The team considered which would translate directly to a digital format, those that could be adapted easily and those that were unlikely to work well on a digital platform. During the process, it became apparent that for a digital development, it was possible to identify some standard functions for which the information could be amended for a relevant activity. One such example is a matching format that could be applied to different examples of cognition. In a food session, for example, participants might associate 'fish' with 'chips', animals could connect 'horse' and 'cart'. Other core functions identified included image prompts, word prompts, number games or sound bingo. The benefit of this approach allowed a finite number of formats to be coded in the app, but easily adapted through uploading text, image or sound files.

One of the core principles underpinning cognition-based therapies is response validation (Neal and Briggs 2002). Rather than testing memory recall and finding the 'correct' answer, validation focusses on cognition. The technique is empathetic and reassuring for the person with dementia and connects the carer to their world. Clearly, there is resonance with creative education. When teaching creative endeavours, we are not looking for a correct response. There are no 'wrong' answers. However, it was interesting to note that the co-design method was the differences in understanding of the process between the app developers and the CST practitioners. This was significant in how validation would be utilised in the working version of the app (Neal 2002). The initial thinking was that it would be necessary to populate the software with some likely answers that the facilitator could select. However, in a pairing exercise 'fish and bacon' would be an equally valid response as 'fish and chips'. It became apparent that trying to predict likely responses was not appropriate in this context. A text entry box for facilitators was introduced instead of a series of set answers. This would ensure validation of all possible answers, no matter how unlikely they could be.

Some activities did not require a game-like structure in the app, but rather simple prompts for a physical activity, such as exercise, creative or life story sessions. Whilst these are straight forward to deliver in face-to-face sessions, for digital CST, the challenge was to identify methods that were both practical and safe for remote participants. For exercise, it was necessary to ensure that the participants remained seated, following simple movements directed by the facilitator. Creative sessions were largely designed to utilise materials easily available to the participants. An example of this is an activity on the theme of Jacometti's sculpture. The facilitator shows work from the artist or takes the participants on a virtual gallery tour, followed by an activity, in which they create their own Jacometti-inspired sculptures using household aluminium foil. For lifestory activities, participants are asked to bring objects or photographs that resonate with them. In this context, the home environment offers a clear advantage as the artefacts are easily available.

Creativity, Ageing and Intersectionality

During the development of the Memory Matters project, a number of broader questions were raised that led to further investigations by the author in academic research and cross-organisational practice. Members of the project had observed and noted the importance of cultural diversity in delivering a cognitive programme for older adults. It led to the question of intersectionality in adults with dementia. Thomas and Milligan (2015) explored intersectionality in the context of ageing and dementia, through a social model of disability. Alongside ageism, social patterns within intersectionality may amplify the impact of living with dementia. Therefore, in developing appropriate CST activities, a greater understanding of social-economic, gender, ethnic and cultural backgrounds was highlighted as key considerations. As a cognitive therapy, the app will utilise activities that reference culture, food, education, language or historical events within the lifetime of the participants. Cultural relevance was previously noted during the Memory Tracks study, conducted with participants in North Wales (Cunningham et al., 2019). Here, the need was to identify musical reminiscence triggers for research subjects (Baird and Thompson, 2018). Those that had spent their early years in this region were often Welsh-language speakers who would have a memory of Welsh songs. As a result, the Memory Tracks app was populated with appropriate music for the study. Whilst the Memory Tracks study was working with a small cohort and just music, delivering digital CST sessions includes a broader range of activities and a considerably larger cohort. A current research project at the University of Bristol, Connecting Through Culture as We Age (2022) is considering digital participation in arts and culture. The focus of this project has been a co-design process with older adults who the researchers describe as those 'with disability and or identify as socioeconomically or racially minoritised' (Willatt, 2022).

In the context of co-design, the participants are co-researchers working in collaboration with the academic team. They utilise a creative process across different media formats, such as photography, collage and creative writing to produce an album of their lives. This is followed by interviews with the participants to further understand their album and as a point for further discussion. As co-researchers, they were able to bring lived experience to the design of digital cultural experiences. The University of Bristol team has also identified concepts of intersectional life course to bring greater understanding of inequalities in ageing (Holman and Walker, 2021). This creative, reflective approach is pertinent to the cognition and validation techniques in CST, especially in the context of intersectionality.

A second area of collaboration was closely connected with the creative industries is project for people with dementia called Living Brands (Museum of Brands, n.d.). This is a three-year funded project by the Museum of Brands that applies sensory remembrance to support cognition for people living with dementia. The museum has a significant repository of brand material dating back to the early twentieth century that consists of packaging, audio and visual material, as well as example products. The Living Brands project is delivered through reminiscence sessions with people living with dementia supported 'sensory boxes' that offers a tactile, olfactory experience. Though different to CST, the approach is similar in the way in which it engages a range of senses to development cognition in people living with dementia. There has been a lack of research into sensory remembrance in the context of people living with dementia and brands, Memory Matters CST practitioners had observed benefits of this type of activity. For example, activities relating to products from CST participants' earlier years have shown a high level of engagement in sessions. As a result Memory Matters have created a partnership with The Museum of Brands that will enable them to include relevant digital materials in the app. The author has also proposed further co-organisational research study that will consider dementia, sensory remembrance in products and brand advertising.

Discussion and Conclusion

The case studies presented here outline a broad range of themes, disciplines and practice, in which creative business education has played a role in addressing a societal challenge to support older adults living with dementia. Academic research has been fundamental in driving both projects forwards. In the first example, Memory Tracks, the initiative began with a music student's thesis, and subsequent research by a team of three academics in creatively led subjects in music, design and user experience. This led to an initial study and published peer-reviewed paper. This research was also underpinned by an inclusive, cross-organisational approach that brought care practitioners into the research, design, and development process. In the second example, the development of a CST app, it was the large evidence base of academic research that supported the funding application, in addition to informing the app development itself. Whilst the core evidence base was researched by health and psychology academics, creative academics and practitioners interpreted this work into design-driven content. Significantly, as the project developed, the need for further studies and research collaborations became apparent. These themes include an additional understanding of intersectionality in older adults and the application of creative activities for people with dementia.

The role of creative business education may be less apparent in these case studies, yet, as with the research, it was important in the progression of these applications. Led by the author, pedagogic techniques in concept development, co-design and user experience were utilised by the development teams to realise the digital tools. Furthermore, the approach to cognition in people with dementia, specifically the technique of validation resonated with approaches to creative pedagogy. This was most apparent in the creation of CST activities in the context of digital media. The experience of teaching creative subjects online during the Pandemic proved invaluable for the delivery of comparable exercises in CST. There is also a recognisable role for creative business education, that of student involvement. In addition to student research, themes on design, enterprise and business development bring learning opportunities in the form of case studies or briefs. In particular, challenges with the business and marketing models for both projects can be areas in which creative business education can provide insight and support.

Creative business education can also bring considerations of intersectionality into practice, to better understand the lived experience of people with dementia. Theory and knowledge gained through education can be associated with older adults living with dementia. Throughout both examples, and especially in the development of CST, this knowledge has informed an understanding of age, culture, ethnicity, gender and sexuality to help create relevant and inclusive projects. There is one recurring strand throughout the research and practice of these projects, that of interdisciplinarity. The innovative nature of new, digital concepts that support healthy ageing through cross-organisational practice requires adaptability and applications that are consistent with approaches in creative business education. The need for adaptive and holistic thinking sits at the core of both. Considered together, there is the potential for reciprocal enrichment between practice, the creative industries and creative business education that can bring a positive impact on real-world solutions.

References

Anderson, F. (2016). *Linking memorable songs to daily routines to helping those with dementia lead more independent lives, Bachelor's Thesis.* Liverpool Hope University.

Baird, A., & Thompson, W. F. (2018). The impact of music on the self in dementia. *Journal of Alzheimer's Disease, 61*(3), 827–841.

Betts, L. R., Hill, R., & Gardner, S. E. (2019). "There's not enough knowledge out there": Examining older adults' perceptions of digital technology use and digital inclusion classes. *Journal of Applied Gerontology, 38*(8), 1147–1166.

Carlgren, L., Rauth, I., & Elmquist, M. (2016). Framing design thinking: The concept in idea and enactment. *Creativity and Innovation Management, 25*(1), 38–57.

Centre for Better Ageing. (2020). *Doddery but dear? Examining age-related stereotypes.* Retrieved from https://ageing-better.org.uk/resources/doddery-dear-examining-age-related-stereotypes

Cognitive Stimulation Therapy. (n.d.). Retrieved from http://www.cstdementia.com/page/sessions

Connecting Through Culture As We Age. (2022). Retrieved from https://connectingthroughcultureasweage.info/

Crook, C., & Harrison, C. (2008). *Web 2.0 technologies for learning at key stages 3 and 4, becta, coventry.* https://dera.ioe.ac.uk/id/eprint/8291/2/web2_technologies_supplementary.pdf

Cunningham, S., Brill, M., Whalley, H., Read, R., Anderson, G., Edwards, S., & Picking, R. (2019). Assessing wellbeing in people living with dementia using reminiscence music with a mobile app (memory tracks): A mixed methods cohort study. *Journal of Healthcare Engineering* [online], 10. Retrieved from https://www.hindawi.com/journals/jhe/2019/8924273/

Czaja, S. J., & Lee, C. C. (2014). The impact of digital technology on the lives of older adults. In C. C. Lee & S. J. Czaja (Eds.), *Human-computer interaction and aging* (pp. 3–24). Springer.

DEEP: The UK Network of Dementia Voices. (n.d.). *Evaluation report for zoomettes peer support group for women with dementia.* Retrieved from https://www.dementiavoices.org.uk/wp-content/uploads/2019/10/Evaluation-Report-for-Zoomettes-Peer-Support-Group-for-Women-with-dementia.pdf

Gasparini, A. (2015, February). *Perspective and use of empathy in design thinking.* In ACHI, the eight international conference on advances in computer-human interactions (pp 49–54).

Golding, P. (2000). Forthcoming features: Information and communications technologies and the sociology of the future. *Sociology, 34*(1), 165–184.

Holman, D., & Walker, A. (2021). Understanding unequal ageing: Towards a synthesis of intersectionality and life course analyses. *European Journal of Ageing, 18,* 239–255.

Isaacs, F. (2019). *How to use ZOOM.* Retrieved from https://www.youtube.com/watch?v=ilK0WAS3Kt4at].

Luka, I. (2014). Design thinking in pedagogy. *Journal of Education Culture and Society, 2,* 63–74.

Memory Matters. (n.d.). *Therapeutic approaches to memory loss & Dementia.* Retrieved from https://memorymatters.org.uk/

Memory Tracks. (n.d.). *Memory tracks is a caregiver-support app that links memorable songs to care tasks.* Retrieved from https://www.memorytracks.net/

Museum of Brands. (n.d.). *Wellbeing programme.* Retrieved from https://museumofbrands.com/living-brands/

Neal, M., & Briggs, M. (2002). *Validation therapy for dementia.* Cochrane Library (3).

NICE. (2018). *Dementia: Assessment, management and support for people living with dementia and their carers.* Retrieved from https://www.nice.org.uk/guidance/ng97

Norman, D. A. (2013). *The design of everyday things.* MIT Press.

Pendine Park. (n.d.). *Pendine park, inspiring care.* Retrieved from https://pendinepark.com/

Perkins, L., et al. (2022). Delivering cognitive stimulation therapy (CST) virtually. *Clinical Interventions in Ageing, 2022*(17), 97–116.

Prenksy, M. (2001). Digital natives, digital immigrants. *On the Horizon, 9*(5), 1–6.

Selwyn, N. (2009). The digital native–Myth and reality. *Aslib Proceedings, 61,* 364–379.

Simmons-Stern, N. R., Deason, R. G., Brandler, B. J., et al. (2012). Music-based memory enhancement in Alzheimer's disease: Promise and limitations. *Neuropsychologia, 50*(14), 3295–3303.

Spector, P. E., Zapf, D., Chen, P. Y., & Frese, M. (2000). Why negative affectivity should not be controlled in job stress research: Don't throw out the baby with the bath water. *Journal of Organizational Behavior, 21*(1), 79–95.

The Sandpit. (n.d.). Retrieved from https://thesandpitpilot.wordpress.com/

Thomas, C., & Milligan, C. (2015). *How can and should UK Society adjust to dementia*. Joseph Rowntree Foundation.

UKRI. (n.d.). *Healthy ageing*. Retrieved from https://www.ukri.org/what-we-offer/browse-our-areas-of-investment-and-support/healthy-ageing/

Willatt, A. (2022). *How to use creative and participatory methods within and beyond research settings–connecting through culture as we age*. Retrieved from https://connectingthroughcultureasweage.info/3518-2/

9

Showbiz Kids Class, Art and Education

S. T. Dancey

Show biz kids making movies of themselves you know they don't give a
fuck about anybody else.
(Showbiz Kids—Steely Dan, 1973)

Introduction

The relationship between class, education and the creative and cultural
sector in the UK is often problematic, complex and contested. In researching and reviewing existing research, a number of initial recurrent themes
became apparent. Firstly, the general lack of research, until relatively
recently, in the areas of class and the creative and cultural sectors; secondly, the lack of mobility from those from working-class backgrounds
into the sector, hampered by lifelong reduced chances for mobility in
school, higher education and the creative and cultural sector; finally, a

S. T. Dancey (✉)
Business School for the Creative Industries, University for the Creative Arts,
Epsom, UK
e-mail: simon.dancey@uca.ac.uk

© The Author(s), under exclusive license to Springer Nature Switzerland AG 2023 **181**
B. S. Nayak (ed.), *Intersectionality and Creative Business Education*,
https://doi.org/10.1007/978-3-031-29952-0_9

picture revealed by recent research (Carey et al., 2020) of a creative and cultural sector that is dominated by the privileged, shaped by their values and their visions and fed back to broader society as art. Their art.

Higher education is a part of the matrix that lets this happen. To understand its role in perpetuating inequality, it needs to be explored within the context of wider structural, socially constructed hierarchies and, as Foucault would say, *Regimes of Truth* (Rabinow, 1991). Rather than simply just restate these issues, this chapter will combine personal, lived and often place-based experiences of these areas, alongside presenting a theoretical sociological conceptualisation of them. Structurally, this chapter will fall into two sections firstly providing an overview of the key issues and mainly, quantitative analysis of class, education and the creative and cultural sector and secondly applying a theoretical sociological framework and approach to the areas in question, exploring social imaginaries, hegemony, field theory and hybridity.

My background within the creative and cultural sector falls into three main areas, and I will also bring these experiences to bear on the analysis and discussions that follow. Firstly, as a practitioner and cultural producer, I began working as a musician and events and concert promoter, including work with radio and TV. Secondly, as a community arts director, I focussed on vocational skills training for disadvantaged groups, then cultural skills global director at the British Council and latterly as chief executive officer (CEO) of the UK Skills Council Creative & Cultural Skills. Finally, as a research academic and university senior lecturer and assistant deputy vice-chancellor, I focussed on careers, employability and social justice.

Overview

To understand the role of higher education in what Bourdieu would identify as the Cultural Field (1993), one most also look more widely at that field. Quite simply, the creative and cultural sector is dominated by the privileged and those from working-class backgrounds are underrepresented and less likely to enter the majority of occupations available. There has been a considerable amount of new research over the last few years.

The NESTA/Policy & Evidence Centre (Carey et al., 2020) review, *Class, participation and job quality in the UK Creative Industries*, a comprehensive overview of occupational data and class and the creative and cultural sector, paints a depressing picture. The privileged have double the chance of securing the job, with that figures jumping to 5.5 as likely when adding a degree to that privilege, a situation that has remained unimproved since 2014, with class disparities occurring across every part of the creative and cultural sector with the exception of Craft and with Publishing and Architecture being the most elite:

> Those from privileged backgrounds are more than twice as likely to land a job in a creative occupation. They dominate key creative roles in the sector, shaping what goes on stage, page and screen…We also find that class interacts with other factors—such as gender, ethnicity, disability and skill levels—to create 'double disadvantage'.…The intersection of class and skills has a particularly pronounced impact on the likelihood of landing a creative job, where those from a privileged background who are qualified to degree-level or above are 5.5 times as likely to secure a creative role than those of working-class background who are only skilled to GCSE-level. (Carey et al., 2020 p. 2)

When exploring the role of education, particularly in relation to skills, those from privileged background who also obtain a degree are 5.6% more likely to secure a position in the creative and cultural sector than those form a working-class background (p. 21). The full scale of the picture is detailed in the *Social Mobility in the Creative Economy* report of 2021:

> The scale of this class crisis is significant: If the Creative Industries were as socio-economically diverse as the rest of the economy, there would be more than 250,000 more working-class people employed in the sector. This deficit is equivalent to the size of the creative workforce in Scotland, Wales and Northern Ireland combined…Growth of the Creative Industries is mostly benefitting the privileged: Two thirds of the increase in employment in the sector over the past five years was taken by those from privileged backgrounds. In contrast, the relative likelihood of someone from a working-

class background ending up in the Creative Industries remains largely unchanged since 2014. (Carey, H. O Brien, D. and Gable, O., p. 2)

What then of the role of education in relation to education and education policy across the UK, remembering the devolved status of both culture and education?

Education and Policy

Arts and culture have been increasingly downgraded in terms of policy priorities, with successive UK governments in thrall to the central tenets of global neoliberalism, placing the value of arts and education clearly on the altar of neoliberalism. Alongside this obsession with markets, measurement and economics, the concept of the *Creative Industries* for some appeared to be an opportunity to place artistic and creative activity back at the forefront of both economic development and innovation, with increased public and private funds for development. The collision of these elements has led to a complex picture and there is a need to unpick these concepts of neoliberalism and creative industries, in relation to policy, to gain a clearer understanding of the current landscape of education and the creative and cultural sector.

Ashton and Ashton explore the impact of policy and values in their paper 'Creativity and the Curriculum: Educational Apartheid in 21st Century England, a European Outlier?' (2022). They point to the overarching education policy and the two-tier public and state school system in the UK as a potent effect on class.

> The underlying philosophy is a fundamental disregard and lack of value ascribed to arts and culture in the state education system, which is more tightly controlled than the private sector that has been free to pursue a more holistic approach. (p. 13)

Whilst there has been considerable devaluing and investment in the arts at state school, in contrast, the private sector has invested heavily and prioritises creative industries within their curriculum. These pupils in turn move to elite universities and elite positions in UK society.

> One consequence of this is that the products of these private schools have started to play not just a disproportionate part in the leadership of the creative arts but in many respects to dominate the sector (Brook et al., 2020). For example, in the post war years we witnessed a significant influence of the local authority state funded fine art colleges in the rock music industry (Frith and Horne 1987; Beck and Cornford 2012) but by 2014, 60% of rock music chart acts were privately educated compared with 1% 20 years before (Burchill 2014). More recently, in 2019, 38% of the richest individuals in TV, film and music attended private schools as did 20% of pop stars. (p. 12)

What then of the role of Universities? In the PEC paper on Social Mobility (Carey et al., 2021a, 2021b), they identify the potential of education to be the great leveller of opportunity. As with other structures in society, access to higher education to those from low socio-economic backgrounds is limited, with cost and mobility hampering participation. This unequal access to education is further evidenced in 'Screened Out' paper (Carey et al., 2021a, 2021b). Looking at the screen industry, it details a highly qualified talent pool with seven out of ten workers holding degree or higher qualifications, yet the access to university for working-class students is restricted by their previous life experiences:

> Yet we know educational achievement in school, and relatedly class origin, is a significant predictor of access to university and in particular to elite institutions (Anders et al 2017). Research by the Sutton Trust found that students from lower socio-economic backgrounds and from state schools are much less likely to apply to Russell Group universities than their more privileged or private-school counterparts. This is the case, even when they had comparable qualifications—including the same A-level grades and subjects (Wyness 2017). Similarly, analysis of data from the Next Steps survey, found that the most advantaged students were twelve times more likely to attend a Russell Group university (Anders et al 2017). (p. 21)

Thus, we are left with a picture of a creative and cultural sector, dominated by the privileged and the role of education at all levels mitigating against those from poor socio-economic backgrounds. This is further compounded by a host of other biases and prejudices. As per a recent paper from the British Psychological Society on psychological impacts of class inequalities:

> Social class—defined as a social category into which we are socialised that affords differing amounts of economic, social, and cultural resources—is conceptualised and measured as being composed of both objective and subjective components. In the context of education, health and work, findings illustrate that psychological dimensions of prejudice and discrimination contribute to class-based inequalities which, in turn, can further influence classism, the experience of which has a significant and detrimental psychological impact on working class and low socioeconomic status people. Social class identity and psychological responses to socioeconomic conditions start to take shape in early childhood and continue throughout the lifespan, affecting how an individual experiences their daily life, their relationships, how they perceive themselves and how they are treated by others, including educational institutions, public services, and professional organisations. (Rickett et al., 2022, p. 4)

What then can applying a theoretical lens tell us about these structures of inequality, dominance of certain values and the suppression of the subaltern? We have noted the role of education across a lifetime, but what can we learn from this and how can we respond and create more equitable structures.

Theoretical Framework

A broad sociological approach has been used to explore the constituent areas detailed in this chapter. The approach utilises a *Quadruple Helix* (Dancey, 2019) framework that employs four interlinked strands. First is hegemony and counterhegemony (Gramsci, 1999) focusing on the mediation of power and exploring notions of how certain groups dominate and how their values are voluntarily and actively adopted by subaltern groups. Gramsci's work moves away from a simplistic binary notion of a dominant paradigm and the dominated. It explores how power is in flux and negotiated and how dominant values become part of our internal belief systems. Second is the cultural field, building on Gramsci's work. Bourdieu (1993, 1998) examined the role of culture in the reproduction of social structures and the way unseen, unequal power relations are legitimised and embedded in everyday cultural practices. Elements of his work are utilised, including concepts of the cultural field, Doxa and heterodoxy. Bourdieu's work offers an analytical framework to examine contemporary dominant models of cultural policy and activity, especially when married to Gramsci's work on hegemony. Third is the area of imaginaries. This mainly references to the work of Anderson on imaginaries (2016), exploring the shared values and collective understanding of reality within respective. The work of Lacan (2007) on the real, the imagined and the symbolic is also included. Finally, building on the work of Gramsci and Bourdieu, Canclini's (2014) work on hybridity in relation to culture, notions of identity and modernity, and particularly in relation to the concept of hegemonies and high and low cultural concepts.

None of these areas are hermetically sealed from each other but intertwine like DNA strands within the social fields and structures created and inhabited by social actors. Together they provide a powerful tool for exploring social phenomena.

Discussion

In the previous section, the research detailed presents a picture of a very distorted UK creative and cultural sector, using data available to provide evidence of social phenomena. In this section, a number of these phenomena will be explored through alternative theoretical lenses. These explorations are not intended to be exhaustive, replicable or final analysis. They are intended to be discursive, theoretical and ongoing.

Social Imaginaries: Everything Counts in Large Amounts

The concept of imaginary is informed by a number of different thinkers including Sartre, Lacan and Castoriadis. In Castoriadis's *the Imaginary Institution of Society* (1975), he argues that the imaginary of the society creates for each historical period its particular way of living, seeing and making its own existence:

> Each country chooses its symbolism; each society is instituted in its own way. The specificity of each society is homologous to a central core of imaginary meanings through which that society creates, organizes and gives meaning to the world. Each society 'institutes' its real. A web of meanings is created that paves the country's existence. This is the imaginary institution of the society. (Arruda, 2014, p. 3)

When considering the earlier findings and the disproportionate number of people from working-class backgrounds in the creative and cultural sector, the works of Lacan (2007) and Anderson (2016) on social and community imaginaries are a useful starting point for a conceptual analysis of the phenomena. These include understanding working-class notions of the self and their communities, their aspirations and ties to place.

These social constructions and knowledge of work, education and opportunities available in turn shape the representation of those from working-class backgrounds in the creative and cultural sector. These representations of self are laid down in the early socialisation process and reinforced through early life with school friends and media. Here the social imaginary is delimiting and restrictive in terms of aspiration. Knowledge of the technical apprenticeship or career paths of the creative and cultural sector are at best opaque (Carey et al., 2021a, 2021b), alongside an often unwillingness to move away from known community support and ties. This phenomenon can be found in many differing parts of the UK, in the South Wales valleys where there is very little movement longitudinally across valleys to attend cultural events and in the East End of London, in places such as Tower Hamlets where research (Dancey,

2023) shows individuals tend to want to work and participate in University education locally (that is if they participate at all).

When these social imaginaries are layered across the spatial distribution of both the creative and cultural sector, with London and the South East dominating and the distribution of university creative education, a picture of lack of UK-based working-class students is no surprise.

Finally, the social imaginary of artistic activity has often been shaped by the construct of success being firmly based on commercial success and wealth. This is the notion that also dominates education and particularly the social imaginary of creative business education. Where is the art? As an arts practitioner, I have seen over the last 20 years the dominant narrative that artists must also be entrepreneurs, bookkeepers and fundraisers all at once. This isn't just the voice of higher education, but throughout the cultural field and including institutions like the four UK Arts Councils whose focus is often dominated by notions of innovation, entrepreneurship and fundraising. Not art. The staffing of these institutions also reflects the values of the middle-class elites, creating their rules and exclusive regimes of truth. But before we explore elite hegemonic dominance, it is important to first deconstruct the imaginary of 'the working class', challenging the idea of a monolithic identity and reductive set of characteristics. To do this, the notion of hybridity will be utilised as a lens.

Hybridity

Garcia Canclini (2005, 2014) adopts an interdisciplinary methodology that also embraces the notion of 'imaginaries'. Imagined communities are seen as structures of feeling where meanings and values are actively lived and felt. The notion builds on Williams notions of *feeling*, expanding the concept to capture:

> The multiple worlds that are constituted by the historically situated imaginations of persons and groups spread around the globe. (Appadurai 1996:33, quoted in Canclini, 2014 p. 98)

Hybridity is seen by Canclini as not being a synonym for fusion. He distinguishes between hybridity and hybridisation, with the emphasis of sociological enquiry resting on hybridisation, the process of hybridity. He defines it as follows:

> I understand for hybridization sociocultural processes in which discrete structures of practice, previously existing in separate form, are combined to generate new structures, objects and practices. In turn, it bears noting that so-called discrete structures were a result of prior hybridizations and therefore cannot be considered pure points of origin. (2005, p. xxv)

A cycle of hybridisation is seen to occur with the continual movement from the discrete to the hybrid to the new discrete: a historical heterogeneous to homogenous movement. This process generates new social structures and practices through the process of reconversion and reconversion strategies with the old being adapted in culture, technology, economic and symbolic areas to create new hybridities (p.XXVII). Canclini argues that this process is antithetic to the notion of pure or authentic identities:

> It is not possible to speak of identities as if they were simply a matter of fixed characteristics, or to posit them as the essence of an ethnicity or a nation. The history of identitarian movements reveals a series of operations for the selection of elements from different historical periods and their articulation by hegemonic groups in a story that gives them coherence, drama and eloquence. (2005, p. 28)

From this perspective, the notion of 'the working class' is a reductive social imaginary, constructed over and selecting elements that reinforce a view mediated by elite groups. The imaginary doesn't take into account the multiple hybridised and fluxing notion of individuals social reality. This has implications beyond the theoretical, for example, in terms of designing education policy with a 'one-size-fits-all' modality. This is not to argue for only individual approaches to education, but rather to create a structure that is reflexive and dialectical.

Hegemony and Counterhegemony

The Gramscian notion of hegemony and counterhegemony provides a useful lens to explore the cultural field education sits in. We have noted the dominance of neoliberalism in terms of educational policy, which shapes the UK system, but also exposes the disjuncture between art and business, culture and creative industries and the ongoing instrumentalising of art and culture. Firstly though, it is useful to look at the hegemonic project that is neoliberalism.

If a hegemonic project (such as neoliberalism) is to be successful and expansive, it needs to develop a strong association between its values, with other groups within the power bloc (Jones, 2006, p. 59). This forging of identity is complex, but in part shaped within the hegemonic process. In an exploration of the middle classes, Du Gay (cited in Jones, 2006) develops the Gramscian notion of the 'self-governing individual' through an exploration of 'enterprise culture' or 'being excellent'.

> A set of discourses and practices, initially emerging in the world of work and gradually spreading into other areas of social and cultural life, has explicitly sought to bind this class of workers and consumers to a moral, political and economic project that coheres around the terms 'enterprise' and 'excellence'. (cited in Jones, 2006, p. 59)

Emerging initially in response to the economic downturn of the 1970s, this concept focused on two main areas, the rollback of the welfare state and the inculcation of the concept of enterprise into all institutions. Du Gay argues, has also led to the individual uptake of enterprise culture where 'taking risks', 'standing on your own two feet' and to compete and challenge. Work is seen as a means to self-fulfilment and chance for individual growth and development. Rather than imposing these values, workers are asked to participate, help set goals and make decisions. Through tying individuals and groups into company values, they are more likely to feel ownership and a vested interest in its success. It is with the group who are themselves managers that this culture of enterprise mostly resonates. It has become what Gramsci describes as a 'common sense notion'. This notion has been central to the separation out of creative industries and cultural activity.

This artificial separation and dominance of the economic is reflected in the concept of creative industries, seen as separate from publicly funded art. This is best observed in policy and structure, with the separation of institutions such as the UK Arts Councils and Creative Industries institutions (e.g. Arts Council of England/Creative Industries Federation; Arts Council of Wales/Creative Wales). In reality, there is a constant move of individuals working and creating between industry and publicly subsidised arts, for example, Holden (2007), but the policy is enacted often in silos, with the social construct of the creative industries always dominating.

The influence of the creative industries is worth deconstructing more here. To see the creative industries conceptualisation as a reflection of a neoliberalist paradigmatic dominance is too simplistic, whilst dismissing neoliberalism entirely is to miss the subtle, dynamic Gramscian power relationships at play, with the move from cultural to creative being accompanied by the move to the neoliberalist language of markets and competition growing within the language of cultural policy, social actors and the increasing rise of a consultocracy of experts. Alongside this, the role of UK key institutions including the UK Arts Council's and British Council at this time moved to a similar discourse of competition, marketisation and the dominance of the economics of culture. As (at least theoretically) arms-length bodies from the government, they provided a bridge to civil society and acted as a repository for experts (or Gramscian intellectuals), legitimising this discourse. Globally, this concept of creative industries, measurement, markets and competition has gained purchase in cultural policy discourse (Bell & Oakley, 2015). Whilst not a simple proxy for neoliberalism, as discussed earlier, it does share common themes and the concept has gained an international ubiquity. In terms of differing discourses.

We not only have the reification of the often neoliberalist social construct that is the creative industries here, but the marketisation of higher education as well (e.g. Kleibert, 2021) Together these create a conceptualisation of creative industries education based on crude metrics and 'bums on seats' and units sold. The focus on the introduction of widening participation, outreach and university civic missions need to be weighted carefully, with some of these elements potential being counter-hegemonic moves, neutralising criticism and legitimising other activity. The university here is seen as purely a business. From this perspective, the idea of the business school itself further pushes the notion of capitalist commerce into the heart of the artistic practice, reducing art purely to commerce. This echoes the Marxian notion of dialectical materialism, with economics shaping a superstructure that includes art.

The other side to this dominance is the subjugation of other ways of knowing, seeing and learning. This is what Boaventura de Sousa Santos terms 'Epistemicide' (2014). Epistemologies of particularly non-Global North are erased and delegitimised in favour of the dominant Global North Economic model.

Cultural Field and Sans Practique: Whose Game Is This and Who Is Allowed to Play?

In any given field, actors compete for positions; in the cultural field, this takes shape in the authority ascribed to recognition, consecration and prestige and is a *symbolic power* not reducible to economic capital. One such symbolic power takes shape in the concept of *cultural capital*, a formulation of cultural knowledge and competencies defined by Bourdieu as:

> A form of knowledge, an internalized code or a cognitive acquisition which equips the social agent with empathy towards appreciation for or competence in deciphering cultural relations and cultural artefacts...like economic capital, the other forms of capital are unequally distributed among social classes. (p. 7)

Specific interests are at stake in different fields as well as different kinds of capital invested in different fields—shown in the cultural field with cultural capital and symbolic capital unequally distributed throughout society.

Much has been made of research highlighting the lack of both networks and the cultural capital of working-class individuals and the creative and cultural sector (Carey et al., 2020). In the UK, the cultural field which encompasses these notions has been shaped in a large part by the two hands of industry and empire. This is reflected in the obscenely immoral public school system, designed to train bureaucrats, managers and leaders to administer and run empire, whilst the working classes provided labour to help the ruling classes asset strip the world.

To find these power structures replicated with the creative and cultural sector is at best perverse. The rules of the game are dictated by the public school elite in most walks of life within the UK. They hold the cultural capital instilled at prep school and the ubiquitous Oxbridge attendance. They have the networks and the right accent and reference point. Research has also shown how many from elite backgrounds play down their privilege and identify their origins as working class (Friedeman et al., 2021):

> (They) able to tell an upward story of career success 'against the odds' that simultaneously casts their progression as unusually meritocratically legitimate while erasing the structural privileges that have shaped key moments in their trajectory. (p. 1)

At the same time those from working-class backgrounds are told to learn the rules of the game, adopt the manners and tastes of the elites and stand a chance of playing. This doesn't sound like a game I would want to play. It leaves the rules intact and forces value change onto the working class, where their values are seen as undesirable. This model sees social mobility as a desirable outcome and reinforces the myths of meritocracy, where the best always rise to the top, the neoliberalist self-improved individual in a fair market place, even if they are from a working-class background.

Conclusion

As a young man studying sociology at university, I remember being appalled reading the extremely famous *Oxford Mobility Study* of 1980 (Goldthorpe et al., 2016). The study proposed that *the service class was engaging within itself, becoming more closed off to new members from lower social classes.*

Recent research on the creative and discussed earlier paints a very similar pattern 43 years on.

Applying the theoretical framework detailed earlier helps to expose the complex power relations and ambiguities in the areas of class, education and the creative and cultural sector. School, university, industry and other institutions in the cultural sector all shape the dominance of elite groups. That is not to say that all activities and individuals perpetuate inequality. Hegemony is messy, fluid and constantly in tension. In terms of university activity, the civic university approach is a potentially exciting one, a move that rethinks the university and connects in to the real lives of people. Similarly, the huge success of some universities, such as Queen Mary University London, in attracting people from working-class backgrounds into university through sponsorship of schools, bursaries and mentoring networks is exciting, but is in constant tension with the commercial nature of modern universities. (Dancey, 2023). Nevertheless, this approach need to be mirrored in other university institutions focussed on the arts. The challenge as with all interventions is that the wider economic model and societal inequalities mitigate against this.

This is also true in the UK. Many recommendations to change the situation of class in relation to the creative and cultural sector are positive and to be welcomed (detailed in PEC Social Mobility Report, 2021) and I have been involved in a number of them professionally, including the Creative Careers Programme and Cultural ambition programme. The challenge is that the hegemonic system mitigates against their success, and they can often support the existing status quo as a legitimising social mobility project (Brook et al., 2020):

> Current career development schemes and many diversity policies do nothing to challenge the somatic norm… they focus on adapting underrepresented groups to be more like that norm…rather than lifting groups out of their underprivileged state, rather than challenging how privilege is constructed and misrecognised as legitimacy. (Brook et al., 2020, p. 16)

Gramsci's work helps show us how this process happens; they are counterhegemonic movements that are neutralised. Theoretical investigation of class, education and the creative and cultural sector helps reveal the hidden power structures, socially constructed imaginaries and hybrid fluid identities. It is only through a radical rethink and a move to a more egalitarian and communitarian approach to arts and education that we will impact class. The first thing though is to remember that people build social structures and new ones can replace the ones we have, or we can remove them. This is also true of what we value from an epistemological view, with non-western, non-neoliberal ways of knowing, learning and meaning offering the potential for reimagining the artistic and creative and cultural field. In the words of Boaventura de Sousa Santos (2014), *Another World is Possible.*

> But no one ever changed the church by pulling down a steepleAnd you'll never change the system by bombing number tenSystems just aren't made of bricks they're mostly made of peopleYou may send them into hiding, but they'll be back again.
>   If you don't like the life you live, change it now it's yoursNothing has effects if you don't recognize the causeIf the programme's not the one you want, get up, turn off the setIt's only you that can decide what life you're gonna get.
>   (Big A, Little A—Crass, 1982)

References

Anderson, B. (2016). *Imagined communities.* Verso.

Arruda, A. (2014). Social imaginary and social representations of Brazil. *Papers on Social Representations, 23,* 13.1–13.22.

Ashton, H., & Ashton, D. (2022). Creativity and the curriculum: Educational apartheid in 21st century England, a European outlier? *International Journal of Cultural Policy.* https://doi.org/10.1080/10286632.2022.2058497

Bell, D., & Oakley, K. (2015). *Cultural policy.* Routledge.

Bourdieu, P. (1993). *The field of cultural production.* Polity.

Bourdieu, P. (1998). *Acts of resistance: Against the new myths of our time.* Polity.

Brook, O., O'Brien, D., & Taylor, M. (2020). *Culture is bad for you.* Manchester University Press.

Canclini, N. (2005). *Hybrid culture.* University of Minnesota Press.

Canclini, N. J. (2014). *Imagined globalisations*. Duke University Press.

Carey, H., et al. (2020). *Getting in and getting on: Class, participation and job quality in the UK creative industries*. Policy & Evidence Centre (NESTA) paper 1. Class & the Creative Industries.

Carey, H. O'Brien, D., & Gable, O. (2021a). *Screened out: Tackling class inequality in the UK screen industries*. Policy & Evidence Centre (NESTA) Paper 2. Class & the Creative Industries.

Carey, H., O'Brien, D., & Gable, O. (2021b). *Social mobility in the creative economy rebuilding and levelling up?* Policy & Evidence Centre (NESTA).

Castoriadis, C. (1975). *The imaginary institution of Society*. Polity Press.

Dancey, S. T. (2019). *Transnational cultural policy*. PhD Thesis. University of South Wales.

Dancey, S. T. (2023). *Internal research document on civic agreement*. Queen Mary University.

De Sousa Santos, B. (2014). *Epistemologies of the south*. Routledge.

Friedeman, S., et al. (2021). Deflecting privilege: Class identity and the intergenerational self. *Sociology, 55*(4), 716–733.

Goldthorpe, J., et al. (2016). Social class mobility in modern Britain: Changing structure, constant process. *Journal of British Academy, 4*, 89–111. https://doi.org/10.5871/jba/004.089

Gramsci, A. (1999). *Selections from the prison notebooks* (online). Retrieved from http://abahlali.org/files/gramsci.pdf

Holden, J. (2007). *Publicly-funded culture and the creative industries*. Arts Council England, Demo.

Jones, S. (2006). *Antonio Gramsci*. Routledge.

Kleibert, J. M. (2021). Geographies of marketization in higher education: Branch campuses as territorial and symbolic fixes. *Economic Geography, 97*(4), 315–337. https://doi.org/10.1080/00130095.2021.1933937

Lacan, J. (2007). *Ecrits*. W. W. Norton.

Rabinow, P. (Ed.). (1991). *The foucault reader*. Penguin.

Rickett, B., et al. (2022). *Psychology of social class-based inequalities policy implications for a revised (2010) UK equality act*. British Psychological Society.

10

Limits of Intersectionality as a Theoretical Framework

Bhabani Shankar Nayak

Introduction

'Who exploits, whom, what, when and how' are crucial questions to understand the rise of 'intersectionality' as theoretical framework to understand and analyse different forms and levels of discrimination and struggles against it. The answers to these questions are central to design, direct and determine the nature and structure of radical and emancipatory politics in search of alternatives to end all forms of exploitation and discrimination. The objective understanding of issues of exploitation and discrimination is based on normative empirical evidence and subjective analysis with relativist outlook remaining important. The historical and broad overview of specific contexts and contemporary conditions of capitalism and all its traditional and neotraditional apparatus is central to shape all struggles against all forms of discrimination, injustice and

B. S. Nayak (✉)
Business School for the Creative Industries, University for the Creative Arts, Epsom, UK
e-mail: bhabani.nayak@uca.ac.uk

© The Author(s), under exclusive license to Springer Nature Switzerland AG 2023
B. S. Nayak (ed.), *Intersectionality and Creative Business Education*,
https://doi.org/10.1007/978-3-031-29952-0_10

exploitation. Berger and Guidroz (2010: 7) locate intersectionality as a form of "social literacy." It helps to guide emancipatory struggles by providing insights into people's experience.

The identity-centric political conceptualisation and individualising nature of intersectionality theory (Grabham et al., 2009) is reductionist. Therefore, it is important for the theory of intersectionality questions absolute nature of identity and challenges homogenous categorisation of people and their multiple experiences by engaging with diversities of social, political, economic, cultural, sexual, social, gender, regional and religious identities. The multiple experiences produced by multiple forms of marginalisation, exploitation and power relations based on access and ownership over resources. Intersectionality acknowledges diversity, celebrates differences and encourages to examine different layers of marginalisation and experiences by critically examining hierarchies of power within different forms of capitalistic hegemony. Crenshaw argues that intersectionality is not a "totalizing theory of identity" (1991: 1244). The idea is to highlight the significance of understanding different social divisions under different conditions of subjective construction of identities (Yuval-Davis, 2006).

The politics of intersectionality transcends the narrow identities by looking at intersection of people's experience with power. It helps to understand different forms of inequalities "routed through one another and which cannot be untangled to reveal a single cause" (Grabham et al., 2009: 1). In this process, it provides leeway to different forms of capitalism and all its processes and structures that produce all forms of inequalities and exploitation. Intersectionality operates within social, political, religious, cultural, racial, regional, sexual, economic and gender-entrenched conditions produced and reproduced by capitalism. Therefore, the articulation of intersectionality can't be separated from capitalism.

Intersectionality as a Theoretical Framework

Intersectionality emerged as a powerful analytical tool in the writing of Crenshaw to understand racial discrimination of Black women (1989) and domestic violence (1991). Her writings continue to provide directions to debates around intersectionality. Intersectionality as a theoretical framework is embedded with egalitarian imperatives in a world of entrenched inequalities and discrimination. It is a theory of life circumstances shaped by various factors. These factors are linked with various forms of capitalism in one way or the other. Intersectionality overcomes its essentialism around the experience of people and their life circumstances by engaging with multiple forms of experiences and their commonness exists among various groups in the society (Hancock, 2007, 2011). She argued that intersectional approach "changes the relationship between the categories of investigation from one that is determined a priori to one of empirical investigation" (Hancock, 2007: 67). Such an empiricist approach is not only reductionist but also reduces human experiences into interconnected or independent categories. Such categorisation is simply impossible without understanding the conditions shat shapes human experiences and their categorisations. As Prins puts it as people are "both actor in and co-author of our own life story" (2006: 281). Valentine questions such a conceptualisation and argues that "the existing theorization of the concept of intersectionality overemphasizes the abilities of individuals to actively produce their own lives and underestimates how the ability to enact some identities or realities rather than others is highly contingent on the power-laden spaces in and through which our experiences are lived" (2007: 19). The place, time, power, processes and people are five pillars to understand and apply intersectionality as an analytical tool to explain different forms of exploitation and inequalities.

Intersectionality as a critical analytical tool in social inquiry has remained crucial for the politics of transformation. The theoretical and political agenda is to understand 'inequalities' are dissimilar means that such 'equality' mainstreaming cannot be a simple adaptation of current tools of gender mainstreaming. Whether one thinks of checklists, training, impact assessment or expert meetings, a clear conceptualisation of how intersectionality operates, a theory of the power dynamics of a specific inequality as well as a choice for a clear political goal will be needed. Moreover, the fact that multiple inequalities are not independent means that such 'equality' mainstreaming cannot be a simple extrapolation of gender mainstreaming. If intersectionality is at work in strategies against inequalities, then new and more comprehensive analytical methods are needed and methods of education, training and consultation will have to be rethought (Verloo, 2006: 222). Such analysis carries a tenet of essentialism and ignores structural transformation of society to end deep-rooted exploitative and unequal systems and processes at work. Therefore, "it is not at all clear whether intersectionality should be limited to understanding individual experiences, to theorizing identity, or whether it should be taken as a property of social structures and cultural discourses" (Davis, 2008: 68).

Limits of Intersectionality

Intersectionality needs to be celebrated as a critical theory embedded with emancipatory politics. It is also important to outline limits of intersectionality. The existing architype of intersectionality debates and discourses have failed to locate the fluidity of power relations and sites of struggles against identity-based violence, exploitations, dominance and discriminations within and outside the communities. The intersectionality approach to movement is ahistorical as it does not look at the inherent and historical roots of different forms of exploitation with capitalism. Intersectionality as a theoretical framework has failed to identify difference between the struggles of marginalised and majoritarian dominance. The marginalised identities and their struggles are emancipatory struggles, whereas majoritarian identity politics is the politics of dominance. So, deradicalisation is an inadvertent outcome of intersectionality as a political approach to emancipatory struggles.

The intersectionality of race, gender, class, caste, sexuality and other marginalised communities is an important indicator to understand different layers of exploitations and oppressions within the hierarchy of capitalist systems. The different forms of identities-based discrimination, oppression and exploitation exist not in separation but in unity with different structures and processes of capitalism. The politics of intersectionality ignores the role of pre-existing unequal social relations in shaping conditions of production and reproduction within capitalism. The failure of class politics and defeat of revolutionary movements during the 1990s led to the rise of intersectionality as an approach to understand exploitation and discrimination based on personal characteristics of individuals, that is race, gender, sexuality, caste, region, territoriality and ethnicity. The post-modern and post-structural theories provide the ideological foundation to intersectionality identity politics.

The idea of intersectionality attempts to find alternatives within existing capitalist system that reproduces the gender, caste and race-based inequalities and exploitations that result in precarity and proletarianisation. The existing architype of intersectionality debates and discourses have failed to locate the fluidity of power relations and sites of struggles against identity-based violence, exploitations, dominance and discriminations within and outside the communities. The intersectionality approach to movement is ahistorical as it does not look at the inherent and historical roots of different forms of exploitation with capitalism. So, deradicalisation is an inadvertent outcome of intersectionality as a political approach to emancipatory struggles.

The critiques of intersectionality do not reject and disregard the realities of multiple forms of power structure that exploits, discriminates and kills on the basis of individual identities. The ideas of identities are not just about atomised, abstract and individual self-reflections. It also involves individual identity's organic relationship and interactions with environment and fellow beings. The individuals build relationships with others to fulfil one's own desires and needs that give meaning to their lives. This generates the foundation of collective identity based on voluntary but natural relationships. These relationships are territorialised and de-territorialised by multiple identities created and destroyed as per the requirements of the neoliberal capitalism under globalisation. For example, the identity issues of displaced person, refugees, internal and external migrants and so forth are direct or indirect products of capitalism. So, there are material conditions that shape identity politics. The mindless criticisms of identity politics are also dangerous. It is important to separate two different ideological trends of identity politics.

The growth of European reactionary nationalist politics led by the British Nationalist Party and English Defence League in United Kingdom, UK Independence Party (UKIP) in England, the National Front in France, New Dawn in Greece and Jobbik in Hungary are classic examples of reactionary identity politics that promotes cultural logic of failed capitalism. The politics of higher-caste Hindus led by the Bharatiya Janata Party (BJP) in India and white supremacists in Europe and America are reactionary identity politics, which needs to be discarded. The Scottish Nationalist Party (SNP) follows both regressive and progressive aspects of identity politics which adds to the complexities of identity politics. The four centuries of globalisation led to the normalisation of precarity, and the emancipatory labour and trade union movements have become wage bargaining movements promoting representative careerism in the name of affirmative actions. Such approach helps in hiding the institutional discriminatory practices of capitalist structures led by the patriarchy of white supremacists in Europe and Americas and Brahmanical Hindu caste order in Indian subcontinents.

The Dalit and tribal movements in India, LGBTQ movements, anti-racist movements, women's movements and indigenous communities' movements to save their land, livelihood and forests are emancipatory identity politics. Therefore, it is important to embrace progressive aspects of identity politics, develop intersectionality and transcend differences as a political strategy to strengthen emancipatory struggles for liberty, equality, justice and fraternity. The progressive ideological engagements with intersectionality politics can reduce the isolationist approach of identity politics. It is impossible to fight racial, gender and caste discrimination without fighting capitalism. The academic left and their privileged politics must get on with it without creating further mirage of theoretical complexities. The struggle against racism, patriarchy, caste, sexism and all other forms of discriminations and exploitations are struggles against capitalism.

Conclusion

It is time for the politics and theory of intersectionality to reflect on the everyday realities of people with their subjective and objective conditions guide an organised and united struggle for alternatives to all dehumanising structures of capitalism. Finally, as the significance of the #BlackLivesMatter movement goes global with its open and inclusive approach, it is important to call for a borderless revolutionary internationalism based on experiences of local sites of struggles against all forms of inequalities, injustices and exploitations. The local, national, regional and global alliance of revolutionary collectives can only help in democratising the world and ensure peace and prosperity for one and all.

References

Berger, M. T., & Guidroz, K. (2010). Introduction. In M. T. Berger & K. Guidroz (Eds.), *The intersectional approach: Transforming the academy through race, class, and gender*. University of North Carolina Press.

Crenshaw, K. (1989). Demarginalizing the intersection of race and sex: A black feminist critique of antidiscrimination doctrine, feminist theory and antiracist politics. *University of Chicago Legal Forum, 139*, 139–167.

Crenshaw, K. (1991). Mapping the margins: Intersectionality, identity politics, and violence against women of color. *Stanford Law Review, 43*(6), 1241–1299.

Davis, K. (2008). Intersectionality as buzzword: A sociology of science perspective on what makes a feminist theory successful. *Feminist Theory, 9*(1), 67–85.

Grabham, E., Herman, D., Cooper, D., & Krishnadas, J. (2009). Introduction. In E. Grabham, D. Cooper, J. Krishnadas, & D. Herman (Eds.), *Intersectionality and beyond: Law, power and the politics of location*. Routledge-Cavendish.

Hancock, A.-M. (2007). When multiplication doesn't equal quick addition: Examining intersectionality as a research paradigm. *Perspectives on Politics, 5*, 63–79.

Hancock, A.-M. (2011). *Solidarity politics for millennials: A guide to ending the oppression Olympics*. Palgrave Macmillan.

Prins, B. (2006). Narrative accounts of origins: A blind spot in the intersectional approach? *European Journal of Women's Studies, 13*(3), 277–290.

Valentine, G. (2007). Theorizing and researching intersectionality: A challenge for feminist geography. *The Professional Geographer, 59*(1), 10–21.

Verloo, M. (2006). Multiple inequalities, intersectionality and the European Union. *European Journal of Women's Studies, 13*(3), 211–228.

Yuval-Davis, N. (2006). Intersectionality and feminist politics. *European Journal of Women's Studies, 13*(3), 193–209.

Index

© The Author(s), under exclusive license to Springer Nature Switzerland AG 2023
B. S. Nayak (ed.), *Intersectionality and Creative Business Education*,
https://doi.org/10.1007/978-3-031-29952-0